Rockin' out of the Box

Purchased through
generous contributions to the
NDSU Development Foundation
Parents Fund

ROCKIN' OUT OF THE BOX

Gender Maneuvering in Alternative Hard Rock

MIMI SCHIPPERS

RUTGERS UNIVERSITY PRESS
New Brunswick, New Jersey, and London

•

Library of Congress Cataloguing-in-Publication Data

Schippers, Mimi, 1964–
    Rockin' out of the box : gender maneuvering in alternative hard rock /
Mimi Schippers.
      p. cm.
    Includes bibliographical references and index.
    ISBN 0–8135–3074–1 (cloth : alk. paper) – ISBN 0–8135–3075-X
(pbk. : alk. paper)
    1. Rock music—Social aspects. 2. Rock music—Sex differences. I. Title.

ML3918.R63 S35 2002
306.4'84–dc21

                               2001048791

British Cataloging-in-Publication data for this book is available from the British
Library.

Manufactured in the United States of America

For Marnie

Contents

Preface

This is, first and foremost, a book about gender. My main goal for the research reported here was to explore how people use everyday interactions and activities to push, pull, challenge, and fortify the rules for gender and sexuality. In order to do this, from late 1992 to the spring of 1995 I conducted an ethnographic study of a rock music subculture. As I will discuss later in detail, the rock music subculture is of particular interest to me because it consists of a group of both women and men who seem to be using what I have identified as a feminist or antisexist sensibility in their approach to rock and roll. This is of interest for two reasons. First, this subculture consists of men as well as women who seem to be explicitly challenging the sexism of mainstream rock in their performances and interviews. Since I am interested in better understanding how all people negotiate gender within face-to-face interaction, I thought it likely that I'd find some men who were approaching rock from an antisexist perspective. Unlike previous research on gender in everyday life, this subculture provided a golden opportunity to see antisexist women and men in everyday interactions and, importantly, how others responded to them. The second reason I chose this subculture was that hard rock has always been a largely male dominant cultural form. I thought this subculture might provide some insight into the everyday processes by which people incorporate alternative ideas about sexuality and gender into what had been, before the early 1990s, a rather exclusive boys' club.

By immersing myself in this alternative to mainstream rock I have come to understand the strategies that members of this subculture use to transform the culture of rock into one that is not sexist, and how they encourage others to follow along. I call the use of these strategies *gender maneuvering*.

Like most ethnographic researchers, when I first entered the field and became part of the subculture I was equipped with a conceptual apparatus that included particular ways of thinking about gender, sexuality, and social relations. What I found in the process of the fieldwork was that the conceptual apparatus was quite useful, but in the end not enough to fully understand what I was seeing. To reconcile this, I used the theories and concepts developed by people before me as building blocks for developing a new conceptual framework for the interactive processes by which individuals or groups negotiate gender and sexuality in their everyday lives.

Though the ethnographic research came before I developed the conceptual framework I present in this book, I want to provide the reader with a brief introduction to the concepts and theories of gender, sexuality, and society that served as the conceptual apparatus with which I started the project and that were eventually the building blocks for my own theoretical perspective. This will hopefully orient readers to my general approach and prepare uninitiated readers by defining and explaining some of the terminology used throughout the book.

This book is written from a sociological perspective, which means that I am most interested in the patterns or trends of behavior, beliefs, and interactions. Specifically, I will rely heavily on structuration theory as developed by sociologist Anthony Giddens. *Structuration* is the process by which the rules for how to act, interact, and understand the world in any given society or social setting are produced, sustained, and transformed. There are preexisting rules for how to act and interact in any social setting. According to Giddens, those rules continue to hold sway only to the extent that we all go along with and continue to follow them. As people begin to change their modes of action and interaction, the patterns themselves begin to shift. Using this concept, I suggest that *gender structuration* and *sexual structuration* are the specific processes by which the rules and patterns for gender and sexuality get produced, sustained, and transformed in our everyday activities and interactions.

Candace West and Don Zimmerman provide the conceptual framework for gender as not simply an identity or a character type, but also a form of "doing." According to West and Zimmerman, we "do" masculinity and femininity as we perform other social roles. All day, every day, as we occupy different roles as students, teachers, parents, or friends, we are expected to also perform gender. We all continue to "do" masculinity and femininity because we are rewarded in our everyday interactions by others for doing so. Thus, we are compelled, through interactions with others, to follow the established patterns—that is, gender structuration is an interactive process. It is because of this interactive requirement to do gender that West and Zimmerman suggest that gender relations are an emergent feature of face-to-face interactions. As we do gender we produce gender relations, including relations of inequality, power, and domination.

Judith Butler also suggests that gender is performative. However, Butler is less concerned with how gender emerges from interaction and more interested in how gender relations of inequality are symbolically produced and maintained. That is, she is concerned with how the meaning of gender difference is produced through all kinds of practices including speaking, writing, and moving about the world. According to Butler, in contemporary Western societies, gender difference is defined as a hierarchical, binary opposition. This means that masculinity and femininity are paired together as complementary opposites, defined as mutually exclusive categories that play off each other. According to Butler, the symbolic relationship between masculinity and femininity is a hierarchical one in which the masculine is favored over the feminine.

Butler adds that masculinity and femininity are always relational and that doing gender is always embedded within this symbolic understanding of gender difference. Gender is not simply a performance of masculinities and femininities by individuals, but also consists of the *relationship* created between masculinity and femininity as we perform gender. Butler also adds that this relationship structures erotic desire, normalizing heterosexuality as natural and inevitable; it is thus implicated in heterosexism.

Placing Butler's notion of gender as relational within the concrete world of face-to-face interaction suggests that, as we interact with each other, the way we do gender as individuals is always embedded in a relationship to others' performances of gender. That is, any individual performance of gender calls out a complementary performance in others. In addition to giving each other feedback about how well we are doing gender through our own performance of it, we send messages to others about who we are—and, importantly, who we expect others to be—in the interaction. Through our performances of gender we establish meanings for our relationships to others and for the interaction itself.

In different settings and among different groups of people, the rules vary as to what is the appropriate way to do masculinity and femininity. R.W. Connell's suggestion that there are *multiple masculinities* is useful here. According to Connell, there are many different forms of masculinity. For instance, the rules and expectations for doing an upper-class, suburban, white masculinity differ from those for a lower-class, urban, black masculinity; the rules and expectations for doing gay masculinity differ from those for straight masculinity. As we go about our daily lives, gender structuration consists of doing masculinities, doing femininities, and, importantly, creating and sustaining relationships between and among masculinities and femininities.

Within the current gender order that defines masculinity and femininity as hierarchical opposites, following the rules constitutes hegemonic gender structuration. That is, male dominant power relations are continually reproduced in the normal, "commonsense" ways of going about our daily lives. If, however, we decide to buck the rules and refuse to follow the expectations for femininity and masculinity in a given setting, we could possibly disrupt the relationship between masculinity and femininity. If done collectively, a group of people could possibly set a new course for gender structuration. This is what I call *gender maneuvering*.

Gender maneuvering is a specific kind of interaction. When one or more people manipulate their own gender performance or manipulate the meaning of their own or others' gender performances in order to establish, disrupt, or change the relationship between and among masculinities and femininities, they are gender maneuvering. *Interactive gender maneuvering* refers to the process by which one or more people manipulate the relationship between masculinity and femininity within the relatively brief moments of a situated interaction. *Cultural gender maneuvering* refers to the actions and interactions taken by a group of people to manipulate the relationship between masculinity and femininity as it has been established in the accepted patterns of beliefs and activities in an enduring cultural setting—in, for instance, rock music culture.

Though in reality it was the activities I observed within the rock music culture that led to my theoretical innovations, for the purposes of the book, the subculture of rock music that I studied, which I call *alternative hard rock*, serves as one case study or empirical example of how gender maneuvering works in the real world. Thus, in addition to being about gender, sexuality, and social relations, this book is also about a rock music subculture in which both women and men deploy different strategies of cultural gender maneuvering to replace the sexist, male-dominant, mainstream rock culture with something else. They also use interactive gender maneuvering to establish and sustain particular rules for gender when interacting with people from outside the subculture, and to manipulate interpersonal power relations among themselves. In the following chapters, I will go into much detail about what and who alternative hard rock(ers) are, the specific strategies of both cultural and interactive gender maneuvering used by alternative hard rockers, and the political implications of their maneuvers. While gender maneuvering in alternative hard rock, as the title suggests, is what this book is about, gender maneuvering is not limited to alternative hard rock. As I will suggest throughout the book, gender maneuvering can happen anywhere, anytime, and, I believe, happens all the time in different places. It is, in sociological terms, a patterned form of interaction—a significant part of social structure.

Acknowledgments

I owe many people a great deal of gratitude for their encouragement and assistance before, during, and since I conducted this research. This project never could have happened without each and every one of them. Paul Lichterman at the University of Wisconsin was a constant guide in my experiences as a participant, as an observer, and most importantly, as a sociologist. He, more than anybody else, patiently reminded me to keep one foot in sociology while I became both an alternative hard rocker and a scholar, and for that I thank him. Other people at the University of Wisconsin, including Jane Collins, Pamela Oliver, Jerry Marwell, and Jane Pilliavin provided invaluable feedback on my work. I would also like to thank Ann Orloff, Emily Kane, Renée Monson, Lisa Brush, and Bonnie Brandreth.

I would like to thank Martha Thompson at Northeastern Illinois University in Chicago for being a constant mentor even long after I left NIU. It was her teaching and wise counsel that led me to sociology in the first place. As well, I'd like to thank BarBara Scott, also of NIU, for making the intersection of gender, race, and class not only theoretically interesting but important in my own life. And I would like to thank the Sociologists for Women in Society, especially Barbara Risman.

I have received a great deal of support from people at Albion College. While maintaining a commitment to fine teaching, the faculty and administration at Albion have been supportive of my research; I would like to especially thank Glenn Perusek, but also my colleagues in the Department of Anthropology and Sociology, including Liz Brumfiel, Len Berkey, Molly Mullin, Amy Tertstriep, and D'emiji Togunde.

I also would like to thank David Myers, my editor at Rutgers University Press, and the reviewers for their guidance and suggestions. David Greenberg at New York University, thank you for forwarding the manuscript to David Myers and for your continuing guidance and support.

The alternative hard rockers who showed me the ropes taught me more about gender and rock 'n' roll than any book could. I would like to especially thank Brendan Murphy, but also Ian MacKaye of Fugazi, Eddie Vedder of Pearl Jam, Kim Thayil of Soundgarden, Donita Sparks and Jennifer Finch of L7, Kat Bjelland and Lori Barbero of Babes in Toyland, Rose of Poster Children, Louise Post and Nina Gordon of Veruca Salt, and Liz Davis and Valerie Agnew of 7 Year Bitch. All were gracious in sharing their knowledge about feminism, rock music, and their own experiences as rock musicians.

I would also like to thank my family. Each and every one of them has taught me and continues to teach me that standing up for what I believe in, despite adversity, is not only noble and worthwhile but absolutely necessary for survival. This includes first and foremost my parents, Jackie Schippers and David Schippers Jr. My sisters, Kate TeWinkle, Tiyi Schippers, Ann Winter, and Colleen Margolis, have been a source of strength and support since I was born. They've taught me so much about gender justice, fighting tyranny, and—most importantly—how to laugh. I want to also thank David Schippers, Pat Connor, David Bunce, Bob Winter, Lou Margolis, Tom Schippers, Carol Schippers, Kevin Schippers, Beth Schippers, Patrick Schippers, Julie Schippers, Peter Schippers, and Colleen Mertes. And to my nieces and nephews, Jamie, Will, Lydia, Dave, AJ, Brian, Valerie, Rachel, Zak, Arra, Ezra, Jake, Mitta, Shannon, Mike, Kali, Allison, Thomas, Scottie, Julie, Katie, Taylor, Mattie,

Isaiah, Jeremiah, and Sophie, thank you for the joy and hope for the future that makes me do this work.

I want to thank the "danishes": Rayna and Sonia, you have taught me how to be a righteous babe and gave me the skills to enter this subculture; Sinead O'Connor, Peter Murphy, and Patti Smith will always remind me of you. Oh yeah—getting men thrown out of bars will, too.

Meredith Berlin and Sarah Austin, thank you for your spiritual sustenance and for providing an oasis in the desert of academia. I never would have made it without you both. For her spiritual guidance, I would like to thank Janet Jacobs, from whom I have learned as much as I have from any teacher. To my cousin, Beth Liautaud: the way you do gender, the way you work a room, the way you shoot pool, and the way you have always been a most-trusted confidante all show in these pages and will be with me forever; thank you for always being there. Thanks also to Tona Williams and John Varda, who kept the rock 'n' roll salient when I was in Madison, and who in trying times were ever-present friends.

I'd also like to thank Stephanie at the Reflections Hair Salon in Madison; she is a hair master. Not only did Stephanie give me the 'dos to do this project, but also showed me that hair is an accessory, and that it does, no matter how much I tried to deny it, make a statement! If you want a good cut, see Dr. Stephanie.

Though you will never read this in this lifetime, Peter, you are a most trusted friend. Such a good, good boy and an even better soul. Your bundies comforted me as much as they did you on those cold, lonely nights in Albion.

To Solon Simmons: your encouragement to be a better scholar and a better person is immeasurable. You have nurtured and encouraged my passion for theory and have shown me how to have a great deal of fun with ideas. You have an unbelievable gift for pointing out and making clear things I had never imagined were there, which makes me a better sociologist, a better friend, and a better citizen of the world. You were a rock of support through much of the writing, and by way of example have taught me that when it comes right down to it, the only real thing that matters is love and compassion. Thank you.

Tara Tremmel, thank you for being both safe and challenging. You have taught me so much about being a feminist, an "outsider" in academia, and a diplomatic pool player. You have more courage than anybody I know, and that courage is a constant inspiration.

I would like to thank Marc Pagani for the cover photo, and for his vision, love, and presence in my life. Marc, let's knock off Everest and finish what we started earlier this century!

There are some people without whom I know I would never have been able to do this project and, more importantly, would not be the person I am today. Marnie Beilin is one of these people. Marnie, you are the strongest, most supportive, funny, fun, girlie, bestest friend in the whole wide world. Your spirit took me by the hand and led me to this path. Every happiness, every success, and every dream that led to or resulted from this research has started with your friendship. Every girl should be so lucky to have such a best friend. Thank you so much.

Rockin' out of the Box

1

GENDER AND ROCK MUSIC
So What's New?

In a *Rolling Stone* interview in 1987, Nikki Sixx, the "chief song writer [and] acknowledged brains" of the glam-metal band Motley Crüe, said, "I want a pool the shape of a pussy."[1] The author of the article also described the Motley Crüe insignia on their private jet as a "bent-over, blond stripper in garters." Sixx wanted the world to know that he was a rock star. He cued us in by telling us that he likes pussy, he likes the idea of diving in when he wants, and the success of his band just might buy him a spot, not so much in the bourgeois world of private pools, but more in that rock 'n' roll world of diving into women when he wants. He was doing rock star with such abandon and zeal that his statement—while interesting if you stop to wonder what shape he was actually imagining for his pool—could only be mundane, rock 'n' roll cliché. (For an explanation of the notion of "doing" rock star, see this volume's preface). Everybody knows that when you become a rock star, you get to jump in when you want, and more importantly, you are always ready and willing to take the dive. Isn't that what being a rock star is all about?

This was 1987, and the tail end of a decade of glam metal. Such bands as Motley Crüe, Poison, Skid Roe, Warrant, White Snake, and others embraced a sort of bad-boy personae that included, among other things, playing the part of the groupie monger. Without exception, these bands were all about "Girls, Girls, Girls," as the Motley Crüe song by this name documents. Women were part of the booty/ie that came with being a rock star.

Five years later, in the winter of 1992, *Rolling Stone* filed a report on a concert performance by three 'alternative' bands.[2] The line-up included the L.A.-based Red Hot Chili Peppers and the Seattle "grunge" bands Nirvana and Pearl Jam. At the time, the Red Hot Chili Peppers were huge, Nirvana was gaining momentum, and Pearl Jam was relatively unknown.

As reported in *Rolling Stone*, during Pearl Jam's set, Eddie Vedder, the lead singer, sang some lines from the punk rock band Fugazi's song "Suggestion" and then said to the crowd, "Don't go partying on anybody's pussy unless they want you to." The song was written by Ian MacKaye of Fugazi, and it is about rape. The lyrics put the singer in the position of a woman walking down the street. She, the voice behind the words, is expressing feelings of being both pissed off about and vulnerable to the threat of sexual violence.

Vedder's statement, "Don't party on anybody's pussy unless they want you to," was a direct reference to the Red Hot Chili Peppers' song "Party on Your Pussy." This was a straightforward counterstance or alternative to the Peppers' song. Vedder was telling the audience to pay attention to the desires of women. When he followed with the Fugazi song, which explicitly takes the subjective perspective of a woman, Vedder situated women in the position of sexual subject rather than as sexual objects of desire. His performance of "Suggestion" also explicitly tied ignoring women's desire or sexually objectifying women with sexual assault. Without saying one word about feminism, about sexism, or even about rape, Eddie Vedder managed to not only politicize the Red Hot Chili Peppers' song but also to remind the audience that women are people deserving of respect and that rape is a problem.

Despite sharing the same bill, and falling under the same rubric of "alternative music," Vedder implicitly distanced himself and his band Pearl Jam from the Red Hot Chili Peppers. Also, by following the reference to the Peppers' song with his own performance of "Suggestion," Vedder drew a connection between Pearl Jam and the edgier, musically less consumable Fugazi, who were already well known within rock circles as a socially conscious band that challenges social injustice. But unlike many socially conscious rock bands, Fugazi is known for explicitly rejecting and speaking out against sexism. While the music of Fugazi and Pearl Jam sounds different, through his performance, Eddie Vedder drew alliances, or at least a common thread, to Fugazi while putting up a boundary of difference between Pearl Jam and the Red Hot Chili Peppers. It struck me as such a completely different—or alternative—relationship to women than the one taken by most mainstream rock guys and so poignantly revealed in the comments made by Nikki Sixx of Motley Crüe.

I had just started listening to *Ten*, Pearl Jam's debut recording, when I read the review in *Rolling Stone* of Vedder's performance. When *Ten* came out, I remember a friend describing Pearl Jam as a "competent rock band." The more I listened, watched, and read, however, the more I began to realize that Pearl Jam was more than simply a competent rock band. Pearl Jam seemed to be doing things a little differently than other rock bands. The cover of *Ten* is a photo of several hands touching with one raising a finger to signify *one*. When you unfold the CD insert, the hands are revealed as those of all five members of the band leaning in, each with one hand raised and grasping the others. It strikes a stark contrast to the scantily clad women or gothic themes of power and violence that made up so much of the hard rock album-cover art of the 1980s. The recording itself starts and ends with the same haunting music and distant sort of moan. I had just read Susan McClary's theory of feminine musical forms as nonlinear, and I was enamored of the circular rather than linear form of *Ten*.[3]

What really caught my attention, however, was that Eddie Vedder was espousing antirape politics in concert. Remember, this was 1992, and glam metal had been the style of rock through the 1980s. Men in rock simply hadn't done such things; instead, they had talked about diving into pussy. I noticed that other all-male bands like Nirvana and Soundgarden were showing signs of what I identified as feminist leanings, that they seemed to be trying to buck the sexist world of mainstream rock.

Soon after reading about Pearl Jam, I was visiting a friend in

Chicago. When I'd visit we would often go dancing at some of the Chicago clubs that featured progressive dance music: the Smart Bar, Club 950, Exit, Circuits, or Avalon. On this particular Saturday night, we were at Avalon, a club with several different rooms in which different sorts of musical themes were featured. There was an acoustic room where one or two people played acoustic music; the live band area; and the dance area, where we tended to spend most of our time. I was in the dance area, probably dancing to "Melt with You" by Modern English, when my friend grabbed me and screamed over the music, "You have to come check out this band! You're going to flip your shit!"

Begrudgingly I gave up the chance to do those catatonic arm waves that are the only possible way to keep moving during the slow part of "Melt with You" and followed her into the live band area. The room was jammed with people who were spilling into the hall. As I walked in I was hit with a wall of sound that seemed to blow my hair back. There were four women on the stage, aggressively pounding out the hardest, loudest rock 'n' roll I'd ever heard. Everyone in the bar (myself included) was completely blown away. When they finished their set, the singer/guitarist jumped into the crowd to be passed along above people's heads. I leaned over to a man standing next to me and asked, "Do you know the name of this band?"

He responded, "They're a band out of L.A.— L7, or something like that. Fuckin' A, they rock." I noticed two T-shirts pinned to one of the amplifier stacks, apparently for sale. On one of the shirts was a photograph of a woman sitting in a chair, her legs spread and a man on all fours with his face in her crotch. *Smell the Magic*, the title of L7's first record, was written on the back of the second shirt. I suddenly thought about what I'd been reading about Nirvana, Pearl Jam, and Soundgarden; Fugazi came to mind. Could it be that feminism had finally arrived in rock music?"

At the time I was a graduate student in sociology at the University of Wisconsin, trying to develop a research project to finish my doctoral degree. As a budding sociologist, I was interested in how people resist or challenge the rules for appropriate masculinity and femininity in their everyday lives. I was particularly interested in theory and research that focused on everyday strategies used by people to challenge their subordinate status. In particular, I was thinking about James Scott's historical explorations of the ways in which members of socially subordinate groups engage in covert practices to sabotage or subvert the power others have over them.[4] I found the notion of everyday strategies of resistance from below intellectually and politically compelling. I was also reading theory and research in the field of cultural studies that focused on how women use popular culture. Angela McRobbie, Janice Radway, Andrea Press, Constance Penley, Julie D'Acci, John Fiske, and others were theorizing and researching how women actively construct meanings out of pop culture and their leisure activities in ways that resist traditional notions of femininity and masculine dominance. These theorists and researchers were talking about how women don't simply passively accept the dominant ideologies of popular culture, but appropriate the images by creating meanings that challenge male dominance, traditional expectations for femininity, and women's subordination.

As a sociologist, I became interested in trying to better understand how resistive understandings of or meanings for gender might take shape in and influence not just women's understandings of their activities but also their social lives as they interact with others. There is ongoing work in gender theory and gender research that focuses on the micro or everyday production of gender difference and inequality among and between women and men.[5] This growing body of work, exemplified by the work of Barrie Thorne, convincingly shows that gender difference and inequality not only shape the social world, but are also emergent features of social relations. Combining this conceptualization of gender with the notion that power and inequality are continuously resisted from below through both practice and meaning production, I became curious about the social processes by which the meanings and rules for gender get created and sustained in face-to-face interaction, and what role resistance from below might play in those sorts of negotiations. Rather than simply focus on the production of resistive meanings or covert practices of resistance from below, I thought it perhaps fruitful to explore the process by which people *interactively negotiate* the production of, maintenance of, and resistance to gender and sexuality as they go about their daily activities. Also, since most of the work in cultural studies at the time focused on the experiences of women and most of the work on everyday practices of resistance focused on subordinate groups, I began wondering about gender resistance in the everyday lives of men. I wondered if men adopted strategies to challenge the gender order, and if they did, how others, including both women and other men, responded to their strategies. That is, I became interested in everyday resistence to male dominance from above as well as from below.[6]

After experiencing L7 for the first time and reading reports of men like Eddie Vedder, I decided that rock music culture might be a good place to begin looking at how women and men use alternative understandings of gender to interactively negotiate the rules of gender. Rock 'n' roll has been one of the few cultural spaces in which men have crossed gender boundaries and not lost status by doing so. There had always been women knocking on the door demanding entrance into the boys club of rock, and it appeared now that a rejection of the sexism in rock was popping up all over. There was a very good chance that in "alternative" rock circles, there would be some face-to-face negotiations of these new antisexist approaches to rock music among and between women and men.

In the fall of 1992, I began an ethnographic study of a rock music subculture in Chicago. I spent two and a half years systematically researching the ways in which people in Chicago talked about, enacted, and negotiated gender and sexuality as they "did" rock music. Most of the research was done in Chicago's Wicker Park music scene. Because I was interested in how people negotiate the rules of gender as they interact with each other and do rock music, most of my time was spent hanging out with active participants in the Wicker Park scene, going to rock clubs, and watching the bands and the audiences.

I spent a lot of time at places like Lounge Ax, The Empty Bottle, Alice's, Phyllis's, Double Door, Avalon, and Cabaret Metro. With the exception of Cabaret Metro and perhaps Avalon, most of these venues were rather dark, dingy, small bars. When I began my research, Wicker Park was a low-rent area of town with largely Hispanic and African-American residents. By the end of my research, a tidal wave of gentrification had hit the neighborhoods with full force. Just five years later, Wicker Park had become Yuppieville with

an edge—a largely white neighborhood where hipsters with a lot
of cash, or hipster-wannabe yuppies live, and where people from
the suburbs go to get a "taste of the big city and alternative culture" by shopping in the boutiques, sipping coffee at an outdor café,
or going to rock shows at Double Door or the Empty Bottle.

I was introduced to the scene in 1992 by a close friend who
lived in Wicker Park at the time and who had become actively involved in the subculture. After some time of going to shows with
my friend, I began to develop independent relationships with other
people involved in the scene and to go to shows on my own.
Though the people in Wicker Park I grew to know spent a lot of
time in these small bars and clubs, the bars themselves were not
hangouts in any straightforward sense, and some of them were not
even in Wicker Park. Decisions about where to go on a typical
evening were determined by the bands playing at the different venues. This was largely because with different bands came different
kinds of music, different sorts of crowds, and different understandings about how to behave. If there were no desirable bands at any
of the usual haunts, people would generally do something like hang
out at someone's apartment and listen to music, see a movie, or
hit a local watering hole that did not feature live music. In other
words, the subculture was not so much attached to a particular location or bar, but was instead a loose friendship network consisting of people who shared similar tastes in music, similar styles, and
similar ideas about what was cool and what was not. Depending
on the kind of music and stage performances of the bands, there
would either be others there who shared their tastes and sensibilities or there would not. Not surprisingly, people would only go to
venues for bands and audiences they liked, and would avoid the
same venues when bands they didn't like were playing. I attended
a handful of shows (at the bars mentioned above) that the people
I was spending time with avoided. These shows were packed with
people, as others were; but with the exception of only a few over-
lapping people, these were different crowds.

For the most part, the people I spent time with were white,
from lower- to upper-middle-class backgrounds, in their mid-twenties
to early thirties, and identified as heterosexual. Exceptions were few
and far between. This was a very homogeneous group of people,

and for the most part they had lived relatively privileged lives in terms of economic and cultural resources. A fairly substantial percentage of the people I met or interviewed, for instance, had some college education. Despite their privileged background, however, most were service sector workers, aspiring musicians, artists, and actors, and thus likely among the ranks of the working poor. Their apartments were small, in disrepair, and inexpensive. The thrift store look was popular, and public transportation was how they got around. The increasing number of yuppies from the suburbs infiltrating the neighborhood was a constant topic of conversation and complaint.

On the nights when there was a band playing that people liked, a group of four or five people would gather at someone's house, listen to music for awhile, often smoke pot, and then head out to the club at around ten or eleven o'clock. There were usually two or three bands who played first, and then the last band played as the "headliner," or main attraction. The first band usually began around ten o'clock. Unless the point was to see the opening band, which was not uncommon because many of the people I was getting to know were in the bands that would get booked to open an evening, there was no real hurry to get to the bar before the second or third band started.

There was limited conversation while the bands played, yet before, between, and after, people would drink, smoke cigarettes, and talk. Once in awhile, after the bar closed, a small group of people might go to an all-night diner or restaurant. A typical night could last until two, three, or sometimes four o'clock in the morning.

On my way home, I recorded my observations on a portable tape recorder. The following morning (or afternoon, depending on what time I had gotten to bed), I relied on the tape recordings to write extensive fieldnotes on what I had experienced and observed. I also interviewed or informally talked with musicians from Chicago, but also from other cities (Seattle; Los Angeles; Minneapolis; Washington, D.C.; and Champaign, Illinois) who were in bands that appeared to be doing gender and/or sexuality in interesting ways and who seemed to have some importance in the lives of the active participants in the Chicago scene.

There were a variety of methods I would employ to gain access to these musicians. For some, especially the more popular bands from other cities, I contacted their managers and requested a formal interview. For others, I sometimes relied on local people who knew people in the band themselves or knew someone who did. For most, however, I simply approached musicians either before or after they played and asked if they'd be willing to talk with me for awhile about feminism and rock music. Especially in the smaller clubs, members of the bands would circulate among the audience when they were not playing, so it was not difficult to request an interview. For the most part, and sometimes to my surprise, people were more than willing to spend some time with me, and most—especially the men—seemed to be very interested in talking about gender and feminism. For instance, when I spoke with the assistant to Susan Silver, who was the manager of Soundgarden, she warned me to have my questions ready; she said that the band's lead guitarist, Kim Thayil, does not like interviews, would probably give me ten, maybe fifteen minutes, and that I shouldn't take it personally if he didn't say much. I went into the interview with my most important questions ready and prepared to cut to the chase. Much to my surprise, Thayil spent almost an hour and a half with me. He had a lot of very interesting things to say, and I never felt like I had trouble evoking responses.

About an hour into our discussion he leaned back and said, "This is probably the most words per minute that I've used in the past month or two. Weird."

I responded, "Well, I feel very fortunate. Caught you on a good day."

"Yeah, 'cause the only thing I've been doing is like 'yes,' 'yeah.'"

I asked, "Do people ask you about this stuff a lot?"

He smiled and said, "No. Maybe that's it. Maybe it's 'cause this issue is important to me."

There was an interesting gender difference, however, in musicians' receptiveness to talking about feminism. On a few occasions, women musicians became somewhat annoyed when I said I was interested in interviewing them about feminism and rock music. Many of them assumed that I wanted to talk about *women* in rock music. Jennifer Finch of L7 politely agreed to do an interview. As we were walking to the stage to find a place to sit and talk, she turned back to me and said, "Just so you know, we're not into the whole 'women in rock' thing. I hope you're not writing your paper on women in rock."

Kat Bjelland of Babes in Toyland informed me that she was tired of talking about feminism because in just about every interview she had ever done, the interviewer asked about feminism. I got similar responses from the women in 7 Year Bitch. It became clear to me that they were tired of making their gender the most salient feature of their careers as musicians. It also became clear that, at least in their eyes, most interviewers wanted to focus on their gender and because of their gender and the kind of music they play, assumed that they were feminist bands. Some of the women I interviewed identified as feminists and some did not. Each rejected the notion of being a member of a "feminist band" as such, yet every single one of them was also interested in undermining male dominance and sexism. Past interviewers, it seemed, tended to conflate being a woman, being in an all-woman band, identifying as a feminist, being in a feminist band, and being committed to subverting sexism and other forms of domination. As I will discuss in chapter 7, for these women few of these things neatly fit together, let alone all of them as a whole. They were tired, as women, of being lumped together, labeled, and dismissed. Despite their frustration, however, the vast majority of women I approached were willing to spend some time with me and were willing to talk about feminism.

Interestingly, several of the men I interviewed made comments similar to the one above made by Kim Thayil. They were almost excited to be able to talk about gender politics and feminism as it relates to their music. Even Ian MacKaye of Fugazi, a musician whose politics are often the focus of attention, never mentioned being tired of talking about gender and feminism and gave me a lot of his time. I found it interesting that the women, regardless of their politics, had often been asked if they were feminists, yet the men, some of whom were pretty vocal about gender inequality and sexism, had rarely been asked the same question. I concluded that the women were tired of people focusing on the fact that they were women and not on their music, while the men were happy for a chance to finally talk about something other than the music.

I tape-recorded most of the interviews. For the rest, I either took handwritten notes or, especially in the informal chats with local musicians, I recorded what we had discussed in my general fieldnotes. The fieldnotes and the interviews are the data upon which this book is based. As I spent more and more time with people in this subculture, all the while writing, reviewing, coding, and again reviewing the notes, fairly clear boundaries around the subculture emerged in the patterned ways in which people acted, interacted, dressed, rocked, the ways they talked about themselves, their friends, the music they like, and the way they played music. When I went to the shows that the people I got to know refused to attend, those boundaries became even more apparent. The differences helped me to identify what was important to these people, and most often, the difference was not in the sound of the music, but in the performance of the band and the behavior of the crowd.

The subcultural boundaries were established and maintained constantly as people interacted with each other before, during, and after these shows. Like most rock music subcultures, the boundaries revolved around the sound of the music, authenticity, and the integrity of bands. The sound was a hybrid of punk and hard rock. Through the use of bass, drum, and guitar syncopation, a sort of Black Sabbath power riff was sped up a notch or two and turned way up. The sorts of bands that musicians cited as important influences included both Black Sabbath and the Ramones. Women musicians also mentioned Patti Smith, Joan Jett, the Raincoats, and Siouxie and the Banshees. While the men talked about current women in rock, like those in L7 and Babes in Toyland, as having a big influence generally and especially on young women who aspire to be musicians, they did not usually mention female rock or punk pioneers as having an influence on their own aspirations or on the kind of music they played.

Authenticity and integrity were defined as they have been in rock culture since its beginning: one had to be doing something different or innovative, and had to be in it for the music, not the money—and certainly not celebrity. In Chicago at the time, this translated into rather bitter disputes over who was and who was not courting major record companies.[7]

The talk on the street and in the mainstream rock press was

that Chicago was the new Seattle. In the early nineties, Seattle had become a hotbed for new bands. Bands like Nirvana, Pearl Jam, Soundgarden, and Alice in Chains were just becoming popular in the mainstream. "Grunge," the term that pigeonholed these bands out of Washington, was steadily rising in its popularity and many Washington bands signed with major recording labels and eventually became huge. When I began my fieldwork, people in Chicago were still pretty excited about what was coming out of Washington and they adopted many aspects of Seattle style, sound, and sensibility. There was, however, already a feeling of "That's mainstream pop, sellout bullshit" among some of the people in Chicago, and there was a general concern over the Chicago scene being gobbled up by the mainstream media machine as—it was becoming increasingly clear—Seattle had. Smashing Pumpkins, a Chicago band, had just hit it big, and there was local buzz about Veruca Salt. In these ways, the subculture was a fairly straightforward rock subculture. There was a thread of similarity in the edgy, hard sound of the music, though most musicians continuously emphasized their differences, and there were genuine concerns about commercialization, selling out, and authenticity.

In the ongoing process of boundary construction, maintenance, and reconstruction, it became clear that the sound and distribution of the music mattered, but it was not the only factor involved in drawing these boundaries. Unlike most rock subcultures prior to the 1990s, the criteria for authenticity and the processes by which these people established and maintained these boundaries tended to revolve around gender. They were trying, like all rock 'n' rollers, to carve out a space of their own that was unique, looking for something that hadn't been done before. However, very much unlike rock genres or subcultures that preceded them, their point of departure was feminism. That is, there were a whole lot of women and men who consciously tried to create a place in the world where rock music did not mean "cock rock"—a place where women were taken seriously as fans and musicians; where men did not exclude, overtly sexually objectify, or otherwise mistreat women; where women did not play traditional parts in rock culture as groupies, teenyboppers, or girlfriends sitting on the side while their boyfriends rocked.

What was most interesting to me as a sociologist, and what I will describe in this book, was how they attempted to transform rock music by doing it differently. Taking quite seriously the cultural criticisms and ideologies of feminism, they consciously rejected the masculinist gender order of rock music and asserted an alternative. In a sort of ideological dialogue with mainstream rock and in face-to-face interaction at rock shows, they encouraged, manipulated, and in some cases forced others to go along with their new model for doing rock. In other words, they forged a new gender order for rock music as an alternative to mainstream rock within the everyday life of the rock club.

This is why I refer to this subculture as *alternative hard rock*. While there is much well-founded suspicion of the term *alternative* to describe rock music, I chose this label purposefully. I feel that *alternative* is a particularly useful word because it always refers to a relationship rather than simply a characteristic. It is a referent not only to the thing being described—for instance, a genre of music—but also points to what it is alternative to; that is, it points a finger at what is accepted, mainstream, dominant, hegemonic. In the past, when someone said that music was "alternative" it meant that it was different from the mainstream, an alternative to what was being served up by the media engine. However, when bands like Pearl Jam, Soundgarden, and REM hit the mainstream, the word lost its meaning. Suddenly, "alternative" referred to a rather nebulous characteristic rather than a relationship: "Alternative *to what?*" became the logical question. This music *was* the mainstream, not an alternative. The label became tiresome, cliché, oversimplistic, and completely meaningless.

Despite the mass marketing of "alternative" music into the pop culture mainstream and the proliferation of countless bands that bore that label, the bands I'm talking about really were alternative rockers—and in some really important ways. They were not alternative so much in terms of their hybrid of punk and hard rock, for that is a sound that eventually became mainstream. But what I will argue and demonstrate throughout this book is that, unlike the many "copy bands" who rode the mainstream wave of "alternative rock," the people I spent time with were on the ground floor of developing and proliferating an *alternatively gendered* rock and roll. Thus, the relationship that the term *alternative* connotes as I use it is not about a style or sound of music; it instead refers to the how these musicians "did" rock music differently from mainstream rock in terms of sexuality and gender. The common thread that runs through all of the bands I will be talking about and the subculture in Chicago is an alternative approach to doing gender and sexuality while doing hard rock.[8]

So you're asking yourself, "What's new here?" Women have been trying to set up spaces like this since Elvis first swiveled his hips, snarled his lips, and sent thousands of young teens (boys included—though we didn't talk about that) squealing and reeling and rocking. I know it. You know it. Countless researchers, culture critics, culture warriors, journalists and rockers themselves have discussed, documented, lamented, and cheered the righteous babes everywhere who don't sit on the side, who have sex with musicians but are not "passive objects" (who is, really, in sex?), and who rock just as well or better than the guys. Though the women I'll be talking about did all this and more, that's not really what's new here.

What's new is that a whole lot of people all over the country, including men, explicitly looked to feminism to develop a *new* genre of rock music. Rockers have, through the years, incorporated other forms of music such as country, soul, gospel, reggae, and so on; they have looked to literature and visual art; they have even adopted the politics of civil rights and socialist movements. But until the early 1990s, no group of rockers had ever seriously looked to and incorporated feminism as their point of departure from mainstream rock. Many individual women in rock, and a handful of notable men, have incorporated feminism into their music and performances, but until the early 1990s there had not been a collective proliferation of genre-defining styles, music, and practices that explicitly incorporated feminism. Of course, this genre was never defined as such in the mainstream press, even though some of the bands reached rock-star status. As happens with most cultural forms, by the time the bands hit the big time their subversive perspectives and resistive activities were ignored and the more marketable angles became the styles of their music, clothing, and performance that now define the genre.

In my effort to help put feminism on the rock map, I will be providing only a small slice of what was going on all over the place. I do not mean to suggest that it was only the bands and people in Chicago who were using feminism to create something new in hard rock. As many have noted, documented, and celebrated, "riot grrrl" bands and subcultures were straightforwardly informed by feminism and incorporated feminist ideals in their vision for punk and hard rock around the same time. I place the riot grrrl subculture under the rubric *alternative* as I've defined it, and as just one part of this cultural phenomenon in the early 1990s. But while it may well fall under the alternative umbrella as I've described it, I have chosen not to focus on the riot grrrl subculture for this project. In the last chapter I will briefly compare the ideological uses of feminism in riot grrrl subculture with that of the people I spent time with and argue that, in many ways, riot grrrls were more effective in challenging the gender order. But this is not a book about riot grrrls because, first, I was most interested in both women's *and* men's uses and negotiations of feminism, gender, and sexuality in face-to-face interaction. Although there were a few men who participated, riot grrrl subcultures were predominantly comprised of young women who, in some cases, went to some lengths to create an all-female space.[9] The second reason I have chose not to focus on the riot grrrl subculture is because I want to tell a story that was not told in the mainstream media about bands like Pearl Jam, Soundgarden, Nirvana, and Fugazi who, despite being all-male bands, publicly embraced feminism and feminist ideals. I was also interested in bands like L7 and 7 Year Bitch, who seemed to be challenging the gender order of mainstream rock but who also explicitly distanced themselves from the "riot grrrl" label and/or a more separatist sensibility. Finally, while I think that riot grrrl rock has a tremendous amount to teach us about sexuality, rock, punk, and transforming gender order, I feel that it could and should be a project unto itself. Fortunately, others have taken up this project and focused exclusively on riot grrrl culture in their own work.[10] My hope is that my project will put one more feminist point on the rock 'n' roll map, alongside the points plotted by those who have studied or written about riot grrrls.

What is also new in this book is my focus on the process by

which these people forged an alternative gender and sexual order for rock music. Rather than simply describe this subculture, I will discuss how the gender order of rock culture was negotiated within the everyday talk and activities of participants as they went about doing rock. As I mentioned in the preface, I call this process *gender maneuvering*. I will try to demonstrate how the overarching gender order of male dominance as an organizing feature of mainstream rock music is constantly being reproduced, challenged, and undermined as people do rock. I will show how challenges to and strategies for resistance to the gender and sexual organization of mainstream rock took shape as individuals alone or sometimes in groups maneuvered within the ongoing cultural practice of rock.

My overall point is that, in any social setting—not just in rock music—people can either go along with the rules for how to do gender or they can do gender in alternative ways. When people go along with the rules, the gender order remains safely in tact. When they don't follow the rules, or even better, make up a new set of rules, sometimes the gender order gets shaken up a bit. The comment by Nikki Sixx in his *Rolling Stone* interview and the performance given by Eddie Vedder are individual examples of gender maneuvering in the ongoing process that is rock culture. In alternative hard rock, however, gender maneuvering is not simply comprised of isolated, individual actions but is instead a strategy for developing an alternative, collective set of rules and meanings for gender and social relations in the context of rock music as well as a strategy for encouraging others to follow along.

In the chapters that follow I will provide many other examples that elaborate not only on gender maneuvering in alternative hard rock, but on gender maneuvering as a general process of social life. That is, I do not think that gender maneuvering was unique to this particular time or to rock music. I will suggest that the general strategy used by alternative hard rockers is used by people, all the time and in different settings. The actual rules and practices might look different depending on who, when, and where the strategies are being used, but the general social process is the same. I will suggest that while the strategies adopted by people in this subculture are specific to the realm of rock music, the process of maneuvering itself is not limited to rock culture, but is an important feature of social life more generally.[11] This means that the term *alternative*, as I use it, does not apply simply to a particular way of doing rock music, but to a way of doing gender more broadly. That is, when individuals or groups in any setting *gender maneuver*, they can potentially produce *alternative* gender and sexual relations. Throughout my discussion of alternative hard rock, then, I will try to make sense of their strategies of gender maneuvering as part of the negotiation of not only rock music but of the gender order more broadly.

So this is a book about rock music and gender. The story of feminism and rock outside of riot grrrl culture in the early 1990s needs to be told. My goal is not to tell the definitive story, but to encourage others, particularly historians and sociologists who are interested in the social history of rock, to include feminism when discussing the genres that spun off from punk and hard rock. Too often, feminism is denied as an important component to the social history of rock.[12] Before the early 1990s this was highly problematic. After the early 1990s, it is simply inaccurate.

My more central goals, however, are twofold. The first is to provide sociologists and other students of gender and sexuality with a useful framework with which to continue thinking about and empirically exploring the social lives of women and men. The second, and in many ways more important goal, is that this book gives people inside and outside of academia a new way to think about and do gender in their own lives. In telling the story of alternative hard rockers, my hope is that more people will consciously look to and develop their own strategies for negotiating gender and sexuality in face-to-face interaction—perhaps even getting some ideas from the pages of this book.

2

THE GENDER ORDER
OF MAINSTREAM
ROCK CULTURE

At about the age of eight, I developed a thing for major league baseball players. It started with Ken Henderson, a tall, blond outfielder
for the Chicago White Sox. Though I grew up in a northern suburb of Chicago—Cubs country—my family were Sox fans. My
father's family were from the northwest side, and working Irish
Catholics. The Comiskys, the original owners of the White Sox,
were Catholic; the Wrigleys, original owners of the Cubs, were Prot-
estant. I was raised a suburban Sox fan with two things that my
suburban friends didn't seem to have: a class consciousness and an
undying love for the Chicago White Sox.

I adored baseball. Everything about it. I loved to watch it, listen to it on the radio, play it. My father still talks about the time
he came home from work, and as he walked in the door, I ran up
to him, beaming and out of breath: "I can finally throw a screwball! I figured it out! I can throw a screwball!" We went into the
backyard, where, to his surprise, I threw him a few. Even with all
the things I have done since, my father still recalls this as the moment he was most proud of me.

And I loved the players. I had a thing for Bucky Dent before
he was traded to the Yankees. Alan Bannister, a scrappy infielder,
was my main crush for years. My crushes on players never seemed

to conflict with my love of playing the game and dreams of one day being the first woman to pitch for the major leagues. It was all mixed up in nebulous feelings of excitement, desire, ambition, and power. It was, quite simply, a passion.

Then, at about the age of fifteen, I discovered rock 'n' roll. I had always listened to pop and rock, but at the age of fifteen I discovered Steve Perry of Journey. Suddenly, men concealed in uniforms hitting and flagging fly balls seemed like children. Steve Perry was sexy—overtly sexual—and had the sort of voice that could make the hair on your arms stand on end. Before long, the drawings and newspaper photographs of baseball players that wallpapered my bedroom were replaced by rock posters, drawings, and album liners. Rock music was now my passion.

I, much like the stereotypical teenybopper, would sit in my room with Journey blasting in the headphones if my father was home, or in the speakers if he wasn't, staring at the pictures in the albums and feeling the first awakenings of lust: deep, exciting, and just a tad terrifying. After staring for awhile, I'd get up, strap on my air guitar, and be Steve Perry. I'd sing at the top of my lungs and strut across an imaginary stage in front of thousands of imaginary fans. My family still talks about the wailing and pounding that would come from upstairs every afternoon and evening. There was nothing that made me feel more powerful, more defiant than getting all worked up and being the rock star in my bedroom: the lust, the power, the defiance would all come pouring out in an embodied fit of rage and joy. When Veruca Salt released their first album in 1994, it was no mystery to me what their song "Seether" was about. Whatever their intentions in writing the song, I knew what they were talking about: I had lived the seether's emergence just about every night from the age of fifteen on.

It was sexual, and it was power. Unlike major league baseball, there were at least some women who had broken into the ranks of rock stardom, and I noticed that a lot of the men were pretty comfortable looking a lot like women. If they could come over to girlhood glam, why couldn't I take a stroll on the rebel side of rock 'n' roll boyhood? Perhaps the most appealing thing about it was that everybody else in my family hated it, especially my father. When I'd talked about marrying and being a ballplayer, he'd smiled with pride and pleasure. But when I started rocking, and the boys of summer were replaced by longhaired men in tight pants singing about fucking, a rift opened between my family and me. And at the age of fifteen, it was exactly what I needed. It was the perfect rebellion.

Since its beginnings in the 1950s, rock music has been about youthful rebellion.[1] It has consistently defined itself in opposition to mainstream, middle-class values, including hard work; conventional norms for dress, behavior, and aspirations; and especially to those who uphold these rules—most notably, adults.[2] Central to rock culture since its emergence has been a pointed opposition to sexual repression and restraint. In its rejection of 1950s middle-class rules and values, rock has always celebrated an explicit, audacious, unattached sexuality.

It was the overt sexuality in rock and its defiance that drew me in as an adolescent girl. Though—or perhaps because—I hadn't really been exposed to a whole lot of women rockers, I identified with the men, whose "fuck you/fuck me" attitude struck a chord. Their embodiment of this pulsing, pounding music made sense to me, and it gave me a refuge from the increasing pressure from peers, family, and harassing assholes on the street to rein in my maturing, girl body.

The overt sex and opposition to mainstream middle-class rules opened space in rock music for "gender-bending" through style, and in fact has been one of the few mass cultural spaces where men have been able to take a walk on the wild side. Beginning perhaps with the Beatles' and James Brown's then shockingly long hair, not to mention Little Richard's eyeliner, rockers have blurred gender boundaries in their appearances. For instance, hippie styles—which included long hair, headbands, army surplus jackets, and bell-bottoms for both women and men alike—very much blurred rigid gender distinctions and were inextricable from the rock 'n' roll styles of the time. In the late 1960s and early 1970s, "glitter rock" was defined by David Bowie's gender-bending makeup; sequined, tight-fitting clothing; scarves; and platform shoes as much as by the music. In the late 1970s and early 1980s, glitter rock was fused with Led Zeppelin's and Black Sabbath's heavy-metal sound to create "glam-metal." Bands like Motley Crüe, Warrant, Aerosmith, Poison, and others took gender-bending in rock style to an extreme and almost to the point of drag. They wore visible makeup like eyeliner, eye shadow, lipstick and mascara; meticulously styled, very large and long hairstyles; and an array of spandex, scarves, and high-heeled boots. Even the mainstream arena rockers, like Steve Perry, had long, flowing hair. (Incidentally, but not coincidentally, this was the part of Steve Perry's performance that I most eroticized. I loved the hair.)

Despite this proclivity for men dressing in drag; despite its sacred place in my own life and the lives of thousands of other girls as a release from the secluded tower of adolescent, feminine sexuality; and despite rockers' claims that it was oppositional to mainstream sexual values, rock music has always been steeped in hegemonic constructions of sexuality and gender. With few exceptions, rockers simply did it louder and with more attitude than others while shrouding themselves in the ostensibly countercultural stance of antirepression. As Michel Foucault has noted, mocking and flouting sexual repression is not necessarily an oppositional approach to sexuality.[3] According to Foucault, the Victorian sexual mores that rockers reject were not simply a clamping down on or repression of sexual expression, as conventional wisdom might suggest. Instead, it was a specific and active construction of sexuality through scientific and medical discourse. What we think of as "repression," or the control of sexual desire and expression, was actually an explicit proliferation and fixing of particular meanings for sexual desire, sexual practice, and sexual identity.[4] The suggestion that sexuality can be freed from repression and expressed without social constraint is based on the false assumption that there is an underlying sexual nature that is held in check by social mores or customs. Historical, anthropological, and sociological work in this area demonstrates how what we understand as sexuality is a product of socially derived sets of rules about sexual desire and practice that arise in specific sociocultural and historical contexts.[5] Social mores and customs don't hold sexuality in check; they actually create sexuality, including appropriate and inappropriate forms of sexual desire, sexual practice, and sexual identity. Because we can never escape or live outside of social relations, we can never be completely "free" from the socially defined requirements or imperatives of sexuality. People can and do deviate from those requirements, but their "deviant" practices are always understood and experienced within already existing, normative expectations.[6] While some practices, desires, and identities might be viewed as outside the norms, it is in fact the social norms and rules for what is legitimate and illegitimate that define the range of possibilities. Any sexual practice or identity, whether "normal" or "deviant," is still defined and understood within already existing, socially constructed meanings of sexuality, sexual desire, and sexual practice. In fact, deviance serves the function of providing a negative comparison against which appropriate practices can be understood and reinforced.[7]

For this reason, Foucault and others suggest that calling for a liberation of sexuality from the restraint of societal repression is simply to reproduce the dominant cultural construction of sexuality as an underlying, natural set of desires and practices that will spring forth if unfettered by social custom. It denies the ways in which what we think is natural and free (having sex with several partners, for instance) is actually a socially constructed and imposed (albeit as perhaps deviant) form of sexuality. This suggests that transforming sexuality will not happen by simply releasing it from social constraint and doing more of it or doing it more publicly, as rockers and many other culture outlaws have claimed. Instead, sexuality can only be transformed by reconstituting or recreating it through the proliferation of different ways of thinking about and doing sexual desire.

Rock 'n' roll rebellion, at least around sexuality, was not so much about reconstituting sexuality as it was about making dominant constructions of sexuality more public. This is particularly clear if one considers dominant rules for *gendered* and *heterosexual* desire. While rockers were "flipping the bird" to repression, they were fully and enthusiastically enacting and re-creating entrenched, normative expectations for sexual desire, practices and identities. So, at the same time that they put on makeup, had coiffured hair, and wore spandex and scarves, the men in rock incessantly talked about how many women they fucked on tour and put out countless videos and record jackets that took the objectification of women to an almost ridiculous extreme. In other words, these boys who dressed up like girls constantly and almost obsessively proved their masculinity by constructing their sexuality as predatory, exploitative, and, above all, heterosexual. In order to not cross the nebulous sexuality line along which all men in a heterosexist culture perilously tiptoe, these drag queens had to publicly embrace masculine and heterosexual dominance with a vengeance. As long as they enacted hegemonic masculinity, especially sexually, they could get away with blurring the gender lines in style. Their clothing played with gender while they enthusiastically and vigorously reproduced male dominant constructions of masculine and feminine sexuality in their music, stage performances, and talk.[8] Although they were feminine on the outside, there was no question that they were all masculine (as deliberately constructed for the public) on the inside. Despite the drag performance in style, through their vigilant enactment and reproduction of heterogender in their practices,[9] most rockers have, with little variation until relatively recently, put everything back in its gendered place.

In fact, far from being countercultural, rock culture more generally has relied upon and reproduced quite mainstream ideas about gender and sexuality. For instance, within popular music, rock music is defined through its difference and superiority to pop. Gender is central to the creation of this symbolic, hierarchical difference between rock and pop in that pop is constructed as the feminine complement to masculine rock. In her book *Gender Trouble: Feminism and the Subversion of Identity*,[10] Judith Butler borrows from Adrienne Rich and calls the contemporary, Western gender/sexual order a *heterosexual matrix*. For Butler, a gender order is first and foremost a symbolic structure or set of meanings about gender difference. According to Butler, the hegemonic gender order is built upon the belief that there are two genders—man and woman—each with a corresponding set of spiritual, psychological, and behavioral proclivities called *masculinity* and *femininity*. Within this symbolic order, the gender identities *man* and *woman* are mapped onto reproductive difference as male and female, and masculinity and femininity are assumed to be the externalized expression of the internal essence of maleness and femaleness. Masculinity and femininity are believed to be complementary or even oppositional with each biological sex, gender identity, and set of characteristics defined by its difference from the others.

Assumptions about gender difference do not simply get mapped onto people, but also onto various forms of cultural expression, including commercial music. Rock music is defined as "hard," "aggressive," and "sexual," while pop is "soft" and "romantic." These characterizations lay a fairly straightforward gender-meaning frame on commercial music. Pop is also constructed as the realm of love and romance, and rock as the realm of sex and rebellion. Rockers are constructed as "bad boys" more interested in unattached, sexual gratification, while pop artists embrace and celebrate rituals of heterosexual love, romance, and commitment. Pop's emphasis on romance, in contrast to rock's focus on sex, has lead to and justified pop's feminization.[11] In this way, the symbolic boundary between rock and pop relies upon and reproduces the boundary separating femininity and masculinity.

Pop has also been femininized and rock masculinized through the construction of skill and authenticity hierarchies. Rock ideology distinguishes rock musicians from pop musicians by asserting that the former generally have more musical skill than the latter.[12] According to this ideology, the pop singer is simply someone who performs and ultimately sells other people's material, while rockers write and perform their own music. For this reason, rock musicians are considered more "authentic" than pop artists, or as more interested in musical expression than commercial success. This, too, parallels the symbolic relationship between masculinity and femininity as outlined by Butler.

The symbolic meaning of gender difference includes not simply a relationship or matrix that binds masculinity with femininity but also presumes a hierarchy of value in which maleness is constructed as superior, more valuable, or better rewarded than femaleness. Any superficial examination of the relationship between masculinity and femininity reveals this: for instance, the label *girl* is commonly used by coaches, drill sergeants, and other men to insult or motivate boys or men to try harder. This only works because to be a girl is to be inferior. The hierarchy becomes clear when we try to reverse the insult by calling women or girls "men" or "boys." There is absolutely no context in which women call each other "men" or "boys" as a put-down or as incentive to try harder; it simply does not make sense as an insult or incentive to try harder because to be masculine is not deemed inferior. For the same reason, it is a much greater injury for a boy to be called "sissy" than for a girl to be called "tomboy." The boy loses status by being girlish while the girl either gains or maintains status by being boyish.

In the same way, feminization and inferiority are coupled in pop and contrasted with the masculine "superiority" of rock. Rock is deemed different from and better than pop because it is masculine, and rock is masculine because it is different from and superior to pop. It is significant and indicative of the parallels to the overarching gender order that a pop star, like the tomboy, does not lose status by crossing the line between rock and pop, while a rocker, like the sissy, does. As femininity connotes a loss of status, pop leanings also mean a loss of status. Bon Jovi, a band led by guitarist and singer Jon Bon Jovi, combines romantic lyrical content with a "harder" rock or heavy-metal sound. Because of the romantic content, Bon Jovi has been marginalized by most "real" rockers as a joke or as a commercial sellout.[13] Bon Jovi crosses the masculine rock/feminine pop boundary; thus, in the cultural reestablishing of that boundary, the band itself and those who really like its music are not considered to be "true rockers." The symbolic boundary created between rock and pop is the rubric by which all rockers and all pop stars, whether men or women, are judged. That is, a woman is masculinized by being a rocker, while a man is feminized by being a pop star.

This is not to say that there are neat content, skill, or authenticity lines that separate pop from rock in practice. Just as gender identity, reproductive anatomy, gender performance, sexual desire, and sexual practices do not neatly match up on one or another side of the gender binary in everyday life, there are, of course, rockers who are not skilled musicians, put romance in their songs and videos, and are certainly in it for the money. Likewise, there are pop stars who are skilled musicians, create their own music, and pay little attention to intimate relationships in their lyrical or video content. The masculine rock/feminine pop structure is a symbolic frame, not a clear marker of actual practices and performances. This symbolic border is created as people talk about and classify pop and rock music.

This hierarchical gender structure is not only the discursive frame that defines the differences between rock and pop, but also a frame for the meanings and expectations that distinguish different positions within mainstream rock. If we think of rock music as an institutionalized, cultural form—that is, as an enduring set of social positions and shared practices, beliefs, styles, and musical sounds that distinguish it from other music[14]—we can begin to look at the different components of rock and see if and how this gender order is manifested. For instance, we can look at the social positions that make up mainstream rock culture.[15] Many social positions within rock are gendered, and the relationship between positions often parallels the relationship between masculinity and femininity described by Butler. For instance, *rock musician* as a social identity is defined as one who plays or perhaps gets paid to play rock music.[16] By *social position*, I mean that the identity label *rock musician* is a set of behavioral expectations attached to a socially recognized position that has a specific relationship to other social positions. Among these expectations are those that define a sexual relationship to others.[17] The sexual complement to the rock musician is the groupie. Mainstream rock discourse constructs the identity label *groupie* as one who is sexually accessible to rock musicians, or someone with whom rock musicians have sex. If we look at the relationship between musician and groupie through the lens of gender, it becomes clear that the groupie is the feminine position that gives the identity label *musician* its masculine valence and status. Femininity is mapped onto and becomes indistinguishable from the social position *groupie*, including the gender identity *woman* and all the practices and characteristics associated with femininity, including making oneself physically desirable and available to men. Rock discourse constructs groupies as sexual objects, as the desirable bodies that rock musicians get to use or possess.

While groupies themselves do not experience their exploits as passive objects and in fact are very active and sometimes ingenious pursuers of the musicians, the point is that mainstream rock discourse constructs groupies as the feminine sexual object of masculine/musician subjective desire. This points to one of the many ways in which rock ideology, as partially structured by gender, masks or distorts the real practices of women and men in order to maintain the overarching gender order. Rock ideology constructs groupies as an exaggeration of the ideal feminine sexual object (nameless, face-less, and available for inconsequential fucking) to complement and make sense of the ideal, masculine sexual subject/musician. How-ever, in reality, groupies are women (and less commonly, men) act-ing on their own sexual desire for the musician. Because being a sexual object is inconsistent with masculinity, rock discourse must construct the groupie as the objectified reward for rock success, not the sexual subject acting on her own desire.

This functions precisely to maintain the hierarchy of value that characterizes a male-dominant gender order. With few exceptions, groupies do not have individual identities nor the public recogni-tion that musicians have. That groupies remain nameless, faceless, ideally sexually attractive women in rock discourse while the mu-sicians are constructed as acting subjects ideologically legitimates male dominant power relations—subjects act upon and control ob-jects. Rock discourse constructs the sexualized position of *musician* as desirable and high in status. No musician loses his place in any gender or rock hierarchy by doing his part in the musician/groupie relationship. In contrast, groupies are constructed as sexually pro-miscuous sluts and thus deserving of contempt, ridicule, or sexual exploitation.[18] Even on the rare occasion when musicians speak highly of groupies, there is always a snicker or implicit joke. As Pe-ter Lyman suggests,[19] the sexual snicker among men is as much about the serious business of differentiating and subordinating the feminine to the masculine as it is about humor.

Because *groupie* is constructed as anyone to whom a rock mu-sician might potentially gain sexual access, all women involved with rock music are potential groupies. For this reason, a symbolic gender line is drawn between rock fans as well, and thus contrasts and defines the groupie in her relationship to the "real" rock fan. To state the obvious, being a real fan means being interested in the musical skill and integrity of musicians. The position of the real fan is necessarily masculine in its difference from the feminine groupie or teenybopper who is more interested in developing real or imagined sexual/romantic relationships with the musicians. As a result and further perpetuation of gender coherence, women and girls have for the most part been relegated to groupie or teenybop-per statuses, respectively, while men and boys have been assumed to be either the real fans of rock music or, as discussed above, the musicians who take advantage of sexual access to women fans. The real fan collects music, acquires insider knowledge about the production and distribution of rock or about the musical roots of particular musicians, aspires to be a rock musician himself, and therefore plays guitar, drums, or bass. The teenybopper collects photographs of her favorite musicians, acquires knowledge about the personal characteristics, especially the relationship status of her favorite musicians, talks about how cute and sexy her favorite musicians are, and aspires to have a relationship with or marry— or simply to fuck in the more liberal post–sexual revolution rock world—a musician.

These gendered meanings attached to rock fandom, like the musician/groupie relationship, reflect and reproduce male dominance by constructing sexual attraction to musicians as inferior to musical appreciation.[20] Collapsing the identity label *groupie* into the identity label *woman* and defining groupies or teenyboppers as those who are only interested in the sexual or romantic attractiveness of musicians and unable to appreciate their musical talents casts women as less-than-serious, or inept, rock fans. The status of the groupie is considered inferior to that of the real fan, so the assumption that women are ultimately interested in the boys in the bands rather than the music sets up a gender hierarchy within rock audiences which places women below men.

Like other gendered social positions and practices, it is far more acceptable and common in rock music for individual women to embrace the masculine position than for men to occupy the feminine. An individual woman can escape the labels *groupie* or *teenybopper* and be an honorary member of the real fan ranks, but only by never expressing sexual desire for musicians and by being knowledgeable about music and musicians, even more so than the men, for she has to overcome the suspicion of being less than serious. She can also escape the groupie trap by being a highly skilled musician herself. However, even the women who were considered competent rockers, like Lita Ford, Pat Benatar, Chrissie Hynde of the Pretenders, or Ann and Nancy Wilson of Heart, were popular for their physical attractiveness as much as their musical skill, especially among adolescent boys. In other words, the masculine counterpart to the woman rocker is not just the man rocker; it is also the boy fan who is the desiring sexual subject in relation to the objectified woman in the video, on the poster, or on the stage. The only real exception to this was Janis Joplin, who more than any other woman rocker managed to remain outside hegemonic feminine sexuality as the object of masculine sexual desire. It is not a coincidence, and illustrative of how gender divides the position *musician* from feminine sexuality, that Joplin is the only woman rocker who is consistently considered a rock legend or genre-defining rock musician. In order for an individual woman to escape the subordinate, feminine position, she must either assume a masculine position—in the way she rocks, in how she comes to know and love the music, and in her desire—or reject conventional standards of feminine sexual attractiveness. The incompatibility of being both the rock musician and a sexually attractive woman suggests that the identity label *rock musician* has been ideologically tied to masculinity.

Finally, there is a hierarchical relationship set up between the rock musician and the real fan. Though both are superior to the groupie or teenybopper, the real fan can be thought of as a form of complicit masculinity as it is defined by R. W. Connell.[21] Connell suggests that the social organization of gender is not simply based on hierarchical distinctions made between masculinity and femininity, but also between different masculinities. He outlines four configurations of masculinity: (1) hegemonic masculinity; (2) subordinate masculinity; (3) complicit masculinity; and (4) marginalized masculinity. According to Connell, these are not character types for individuals, but instead constitute a normative or symbolic framework for evaluating the practices and characteristics of all men and women. Briefly, hegemonic masculinity is a set of practices that are defined as masculine and that work to maintain, reproduce, legitimate, and guarantee male dominance within any given gender order. In the world of rock culture, being a musician, having anonymous sex with countless women, and talking about it in public are some of the practices that constitute hegemonic masculinity. These practices are the specific cultural incarnations of broader requirements of hegemonic masculinity more generally—that is, sexual skill, experience, and boastfulness.

Subordinate masculinity consists of practices and characteristics deemed inferior in relation to hegemonic masculinity, and it is often likened to femininity. For example, men having sex with other men and identifying as gay are associated with subordinate masculinity. In the rock world, the pop star serves as an inferior, feminized point of comparison. There are also marginalized masculinities that circulate among men of subordinate racial or economic classes. The practices of men of color or who are economically disadvantaged are marginalized to maintain the dominant positions of socially privileged men. Marginal masculinities are not feminized, but they are still defined as marginal and therefore less desirable than hegemonic masculinity. I would place the practices associated with rap music under Connell's marginal masculinities in the world of popular music. Rap is in no way feminized like pop, but it is not at the center of the rock world. That all gangsta rap and some hip-hop is demonized as materialistic, misogynist, and violent despite (or perhaps because of) its popularity keeps rock in the center as the ideal form of popular music despite the rampant sexism and violence in rock lyrics, videos, and album-cover art.[22] Like hegemonic masculinity, complicit masculinity is also a set of practices and characteristics that uphold male dominance. However, complicit practices are those that support and/or do not denounce hegemonic practices, reap the benefits of masculine privilege, but are not on "the front lines." One of Connell's examples is the practice of watching football rather than being on the playing field. The real fan of rock music practices complicit masculinity by fully embracing and supporting the practices associated with being a rock musician, including "getting chicks." In many cases, rock fans aspire to climb the ranks in order to some day become rock musicians themselves precisely because they will have access to women. Like the armchair football fan, the rock fan never questions but celebrates and benefits from the entire gender structure of rock music by maintaining heterogender as the ideal form of masculinity. Also, by supporting and celebrating the practices of musicians, even if he does not engage in those practices himself, the rock fan reaps the benefits of masculinity—e.g. higher status in relation to women and girl fans. And like the armchair fan in relation to the football player, the rock fan is implicitly inferior or lower in the status hierarchy than the rock musician. Though constructed as parody, there was more than a hint of truth when the characters Wayne and Garth bowed down to worship Alice Cooper in the film *Wayne's World.*

Despite the inferiority of the real fan in relation to the rock musician, both positions are superior to their respective feminine counterparts, teenybopper and groupie.[23] Similarly, it is not coincident, but indicative of the overarching gender and sexual order described by Butler that the relationship between musicians and women is explicitly sexualized and the relationship between musicians and male fans is not. This reflects and reproduces the sexual complementarity of gender, which places the feminine in a relation of subordination while also maintaining heterosexuality as the normative center. By fusing sexual desire with masculinity and femininity, sexual desire becomes gendered and gender becomes sexualized. Sexual desire directed toward a feminine object is symbolically constructed as masculine desire. To be desired by the masculine is to be femininized. As Butler suggests, the gender order is implicitly heterosexual because it sexualizes masculinity and femininity as naturalized halves that together make a whole. This is why lesbian women are stereotyped as masculine and gay men are assumed to be feminine.[24] For homosexual desire to make sense within the gender order, one's gender orientation must be consistent with her sexual orientation, so the masculine is always paired with the feminine.

Heterosexism, or the construction of heterosexuality as the norm and homosexuality as marginal or deviant, depends on the gender order that naturalizes the pairing of masculine desire with feminine desire. Likewise, the gender order relies on heterosexism to stigmatize desire that conflicts with hegemonic constructions of gender.[25] Thus, in addition to a hierarchy that values men and masculinity, this construction of heterogender supports a hierarchy of sexual identities as well.

In contemporary Western societies, sexuality is constructed as consisting of two, complement/opposite sexual identities—heterosexual and homosexual. Because a heterosexual identity neatly reproduces the heterosexual matrix, or matching complementary genders, it is constructed as normal, desirable, and natural. A homosexual identity, in its difference from heterosexuality, is defined as deviant, undesirable, and unnatural.[26] Within rock culture, blurring the masculine position with the position of sexual object comes dangerously close to opening space for homoeroticism between men. This is particularly true in rock music, where some of the men are already dressing up like women. For similar reasons, while women can, with great effort, get themselves a place as real fans or as musicians by doing masculinity, there is absolutely no cultural space in rock for men to be groupies or teenyboppers. As a result, both masculine and heterosexual dominance simultaneously structure and are reproduced in the symbolic structure of rock music.

According to Butler, the meaning of gender does not simply remain in the realm of the symbolic, but manifests in the performance of gender. We thus not only internalize this structure for gender in our thinking, but act it out through gender performance. Because there are rigid and sometimes harsh sanctions for not performing gender appropriately, most of the time gender identity, biological sex, and gender performance more or less match up. Butler labels this the *myth of gender coherence*. The coherence among sexed bodies, gender identities, and gender performances is created through social processes that enforce the symbolic order. In an article published in 1993 in the feminist fanzine *Bitch: The Women's Rock News Letter with Bite*, Cheryl Cline cites Sheryl Garratt in order to warn women about the dangers of this symbolic structure and the position of the groupie. She writes,

> We might "all be groupies sometimes" but where women are concerned that's all too often meant literally, translating as we're really all sluts. It's best to keep in mind Sheryl Garratt's warning that "the term groupie is a dangerous one, for it is often used as a put down for any woman in the industry." Until the word "'groupie" has stopped being a short-hand term for women involved in Rock & Roll, and until its taken for granted that girl fans, women musicians, and female photographers, publicists, recording engineers and journalists come to Rock & Roll for the same reasons as their male counter-parts [sic], it's well to keep a sharp watch on how the word "groupie" is bandied about.[27]

Cline is suggesting that the significance of the label *groupie* does not remain in the realm of meaning. It translates into an unequal distribution of power, prestige, and resources along the lines of gender that is advantageous to men and disadvantageous to women.[28]

This happens not simply because people believe masculinity is superior to femininity, or even because individuals perform gender coherence, as Butler suggests. The material consequences result from the institutionalization of this symbolic structure in systems of power, prestige, and resource allocation and from how people relate to each other according to these positions in the concrete activities of social life.[29] In rock music culture, it is not simply the belief in this musician/groupie structure nor the individual performance of musician, groupie, or real fan that is of concern; it is the ways in which, by performing these gendered positions, people create relationships to real, particular others with real consequences, and importantly, continue to sustain the institutionalized structure of rock music culture that is built upon this hierarchical relationship between masculinity and femininity and among various masculinities.

According to sociologist Anthony Giddens, social systems, like gender, only exist to the extent that people continue to act out established or already existing patterns of activity. The process by which preexisting patterns of action shape social activity while the social activity itself further perpetuates these patterns is called, in Giddens's term, *structuration*. Giddens stresses how we as members of a society neither make up nor decide anew what to do in each situation; nor do we freely or autonomously choose how to interpret or understand our worlds. Instead, established and accepted patterns of activity and belief are passed from generation to generation and are continuously enforced through social interaction with others. All day and every day, our lives are shaped by these patterns at the same time we re-create them. These patterns include what we do, how we do it, and how we interpret our worlds. Once learned, the patterns are internalized to become a part of us, so our activities seem like personal preferences and choices; yet even though they feel autonomous, our actions are influenced by the already existing rules and, to the extent that we follow those rules, further create the social order.

The gender structure of rock music culture continues as people continue to do rock music in ways that reproduce these patterns.[30] For instance, the practices and behavioral expectations for rock

musicians, including on- and offstage performances, reflect and further create hegemonic requirements for gendered sexual desire
while they create rock culture itself. The rock musician must be
sexually active and, above all else, straight. This is enacted by male
rockers through an overt expression, both verbal and nonverbal,
of an aggressive sexual desire for women. For the few women who
made it as rockers, the requirement to be heterosexual often translates into being sexually desirable to men and limited their chances
to be taken seriously as rock musicians. As men rockers do sexual
desire and women rockers do sexual object, the gender order is created and sustained. Rock culture, then, is one contextually specific
form of gender structuration.

The gender order as a whole is created and maintained through
processes of gender structuration as they take shape in particular
contexts. By performing gender in the process of conducting our
lives, whether in a rock club, at work, or in our families, we continuously reproduce the symbolic meaning of gender and material
inequality along the lines of gender. Everyday practices, as they take
shape in specific social settings, are circumscribed by our ideas about
gender and preexisting patterns of inequality at the same time they
further create and support the symbolic meaning and material consequences of gender difference. As such, complementary social positions like father/mother, boss/secretary, and doctor/nurse are not
simply a set of symbols. They affect what kinds of work women
and men are hired and choose to do and how they do it. With male-
dominated occupations drawing, on average, higher wages, more
prestige, and more authority than female-dominated jobs,[31] the
gendered meaning of employment has very real and very serious
consequences in the material conditions of women's and men's
lives. At the same time, as women and men perform their work,
they do gender and thereby reinforce assumptions about gender.[32]
As we look around and see people engaging in work, because most
people simultaneously do gender we see sex, gender identity, and
gender performances neatly matching up; this then re-creates patterns of meaning for jobs as gendered. The gender structure of employment as social practice results from and reproduces a gendered
division of labor that allocates more power and resources to men
as a group than to women as a group.

There are few, if any, social contexts that are not shaped by gender and in which we are not expected to do gender at the same time we carry out other social activities,[33] including mainstream rock music. Though different from the kinds of doing in other kinds of work and leisure, the symbolic gender hierarchies created between pop and rock, musicians and groupies, real fans and teenyboppers, and musicians and rock fans are similarly constructed as people do and talk about rock music. Thus, mainstream rock culture is one specific part of the bigger picture of gender structuration that keeps the gender order in place.

Importantly, as Butler suggests, the gender order relies on not simply masculinity and femininity as social locations but on the relationship between or the matrix that connects masculinity and femininity. As people go about their daily activities, they do masculinity and they do femininity,[34] but they also do the relationship between masculinity and femininity. Doing rock music is masculine and superior only because people do pop, and the two are connected through discursive processes. The rock musician is the sexual subject only because other individuals collectively construct the identity label *groupie* as the feminine sexual object in their talk, their practices, or in visual imagery; the same is true for the relationships between real fan and teenybopper, rock musician and real fan, and so on. Though these differences are largely constructed through talk and visual imagery, it is precisely the relationship itself that legitimates and motivates others to reproduce the material inequalities that characterize rock. Male dominance, both symbolically and materially, can only be sustained as long as people keep reproducing gender.

I started this chapter discussing rock music as counterculture because of its rejection of repression. The whole groupie phenomenon, which is a defining feature of rock culture, is built upon the so-called rebellion against repression, but it is also one of the most conservative characteristics of rock in the sense that it keeps the gender and sexual orders in place. It not only reproduces, but champions, the status quo of compulsory and compulsive heterogender. Similarly, the use of explicit sex (which in reality means the use of women's scantily clad and sexually alluring bodies) in videos, album-cover art, or in lyrics accomplishes both the rejection of repression and the restructuration of hegemonic gender and sexuality. While framed often as a "liberation" from sexual repression, rockers' approach to sexuality is simply an exaggeration and public display of the already existing forms of sexuality, not an escape from them. Rather than proliferating different understandings and alternative ways of doing erotic desire and gender, these rockers reproduced the gender and sexual orders, both symbolically and materially.

The reproduction of this order, however, is not inevitable. Although preexisting patterns of beliefs and activities guide our actions, in his theory of structuration Giddens is careful not to disregard human agency. Because the social order exists only through human action, it is a constant process, not a fixed structure, and because human beings have agency and can reflect upon their activities, the dominant social order influences, but does not determine, what we do. This is why Giddens offers the concept of *structuration* as a necessary addition to sociological understandings of social life. Unlike the concept of *social structure*, which is a useful label for a snapshot of the already existing rules in any given context,[35] structuration refers to the dynamic process by which reflexive, thinking agents engage in everyday activities to not only produce order and predictability in daily life but also to negotiate and transform order. If the existing social order—which includes gender as a social system of patterned activities—is produced through a dynamic process enacted by thinking, reflexive agents, then the order itself can be manipulated through social action. For instance, ideological or political movements such as feminism, Christianity, or Marxism might question, reestablish, or transform the normative expectations for gender structuration. As people accept these or other ways of thinking about gender, they might begin doing gender differently. Also, as people start to change the way they do gender, new patterns might be established that would then necessitate a transformation in our thinking. Thus, structuration is not simply the reproduction of social order, but also refers to the process by which social order changes over time.

This suggests that new ways of thinking about gender—feminism, for instance—can impact how people think about and do rock music. As people begin to talk about and do rock culture differently, it is possible that gender structure, both symbolically and materially, might change. That is, through a process of alternative gender structuration, or developing patterns for doing gender in ways that do not reproduce the existing patterns, people can potentially impact the gender order. Further, if Butler is correct, and the gender order relies on the re-creation of the hierarchical relationship between masculinity and femininity, then manipulating that relationship through social action is one process by which the gender order of male dominance is maintained, undermined, or transformed. This active manipulation of the relationship between masculinities and femininities through social action is what I'm calling *gender maneuvering.*

Gender maneuvering refers to individual action or patterns of action developed by a group that manipulate the relationship between masculinity and femininity in ways that impact the larger process of gender structuration. That is, gender maneuvering is a process of negotiation in which the meanings and rules for gender get pushed, pulled, transformed, and reestablished. What the concept of gender maneuvering adds that the theories above do not address is how gender structuration—including the production, maintenance, and transformation of the meaning of gender difference, the relationships between genders, and power relations along the lines of gender—can be actively *negotiated* in face-to-face interactions and everyday practices. I am suggesting that not only are there preexisting symbolic meanings and rules for gender that shape and are produced through our activities and performances, as both Butler and Giddens suggest, but that the meanings and rules themselves are constantly volleyed back and forth as individuals and groups try to control the meaning of their activities, their relationships to others, and their place in power relations.

Because gender structuration is a constant feature of social life, gender maneuvering is possible in any social setting and can take many different forms of social activity, including but not limited to the production of mass culture, the development of subcultures, traditional political activism, or as a one-time maneuver in face-to-face interaction.

While maneuvering can take place in any social context, the form of the maneuvering will vary depending on the specific setting.

This will be so because gender takes different forms and the rules for gender performance vary by social context. That is, the rules for doing femininity and masculinity will be different in different institutional settings, such as going out with friends, being at a job interview, or nurturing children. Also, the expectations for doing masculinity and femininity vary by class, by race, by ethnicity, by sexuality, by age, by geographical location, and so on. The practices and rules for masculinity and femininity will vary by context, so the relationship between them will manifest differently depending on context. Because gender maneuvering refers to a negotiation of the process of structuration, it will always be contextually specific.

Thus, any analysis of or strategy for gender maneuvering must begin by identifying the established gender order within a particular setting. What is the institutional setting? Is the activity taking place at school, at home, at work, at a rock concert, at a hip-hop concert? What are the salient social identities of the people involved,[36] and what is the meaning of their relationships to each other? What are their races, their socioeconomic statuses, their genders, their ethnicities, their ages, their sexual identities, their jobs, and so on? All of these factors will impact the rules for gender performance and thus will be implicated in any attempts to manipulate the rules through social action.

I wish to further elaborate the concept of gender maneuvering by way of example. In the following chapters, I will detail the ways in which alternative hard rockers gender maneuver to transform the gender order of mainstream rock culture by transforming the meanings attached to the identity labels *rock musician, groupie, real fan,* and *teenybopper,* and redefine the rules for doing rock music culture. As the meanings for these positions have changed, the relationship between them has shifted. As the meanings for and relationships between the positions are manipulated, the hierarchical, binary relationship between masculinity and femininity has been transformed, and power relations between and among women and men have shifted. The key here is that, unlike during my private rebellion in an adolescent bedroom, these people have acted publicly and collectively.

When I was in high school I wasn't aware of other girls or boys around me who were interested in the sexual rebellion in rock, so I would go up in my room by myself and be the rocker in my own head. Though I was using the raw materials of rather sexist, some-times misogynist rock 'n' roll, I constructed a place where I felt pow-erful, and a way to have fun. My pleasure lay in the feelings in my body and the meanings I constructed out of those feelings. And I suppose that on some level putting on the headphones but still singing about fucking at the top of my lungs so that everybody in my family could hear was resistance from below. But I stayed in my bedroom. It was important in my life, and I think central to developing a rebellious sexuality, but it was my own experience. My pleasure and my resistance from below did little, or perhaps nothing, to change the oppressive gender order of my family, let alone anything outside my suburban home. Alternative hard rock-ers, in contrast, took it public. In the ongoing process of rock cul-ture as social life, they worked together, rather than in isolation, to hold on to what they thought was good in rock—the music, the social rebellion—and to throw out the sexism in order to create something new.

3

THIS IS ALTERNATIVE HARD ROCK
Rock Culture as Gender Maneuvering

In this chapter, I will begin to describe how alternative hard rockers take mainstream rock culture and twist, pull, and push it to create a different set of rules for doing and thinking about rock and being a rocker, a process I call *cultural gender maneuvering*. Cultural gender maneuvering refers to efforts to manipulate the relationship between masculinity and femininity as it takes shape in rules for and the general patterns of social relations within any culturally specific milieu. Stuart Hall defines culture as an enduring set of commonly held beliefs and practices that define or draw boundaries around a group.[1] Included in some patterns of beliefs and practices are rules for doing and thinking about gender. These rules, as part of doing a specific culture, often set up and reflect the heterosexual matrix or the hierarchical, binary relationship between masculinity and femininity. As described in chapter 2, mainstream rock is one example of a culture that is constructed partially around and by gender.

The gender maneuvering I will describe in this chapter is a collective effort by alternative hard rockers to draw cultural boundaries between themselves as a group and other rockers. They do this by proliferating alternative rules for how to do and think about being a musician, a groupie, and a fan so that a straightforward gender hierarchy no longer operates or makes sense. By manipulating the meanings and practices associated with these rock identities, alternative hard rockers can disrupt the relationship between masculinity and femininity. As they manipulate the relationship between masculinity and femininity, in some ways they also disrupt male dominant power relations within the localized setting of the rock show.

In order to fully describe cultural gender maneuvering and its implications for alternative hard rock and for gender relations more generally, I will take you through a typical evening in Chicago as alternative hard rockers do their thing. My focus will be on how they enact and talk about gender as they go about their normal, daily life at the rock show. The one evening I describe here is not a description of a real sequence of events over the real time of one evening. Instead it is a conglomeration of experiences and observations that happened over the two and a half years I spent in the subculture. While I will focus closely on a handful of people, the talk and activities of these people are typical for alternative hard rockers. As I take you through the evening and describe the activities of some of the participants I came to know very well, I will weave other observations and the perspectives of others, including the musicians I interviewed who were from out of town, into the narrative by presenting them as recollections from the past. As I do so, I hope to provide a vivid picture of the subculture while also highlighting the broader theoretical and political importance of what alternative hard rockers do.

Would you like to Go to the Rock Show? Well, climb on in and let's go . . .

It's an exceptionally warm June night on Chicago's near west side. Blaring from Maddie's car speakers is Donita Sparks of the band L7; she's as much howling as she is singing the story of a young woman by the name of Everglade being bullied at a rock show by "some drunk, stupid loser." A cigarette dangles from Maddie's lips as she tries to maintain control of the car, which is turning just a little too quickly onto Western Avenue, while adjusting the volume on the stereo. Veering into another lane and almost sideswiping the car next to her, Maddie responds to the other driver's horn with a quiet yet defensive "fuck you." She then looks over at me and laughs.

Maddie is an interesting combination of girly-girl and badass. She stands about five feet tall, has short, spiked, bleach-blond hair, and will take on any man or woman in a bar who crosses her. I've seen her aggressively stand off with men twice her size and get her way. Most of the time however, she is very friendly, smiles and laughs easily, and can, when she wants to, strike up an amiable conversation with anybody. Maddie, like most of the alternative hard rockers I came into contact with, is white and grew up in a middle-class family setting. And like most alternative hard rockers I spoke with, she describes her adolescence in terms of not fitting in. According to Maddie, she was just too assertive and strong. The popular girls and boys just didn't accept that she wouldn't "take any shit from anybody"; it was not until high school that she found others who accepted her for who she was. By Maddie's account, the kids who accepted her were those listening to both Black Sabbath *and* the Sex Pistols, smoking cigarettes, and experimenting with drugs. Since she has moved from the suburbs to the city, she has worked several different jobs, most of which involving bartending and restaurant service.

We pass The Empty Bottle on our right. The Empty Bottle is a local rock club that serves up strong, cheap drinks and features both local and touring bands for relatively low cover charges. It's one of the places that Maddie and other active participants in the alternative rock scene frequent. However, tonight Veruca Salt, a local band who made it big, is playing to a sold-out crowd. Maddie looks at the people waiting outside to get in and grimaces.

"What a nightmare. Can you imagine being in there? It's probably packed and full of 708ers."

"Seven-oh-eighters?" I ask.

"People from the suburbs. The area code.[2] All those assholes who wouldn't be caught dead in this neighborhood three years ago, but now 'cause Wicker Park is the hip spot, they flock here. Especially for, like, Veruca Salt. Fucking MTV."

As Maddie continues north on Western Avenue and sings along with Donita Sparks, I recall previous conversations I have had with Maddie and others about Veruca Salt.

Not much more than a year earlier Bryan, another alternative hard rocker, was talking about a band called Veruca Salt, supposedly the next big thing out of Wicker Park.

"They're supposed to be pretty good," he said. "I haven't seen 'em, but I guess they're the buzz." (By "the buzz," Bryan meant the hottest local band around.)

"What are they like?" I asked.

"Oh, another chick band." He laughed and continued, "No, I guess there's two women who are pretty good. I've heard they're pretty heavy." ("Heavy" means, among other things, that their sound is loud and aggressive.)

Bryan continued, "I don't really know; I haven't seen 'em. I've heard they're worth checking out, though."

A few months later, Veruca Salt was getting a lot of airplay on the local progressive-rock radio station, Q101. I had seen them once before and really enjoyed the show so, at the time, I told Maddie about it. She said that she really loved the song they were playing on the radio and would like to go to one of their shows.

It wasn't long after that that Veruca Salt hit it big. They secured a spot in MTV's regular rotation with their video for the song "Seether" and were getting written up in the national rock press. With this national attention, the sentiment among those I was spending time with in Chicago changed. I couldn't find anybody who liked Veruca Salt. One night, I was with some of the people in the local scene sitting around Bryan's apartment when the topic of Veruca Salt came up.

Colleen said, "I saw them a long time ago and hated them. It was like someone had taken a string of barbed wire, ran it through one ear and out the other and ripped it back and forth." Colleen demonstrated with an agonizing grimace.

Carrie chimed in, "I never liked Veruca Salt. I never liked Smashing Pumpkins [another local band that made it big]. They're all a bunch of sellouts."

Curious about this shift in sentiment I asked, "What do you mean? What don't you like about them?"

Carrie responded, "Well first, I never liked the music. There's a certain type of band that makes it big, and I tend not to like them. They have a sound that appeals to teenagers. And when good bands make it big they change. They start putting out crap because it has to appeal to yuppies from the suburbs. They cop an attitude like they're better than everybody else. They just become assholes putting out shitty music."

Even though I had heard people's "buzz" about Veruca Salt not three or four months earlier, everybody at Bryan's that night situated themselves as different from those who liked Veruca Salt. The sound of the music hadn't changed; the audience had. Veruca Salt was now part of the mainstream—a rock band doing things to appeal to the masses—and these people would have no part of it. This was a typical rock 'n' roll move: drawing lines between "real" and "inauthentic" fans. Alternative hard rockers hold on to mainstream rock's heavy dose of skepticism toward commercialism and associate poor taste in music with outsiders like "teenagers" and "yuppies from the suburbs." However, in these conversations, the inauthentic fans are "708ers," "yuppies from the suburbs," and "teenagers." Unlike the labels *teenybopper* and *groupie*, there is no gender valence to these terms, but instead geographical and age distinctions. Immaturity and class privilege mark the inept fan, not gender.

So tonight, as Maddie and I pass The Empty Bottle, she is disgusted by the crowd of "708ers." Ironically, she is excited to be heading for Lounge Ax, another local club, to see the Wesley Willis Fiasco, the band that is, on this particular June evening, the buzz in Chicago and Maddie's favorite band.

Because Lounge Ax is on Lincoln Avenue, which has become a hotbed for all types of nightspots, it is always difficult to find parking nearby on a Saturday night. After a few tries, Maddie finally scores a parking spot just a block and a half from Lounge Ax. As we walk along the street toward the bar, a group of three men in their mid- to late twenties approach us on the sidewalk heading the opposite direction. As we pass, none of them step aside, and Maddie sort of plows through, not yielding any ground. One of the men turns and says, "Fucking dyke."

"Fucking asshole 708ers," Maddie says loudly.

I look back as the men disappear into the sports bar on the corner. Maddie also looks back and says, "Now *there's* a big surprise. I never would have guessed they'd be going in there. Assholes."

We both laugh and step into the darkness of Lounge Ax. The doorman collects the cover charge and we make our way into the bar. The volume of the jukebox is, if not at full tilt, damn close, so that the chatter of patrons and Alice in Chains' "Man in a Box" is a well-blended cacophony. A haze of cigarette smoke hangs in the air, yet still doesn't overpower the stale smell of alcohol that has seeped into the wood of the huge bar and the fabric of the sofas that line the wall.

The minute we have stepped in, there is a different feeling from that of the outside world. Maddie's tight, black halter top, cut-off jeans, and engineer boots no longer seem out of place, nor do they draw attention as they had on the street. They don't draw stares because most of the women are dressed a lot like Maddie and would probably draw attention on the street themselves. As we move through the crowd, people for the most part move out of our way; there is no real need for Maddie to plow through anybody here.

Maddie notices Carrie and Nancy sitting at the bar, so we make our way over to them. Carrie says, "Hello you trashy little slut," as she kisses Maddie firmly on the lips. Women in this subculture often use the word *slut* to refer to themselves and to each other. For all women, *slut* is a derogatory label hurled at them when they step out of the bounds of hegemonic femininity by expressing or acting on an overt sexual subjectivity. The label *slut* is fused with the label *groupie* in rock culture. Like other derogatory labels reclaimed by marginalized groups, *slut* has become a mark of solidarity among female alternative hard rockers. Men on the scene, on the other hand, do not refer to women as sluts, at least not in their presence. Like most reclaimed labels, *slut* would take on a completely different meaning when used by someone who is not a member of the marginalized group—in this case, men.

Not just using the label, but also *doing* slut is a central part of this subculture. Overtly expressing sexual desire, talking about sex, and wearing sexual promiscuity as a badge of honor is the way to do alternative hard-rock femininity.

In response to the "trashy slut" comment, Maddie compliments Carrie on her outfit, which is a brightly colored, 1950s-style dress shortened and modified to reveal a lot of skin. Carrie is extremely gregarious and flirts with everybody, men and women alike. She, unlike most of the others, is in her early thirties and has lived in Wicker Park all of her life. In one conversation with her, she articulated the problem with "708ers." I had revealed to her that I had grown up in Northbrook, an upper-middle-class suburb of Chicago.

"Oh, you're from Northbrook," she said. "I know people from Northbrook, or at least that type. That kind of upbringing. I grew up right down the street from here, and to tell you the truth, I really resent people from Northbrook and from the suburbs. Sorry, but that's how I feel."

Feeling like she had just found out that I kill puppies, I quickly said, "You don't have to apologize. I know exactly what you mean."

"You know all those fucks are moving down here because it's like this hip place to live now. Did you know they're putting up a Starbuck's right across the street so the yuppies can get a cup of coffee before they get on the train? The yuppies from the suburbs move in and all my friends have to move out. The rent goes up and people can't afford to live here anymore. I'll be walking down the street and three or four guys from the suburbs go walking by and they're like, 'Freak!' Fuck you, man. If you don't like it, get the fuck out of here. This is what it's all about. It never used to happen."

"Does it happen often?"

"Too often. To all my friends, too. I'm more afraid in the suburbs than in the city. If someone's going to kill me here, they'll just shoot me or stab me. If someone wants to kill you in the suburbs, they chop you up into little pieces and weird shit like that. I hate the fucking suburbs."

Quietly, but knowing exactly what she meant, I agreed, "Me too."

Nancy, on the other hand, is far more soft-spoken and simply says hello to Maddie and me. She is dressed unlike the other women, but as always she is in a very loose-fitting T-shirt, baggy jeans, and motorcycle boots. She wears thick, plastic-framed glasses and sports a chain that runs from one belt-loop of her jeans into her back pocket to her bulky, leather wallet. When I first met her, I immediately assumed that she was a lesbian, which says as much about my own gender lens as it does the consistency of women's styles in the subculture. She is extremely shy and sweet, although at first she comes across as aloof and very tough. Nancy is in her mid-twenties and works at a local coffee shop. Her story is that she was raised by a single mother in the south and moved to Chicago in hopes of finding people with whom she could fit in.

As usual at these shows, the crowd is very gender segregated. Men are for the most part chatting with other men and women are with other women. Once in awhile an individual man will approach a pair or group of women, chat for a few minutes and then walk away. Less often, a woman will approach a pair or group of men. There are a man and woman clearly together standing close to the stage. He has his arm around her shoulder and she is leaning into him. Based on their clothing—he in a short-sleeved, oxford, button-down shirt and khaki shorts and she in a tank top, miniskirt, and white "flats"—I immediately assume they have wandered in and are not part of the alternative rock scene. It's not surprising that they are the only people in the bar that are clearly "coupled." For the most part, the rock show serves as an opportunity for women to spend time with other women and for men to hang out with other men. It is rare to see heterosexual couples together, and even more unusual to see what participants call "scamming" or "schmoozing"—men overtly hitting on women.

Maddie asks Carrie to get the bartender's attention so she can order a drink. Carrie, a bartender herself and friend of the man tending bar tonight, leans forward, snaps her fingers and shouts "Honey! Honey! Could we please have some service down here?" The bartender, along with Carrie and the rest of us, laughs and comes over immediately. It is common for women to exaggerate in order to mock the practices of hegemonic masculinity. By exaggerating taken-for-granted masculine mannerisms or behaviors, women expose the sexism embedded in the practices and make them ridiculous. I have never heard Carrie explicitly talk about her experiences of sexual harassment or degradation as a bartender, but she has never missed an opportunity to expose sexist behavior through her actions or her telling of a story.

As with all Wesley Willis Fiasco shows, the opening act is Wesley Willis himself playing keyboards and singing a few of his songs alone. As he begins, some people move up toward the stage to watch and listen.

When Willis finishes his solo set, Motorhome, another local band, begins to set up their equipment. Maddie and I decide to hit the bathroom before the next band starts. We descend the long stairway into the basement and are relieved to find that there are only two women ahead of us in line. While waiting, we silently read the graffiti on the walls.

INCITEARIOT

Please stop
being helpless
Now we have the
Opportunity
to take what is
OURS
Let's not shy away from it
Let us
embrace
that is which
fully ours
we can
finally
be
WOMAN

Next to this:

Thank you girlfriend

First and foremost love what you have been born with

RESPECT

I'm a slut so what

Next to this:

me too

more power to you sister

Mamma
Pick up an instrument
What do you have to lose

It strikes me that there are no hearts with initials in them, no promises of love lasting forever, no disparaging remarks about a man who did some woman wrong. The emphasis is on action, empowerment, and solidarity. The focus is on women, not men.

I notice Maddie also reading the walls with a slight smile of satisfaction. "I haven't written on bathroom walls since high school. I wish I wrote this shit then. Shit, I wish *anybody* wrote this shit then."

I respond, "I know. I wonder why girls don't come up with this in high school."

"Because you're stupid in high school. All you want to do is fit in. I betcha girls in high school now are writing this shit. All the little alternative kids aren't as stupid as we were. Can't you just see a little riot grrrl writing this shit on the walls?"

Once I get the image in my head, the corners of my mouth curl up in a grin, and I wonder if perhaps this *is* happening outside these rock clubs.

When we climb the stairs, Motorhome is churning out a melodic, hard guitar riff while the only man in the band sings, "I'm just a little man." The drummer has bleached-blond, extremely short hair and the bassist is sporting a T-shirt with the mud-flap decal of the seated, busty silhouette of a woman made famous by the film *Thelma and Louise*. Upon closer inspection I see that it is a 7 Year Bitch band t-shirt.

As Motorhome continues their set, more people move up toward the front of the stage and many of them are moving their bodies to the music. This isn't really anything like what you would call dancing. They are head-banging, which is vigorously throwing or slightly bobbing the head back and forth. Some are gyrating their hips, slapping their thighs, pretending to play an imaginary guitar, an "air guitar." It doesn't look like dancing because, in an effort to respect the space of those around them, they keep their feet relatively still and in place. There are a few women who are doing something that looks more like dancing, but for the most part the crowd moves as they usually do for an opening band—very little.

I move toward the front of the bar and sit next to Bryan on one of the sofas that line the wall. Bryan stands about five feet, seven inches tall and has a medium build. His head is shaved completely and he sports a goatee. He, too, is from a middle-class family;

he lives in Wicker Park, and works at a local record distributing company. It's not exactly clear what he does there because he doesn't like his job, finds it boring, and would prefer not to talk about it. He's also a musician and plays with a local band. The talk on the street and in the local rock press is that his band will probably be signed with a major record company. He is a little shy at first, though once he's comfortable he is hilariously funny and will entertain a room full of people with his visual humor, repertoire of cartoon sounds, and wit. The first thing I noticed about Bryan when I met him was that he laughed with equal enthusiasm at women's jokes as he did at men's.

Right now he is engrossed in a conversation with a woman I don't recognize. When I sit, he introduces me and then continues with the conversation. After a few minutes she gets up and walks away. Bryan informs me that she is someone he "went out with" in high school and hasn't seen in awhile.

"She's so cool, man. She was always one of those people who was like super nice and totally cool. She's a great musician too. I guess the band she's in now is going on tour soon. I've heard they're really good. She could kick my ass in high school."

There is this thing in alternative hard rock about women being able to "kick ass"—especially a man's ass. Even in stories that would make the storyteller seem weak or vulnerable, men still paint a picture of women as physically powerful. During one discussion of high school, one man told a group of four others how he had been harassed by a group of girls.

"It was my first day of school, and I was really fuckin' scared. You know I'd come from a really small town to this huge school and all the kids seemed really tough. So I'm walking down the hall and these three, huge, tough girls come walking by. One of them says, 'Oh baby, I'm gonna fuck your brains out!' Man, that sucked."

Unlike most stories told by alternative hard rockers, this was not meant to be funny. Everybody sort of shook their heads and sighed. While most were probably identifying with the alienation and insecurities of high school, that this man was willing to re-veal not only physical but also sexual vulnerability to girls is illustrative of this subcultural construction of girls as powerful. Bryan's friend from high school was one of those powerful girls who could kick his ass. There is no doubt in the way he speaks about her that he has nothing but respect for her.

Motorhome finishes their set, and the song "Back in Black" by ACDC fills the bar. Bryan stands and breaks into an exaggerated air-guitar riff, straddling his legs and bending backwards. He stops, and we both laugh. Although he is making fun of someone who would take air guitar seriously, it's clear that he is using mockery as an excuse to do it himself.

Jim, another participant, steps up and says hello. He is about five feet, ten inches tall, very thin, and sports moppy, longish dirty-blond hair. Jim is usually very friendly, though he comes across as a bit of an airhead.

The first time I met Jim I was standing with a group of four people, including Bryan. Jim walked up behind Bryan, whispered something in his ear, and Bryan immediately introduced us. My guess, given Bryan's spontaneous introduction, is that Jim asked who I was, or wanted to be introduced. Once introduced, he joined the conversation.

Jim's decision to go through Bryan rather than approach me directly was not out of any lack of confidence or shyness. As I suggested earlier, there is an understanding among alternative hard rockers that schmoozing women is sexist, intrusive, and therefore obnoxious. Because of these subcultural norms, there is almost a hyperawareness of men approaching women they do not know in order to strike up a conversation. In order to get around this, getting to know people is accomplished by going through friendship networks. While going through friends is still often about gaining access to women, the norm against schmoozing leaves women relatively free from being harassed by strangers in the bar.

Jim and Bryan are in the same band, and from what Bryan has told me, Jim's sheepish, airhead persona is an act "to get chicks." Bryan says this because when Jim is around women who are not part of this scene he is not sheepish, and aggressively schmoozes them. Despite Jim's "double personality," as others called it, it is a testament to the subcultural norms that he adopts this mode of interaction to be appealing to women in alternative hard rock.

Not long after I met Jim, I was waiting to see Bryan's band and talking with Maddie and Bryan. At one point, Maddie nudged me and said, "Check it out."

Jim was talking with a woman I did not recognize. She looked rather young, and though dressed in pretty convincing "power-slut" wear, she appeared unsure of herself. Jim was very close to her and doing most of the talking. After a few minutes, the woman walked away, rolling her eyes and shaking her head.

Maddie smiled and said, "If you schmooze, you lose. He's such an asshole sometimes."

To demonstrate his disappointment in Jim or perhaps in his gender, but to distance himself nonetheless, Bryan added, "Oh, I know. Jim can be such an asshole sometimes. It's embarrassing to be with him in public. He totally schmoozes chicks and the way he does it is so fucking obnoxious.

This was news to me, so I asked, "What does he do?"

"Some woman will walk by, and he'll like step in front of her." Bryan mimicked Jim's behavior by getting really close to me, held out his hand, smiled broadly, and said, "Hi, You're cute!"

A little surprised, I responded, "No way!"

"All the fucking time. I just walk away and pretend I don't know him. God, and it works sometimes. I can't believe some women go for that shit. It just makes him do it more. You know, if it works once, he'll keep doing it."

Bryan and others often use stories about Jim to reestablish the norms against schmoozing. However, as Jim approaches us, Bryan acts as if they are the best of friends. Jack, a third member of their band, joins the group. I have heard that Jack has a mean temper when he drinks and has been in several fights. There is some concern that he is physically violent with his girlfriend. Despite their commitment to not reproducing the sexism of mainstream rock, other participants didn't seem to have a way to really talk about Jack's interpersonal violence and Jim's sexual exploits. They simply said, "He's such an asshole sometimes" and left it at that. Or worse, they would say something about how Jack's girlfriend fights back, or how the women Jim schmoozes fall for it. These things were always said in a way to imply the women were at least partially responsible for reproducing these kind of sexist, interpersonal relations. According to the others it was a problem, but an individual, at best interpersonal, problem. This points to one of the weaknesses of alternative hard rockers' overall strategy for countering sexism. As I will discuss in detail in the chapter 7, alternative hard rockers define their politics for the most part in terms of individual, gender display. This leaves little room for thinking about gender in terms of group interests. Women and men both participate in violence or normative sexual scripts, so both women and men are equally responsible. There is little discussion about how those patterns of behavior work in men's interests and against women's. The people who participate, including women and men, are simply "assholes," individuals who simply don't get it.

As Bryan, Jim, and Jack close me out of their conversation, I decide to find Maddie up by the stage. As I move through the mass of people I'm struck by how politely people move out of my way. The Fiasco is about to start their set, so the density of bodies increases the closer I get to the stage. Still, people make an effort to make room to let me through. I locate Maddie, who is talking to Colleen. Colleen's mother died when she was young, which, according to Colleen's account, made her extremely independent and strong and unlike most of the other girls in her hometown.

It seems that every alternative hard rocker has a story about high school years as a time of not fitting in. While this fits nicely with mainstream rock's antiestablishment, cultural outlaw stance, that it most often revolves around gender is a point of departure. Bryan's girlfriend could kick his ass; Colleen was unusually independent; Maddie refused to be passive and therefore didn't fit in with the popular kids. They all describe themselves as the kids in high school who didn't fit in because they didn't want to or were not capable of successfully playing out suburban gender roles. According to their construction of their past, being a jock or a cheerleader was apparently not an option for these people. And so the story goes that, like so many refugees from the politics of high school popularity, they turned to rock music. They could have chosen any story to tell about their past. They could have focused on academics. They could have focused on drug subcultures. Instead, they all told stories about gender.

These people were children in the 1970s, and their gender stories reflected this. When alternative hard rockers were growing up, the cheerleaders cheered, the jocks maneuvered balls into various goals and nets, Ted Nugent's "cock rock" extraordinaire was being marketed to white, teenage boys, and everyone else was being gorged with disco. But in this cacophony of Americana, there were two very loud, very angry rebellions taking shape. One was the second wave of the women's movement and the other was punk rock. Alternative hard rockers, with a lot of help from the feminist critique of male dominance, decided the people doing cock rock were not much different from the jocks and the cheerleaders. In their desire to create something new, they turned to this cultural critique of gender called *feminism*. At this same time, punk music was angrily articulating a fierce cultural opposition to corporate rock and middle-class banality. Punk had the rock roots, but in contrast with mainstream rock, it also had a deep cultural critique, and small glimmers of gender transformation.[3] Alternative hard rockers took the cultural criticism of punk, the gender criticism of feminism, and tried to create a world that was different. Within this world, a story about not fitting in with the jocks and cheerleaders became very important. It was rockers' form of authenticity, and contributed to their status as cultural outsiders.

As I approach Maddie and Colleen, I hear Colleen telling a story about hanging out with Michael Stipe of REM. Maddie is looking around, not paying attention to Colleen's story, and she strikes me as somewhat bored. Maddie takes my presence as an opportunity to change the subject, physically pulling me into their conversation and asking, "So what'd you think of Motorhome?"

Before I met Colleen, Maddie had informed me that she is a "scenester," which means that she is up on all the local bands, knows everybody at the shows, and is a name-dropper. Scenesters often talk about their experiences of "hanging" with more famous rock musicians. In Colleen's case, she often talked about "Michael" (Stipe) and "Kim" (Kim Gordon of Sonic Youth), both of whom she had met. One night I was at Bryan's with some others before a show. Colleen was telling us about a Raincoats concert she went to.

"Raincoats?" Maddie asked.

"They're like one of the first hardcore, all-women bands. They're so good. They haven't put anything out in a long time, but I guess Kurt Cobain was a big fan and got their old stuff reissued, and put together these concerts. There were eight [concerts], and I went to two in New York. Kurt Cobain was supposed to be there, but I guess he had other stuff to attend to. He killed himself, like, the day before the show. It's weird."

Maddie was returning from the kitchen and must have missed part of the story and asked, alarmed, "Who killed himself?"

With a look of tired irritation Colleen said flatly, "Kurt Cobain."

As if shocked, but mocking anyone who didn't know, I said, "Kurt Cobain died?" Everybody laughed. How out of it would you have to be to not know Kurt Cobain died? In a Southern drawl, Colleen nodded her head and confirmed, "Yup. Shot himself right upside the head."

Even though alternative hard rockers consciously try not to reproduce old patterns of gender inequality and explicitly challenge racism or homophobia, their main trope for doing "dumbass" is to adopt a Southern accent. "White trash" is also code for reactionary, conservative, and/or stupid. Their radical agenda is articulated by constructing opponents or political "others." When particular others like Jim were not available, alternative hard rockers, like many middle-class, educated white people, often choose southern, rural, poor white people.

Colleen continued with her story. "So, Kim was there . . . "

Visibly annoyed with having to ask, Maddie interrupted: "Kim?"

"Kim Gordon." (Gordon's band, Sonic Youth, is a favorite of virtually all of the alternative hard rockers I knew.)

Maddie's annoyance transformed to interest: "You met Kim Gordon?!"

"Yeah. We went backstage and . . . "

Maddie's excitement took over once again, "I love her. I really, like, have fallen in love with her. Bryan and I were talking about meeting people just this afternoon, and I was talking about Kim Gordon."

Colleen raised her eyebrows, looked at Bryan and smiled, "And Bryan was listening attentively."

Oblivious to Colleen making fun of the heteromasculine fantasy of having a threesome with two women, Maddie was lost in the thought of Kim Gordon.

"She's so cool. They're so good, and she is just so cool."

Bryan jumped in, "Oh, I know."

Maddie was on roll now, "I love Sonic Youth. I swear, I love her."

Colleen got caught up in Maddie's enthusiasm, "She is totally hot! I thought she'd be taller but she's really little."

A competition began about who knew more about Sonic Youth and Kim Gordon.

Taking the bait, Bryan couldn't resist flexing his cultural capital muscles, "Oh I know. I thought she was really tall until I met her, too."

At this point, Bryan got up and fished out an LP cover from a Sonic Youth album. This demonstrated to everybody that he listened to Sonic Youth before CDs were the norm and that he preferred the better sound quality of albums—major cultural capital.

"Look at this picture. Doesn't she look tall? Thurston [Thurston Moore, another member of Sonic Youth] is, like, huge."

Maddie jumped in, "They're one of those bands that just always puts out good music."

Colleen took the volley, "They also help a lot of other bands, too."

Maddie was back to thinking about Kim Gordon in particular. "She's so hot and so fucking cool."

Colleen decided to finish the story she started, but the focus was now less on the Raincoats and more on insider knowledge about Kim Gordon.

"I didn't really get to talk to her, but I was with this group of people including Thurston and he said something about Kim being pregnant. I already knew, but everybody else was like 'Kim's pregnant?' I didn't know if it was, like, common knowledge or whatever. Did you guys know she's pregnant?"

Bryan practically leapt at the gold ring: " . . . *was* pregnant."

A bit shaken, Colleen asked, "She had her baby?"

Visibly pleased with himself, Bryan confidently said, "Yeah. Like last week. It was a boy I think."

This exchange was much like most struggles over subcultural capital among alternative hard rockers. Men and women participate and compete with and among each other. More interestingly, conversations like this one fairly consistently include not just insider knowledge about the musicians or the bands, but also a lot of admiration of the personal integrity of musicians, and most importantly, a lot of sexual desire and attraction for the musicians. The real fans in alternative hard rock act as groupie wanna-bes. Sexual desire for musicians does not fall into two neat categories that separate fans along the lines of gender identity, as mainstream rock ideology would have it. Instead, sexual desire for musicians is articulated by both men and women, and people who express sexual desire are not considered less-than-serious rock fans.[4]

Cultural gender maneuvering to undermine the groupie/rock-fan dichotomy manifests itself through the creation of one field of appreciation for both women and men that includes but is not limited to sexual desire. This field of appreciation consists of three components—sexual attraction, musical appreciation, and personal admiration, and all are expressed by both women and men in these cultural capital exchanges. The field of appreciation disrupts the groupie/real fan dichotomy by including sexual desire as part of being a serious rock fan. It is a cultural maneuver to eliminate sexual desire for musicians as a factor in any gendered organization of the social space of the rock show.

Bryan often expressed both musical appreciation and personal admiration for James, the singer of a local band. One night after they had played, Bryan approached me with a huge grin.

"So what'd you think?"

"I loved it. It was great."

"How 'bout his voice? I love his voice."

I agreed, "And his guitar. Damn, it sounded so fucking good."

"Yeah, he's got a lot of guitars. He just comes across as so sincere. There's no bullshit about him."

"It was so charming how he would smile when people would clap."

Bryan smiled and tilted his head. "Yeah. He's so real and genuine."

I asked, "Is he always that shy, or is it because they haven't played in awhile?"

"Well, he's nervous 'cause they haven't played, but he's always like that. Even three years ago he'd get really freaked out about shows. God, I love him!"

We both laughed.

I asked, "Do you have any of their recordings?"

"They won't let me dub their tape. But they're coming out with a single, and I'll be sure to get it to you. The cover art is unbelievable. It's like from another time or something. It's just James and it looks like it's from the 1800s or something. I can't wait till it comes out."

The next time that Velvet, James's band, played, Bryan, Maddie, Nancy and I were chatting it up before the band started. Although he had certainly expressed personal admiration and musical appreciation, Bryan had never verbally expressed sexual attraction. However, the way Bryan talked about and watched him appeared to me to be very sexual.

I took this opportunity to ask Bryan outright, "Do you have a crush on James?"

Much to my surprise, Bryan smiled and asked "What do you mean *crush*?"

I sort of shrugged my shoulders and scrunched my face, "You know . . . "

"I think he's an awesome person and a great musician. I have a lot of respect for him."

"Yeah, but do you have a crush on him?"

"You mean do I want to fuck him?"

Going along with his definition of a crush, I simply said, "Okay."

Bryan looked over to James obviously thinking about it, and then turned back to the three of us, "I don't think so . . . "

Maddie was pleased. "Notice he didn't say 'no.'"

She looked over at James, shook her head and said, "You can hardly fucking blame him though."

Nancy was also looking at James and almost whispered, "He's

so great. He's like a poet. What a great musician. Velvet is my favorite band right now."

At another show, Nancy and I were talking about the band we were about to see, Palace Brothers. It was my first time seeing them.

I asked, "So, have you seen them before?"

"No, I haven't. But I'm totally hot for the lead singer."

Wondering how she could be hot for a singer she'd never seen play, I asked, "Have you met him?"

"No, but I've seen pictures, and I've heard his music. He's such a great musician and songwriter."

While being hot for a singer because she'd seen pictures of him smacks of teenybopper, she was quick to add that she had heard his music and that he's a great musician and songwriter. This was typical for alternative hard rockers. Nancy sexualized her relationship to both the singer and his musical ability.

Not ten minutes later, Nick Cave of the Bad Seeds came into the bar. He is an internationally known musician, and very popular among this crowd. I watched as both men and women approached him to talk. Nancy appeared to get visibly uncomfortable.

"What could these fucks possibly be saying to him? 'Hey, I love your music. That first album was so great.' How embarrassing! I would feel so embarrassed."

I said, "What a drag to have to constantly deal with people like that."

Nancy agreed, "No shit!"

We watched as a woman talked with him for a long time. Another woman stood by patiently, waiting to get her turn. The woman talking with him had her hands in her back pockets and was moving her hips back and forth. The woman waiting couldn't keep her eyes off of him. Nick Cave appeared to be listening patiently and periodically offering a word or two.

Shaking her head, Nancy said disappointingly, "I feel sorry for those women."

"What do you mean?"

"Anything to talk with a rock star, you know. Look at her. She wants to fuck him. I mean, whatever. I don't blame her. But, Jesus, you don't have to put yourself in that position."

While it wasn't altogether clear whether or not Nancy's disgust was with the women's behavior or her own inability to be asser-tive enough to go talk to Nick Cave, she was sure to let me know that there was a problem with women simply being interested in rock stars for their sex appeal. She was, in a sense, conveying to me that the rules of the game don't include simply playing the groupie. While it was perfectly legitimate for her to be totally hot for the singer in Palace Brothers because of the way he looked and his music, it was a different story when women put themselves in the position of groupie.

When the one woman finally walked away and the other stepped up to take her turn, I decided to find out what she had talked with him about.

I walked up to her and said, "Excuse me. I'm doing this research project on rock music audiences, and I was wondering if I could ask you a few questions."

She was a bit apprehensive, but responded, "Like what?"

"Well, I'm interested in what you two talked about."

"We talked about music."

"Are you a musician?"

"I'm a musician of sorts. I work in a studio and I ran an idea by him and I got affirmation from him. Sometimes you don't know the truth until you get it from certain sources."

There is really no way I could know what she had really talked about with Nick Cave, but in my interaction with her, she estab-lished that, rather than doing groupie, she was involved in music herself and wanted to get feedback on her work. Whether or not she was sexually interested in Nick Cave, she constructed her in-teraction with him as anything but that of groupie and rock star.

When alternative hard rockers talk about musicians, it is al-ways difficult to distinguish personal admiration, musical appre-ciation, and sexual attraction. Sometimes, alternative hard rockers might articulate an understanding of how these things are gendered but then immediately reject that way of thinking. Carrie and I were once talking about the musician Jon Spenser. Carrie had very strong feelings about him.

"The thing about Jon Spenser is that he's incredibly talented. I mean really talented musically. He's great on stage. And he's very handsome. That's my female side coming out."

She made an exaggerated face of disgust and then laughed.

"He also wears great shirts. They're all really well made and very stylish."

Carrie was well aware of how being sexually attracted to musicians was somehow feminine. But her facial expressions right after she said this, and that she so fluidly moved from his musical talent to his physical appearance, to the quality of his shirts simultaneously invoked, but also dissolved the gender dichotomy that links the identity label *woman* with finding a musician "very handsome."

This field of appreciation comes through as, earlier this evening, I observed the crowd watching Motorhome perform. I noticed two men moving around as if trying to get a better view of the drummer, a woman with bleached-blond, short, spiked hair who wears a tank-top-style T-shirt, boxer shorts, and combat boots. The men finally got a clear view and, as they watched, exchanged words with each other. I moved closer to them, leaning in to try to hear their exchange.

"Look at those shoulders. Holy shit. She's fucking excellent!"

With a nod the other man broke into a little air drumming to imitate her—a bodily nod of respect for her musical abilities.

When Babes in Toyland played Lounge Ax, the men in the audience engaged in a fair amount of behavior that certainly smacked of teenybopper. They yelled things like, "I love you!" and "You're awesome!"

All of this talk about how hot musicians are smacks of doing groupie or teenybopper. In fact, I have heard about people having sex with touring musicians as they came through town. However, femininity and the identity label *woman* are never straightforwardly mapped onto those behaviors or these expressions of sexual desire. For men, getting the women in alternative hard rock bands to stay at their house is always cryptically suggestive of having had sex with them, whether or not they actually had. In other words, both women and men act as both groupie and real fan. By embracing these two positions simultaneously, the gendered meaning and, importantly, the androcentric hierarchy of value that structures mainstream rock was replaced with a nongendered field of appreciation.

This rejection of the musician/groupie gender structure came through in my conversations with touring musicians as well. One of their cultural maneuvers is to talk about the groupie scene as something other people do, but not as part of what they themselves are doing. Kim Thayil, a member of the all-male band Soundgarden said, "I think in the last few years there's been a lot of great bands that have killed that stereotype, that male stereotype . . . initially when I got into [rock music] I was like, yeah, guys are dicks, rock bands are pretty stupid, and I want to be in a rock band that doesn't patronize the sexist and racist aspects of rock. Like punk in that sense. . . . They're normal people. They're not playing some kind of rock dream of dressing up and getting girls or whatever."

Similarly, Ian MacKaye of the band Fugazi talked about trying to do sexuality differently and encouraging others to do the same. He explained, "I wrote a song called 'Out of Step' that said 'don't smoke, don't drink, don't fuck. At least I can fuckin' think.' And it was sort of about guys around me. That was their big thing, to get fucked up and get laid constantly. That wasn't my priority in life. My priority was to be like a person or whatever. . . . [Punk music] was something that gave me access to a whole 'nother world, and I was challenged on so many levels, like politically, sexually. Everything I thought had to be turned upside down and reexamined." MacKaye thus made gender salient by contrasting being one of the "guys" with being a "person."

Their point of departure from mainstream rock's groupie culture sometimes was stated rather straightforwardly. Jennifer Finch of L7 said, "Groupies are mostly a mainstream rock phenomenon. It's a sexist world and groupies are just part of that world. Not any different from any other sexist aspect of society . . . I don't get into that scene myself, but for some people it works."

While she did not condemn the people who participated, Finch was very clear about the groupie scene being a reproduction of the sexist ways of doing gender inside and outside of mainstream rock. Though she presented it as a personal preference, her bandmate Donita Sparks made clear that this was a choice made by many musicians. She talked about this more as a characteristic of the subculture.

"The groupie thing just doesn't happen. It's not part of the sensibility of what we're doing. And the guys that we tour with, you know the Melvins and Wool, it's not like there are groupies back here hanging out with them. It's just not part of what we do."

I asked her, "What is this *sensibility* you keep referring to?"

She responded, "It comes out of punk roots. It's about being more enlightened, having a sense of fairness and not being sexist pigs. You know those guys in rock bands with all the groupies. That's fine, but they're usually fuckin' pigs trying to prove something. We're just here to rock."

Kat Bjelland of Babes in Toyland also talked about how the groupie scene is not part of what her band or its audience does. When I asked her if there is a difference between how men approach her and how women do, she responded, "The guys are never, like, sleazy, groupie-type people. It's always really nice people. We have really nice fans for some reason."

I asked, "Any idea why?"

"Hopefully it's because . . . "

She paused and smiled, looking down.

Stating the obvious, I said, "Because you're smart and you're cool?"

She laughed and filled in, "Yeah. You know, similar minds."

Having "similar minds" meant that both Bjelland and her audience had an understanding that doing musician did not include having sex with fans, and that doing fan did not include trying to gain sexual access to musicians. One might argue that women playing the part of sexually objectifying male fans and using their status as musicians to gain sexual access to men challenges the gender order. After all, it is the woman who is in this case sexually objectifying and exploiting the men. However, as Judith Butler and others have argued, when individual women embrace and do the masculine and when men do femininity, the overall gender structure, or the relationship between masculinity and femininity remains in tact. That is, if women musicians enact the role of musician in the ways men have, they are reproducing and supporting the gender structure of the relationship between musicians and fans. The women would be doing the masculine position in relation to the feminine. It maintains the sexual subject as masculine and the sexual object as feminine. Instead, the women musicians in alternative hard rock, like the men, are committed to transforming the norms for how to do musician. Because it has been a staple of mainstream rock and implicated in the sexism of rock, both the women and the men reject the practices tied to the sexual objectification and exploitation of fans, and by doing so, subvert the hegemonic relationship between masculinity and femininity.

Eddie Vedder extended this to lyrical and video content when he said, "Music videos are so cliché. They all objectify women. Like I was watching Warrant's video for 'Cherry Pie.' That just disgusted me. I know some people try to make fun of the whole use of women in videos, but they end up doing the same thing. I quit my last band over a conflict over a song. It was called 'She's so Sexual.' It was written by someone else in the band, and I just refused to sing it. It seemed like it was from the perspective of a bunch of guys standing around watching a woman go by. It also used words like *baby* and *sweetie*. I didn't write it and that's not how I would express myself, so I quit."

Unlike mainstream rock musicians, as they talk about what they do these musicians redefine what it means to do musician. By claiming that the groupie thing is not part of their scene, they take the identity label *groupie* out as the complement/opposite of *musician*. *Musician* no longer has the sexualized, masculine valence it has in mainstream rock. In a conversation not explicitly about groupies, Ian MacKaye provided some insight into how these musicians think about their relationship to fans, especially women fans:

> For me, music is a big part of my life. Strange but true. Always has been. There's something very immediate, very . . . I don't want to say *visceral*. That's not the right word. Sexual, honest, vulnerable. That's what I like about these shows a lot of times. When I was out there, it kind of reminds me back when I was on a baseball team . . . you would go into the backstop and you have your mitt, and the coach just sits there with a bat, and the coach is just hitting them at you and you have to just run back and forth trying to catch all the balls. And in a way, I like throwing myself in that kind of situation. The stage is like that because there are

a million things comin' from all over the place. And some things are beautiful social lobs and they're just wonderful, and some of them are very agitated, angry things. Like tonight, there was a kid giving me a hard time. But just to the right of me there was a woman dancing and it just made me feel so good. Cause she was just really, like, opening. She just opened. And it made me happy that she felt that kind of comfort or whatever in the music 'cause that's like what I want—to be free. When I see people dance that's like pretty close to being free. And I want to be free too. I'm usually only free when I'm on stage.

The woman, as described by MacKaye, was both a serious fan and responding sexually. In fact, the woman's sexual reaction, as MacKaye saw it, was what indicated to him that she was losing herself in the music, which was the ultimate compliment to a musician's musical ability. However, rather than talking about having sex with her or being sexually attracted to her or even of her being sexually interested in him, he talked about her sexual response to the music, not to him personally. Further, unlike the rock musician who has power over the woman, MacKaye characterized the power relations and gender dynamics very differently. He placed himself in a position of subordination by comparing his relationship to the audience with his relationship to a coach who is in a position of authority. Finally, his construction of this experience played not only with power relations between himself as performer and people in the audience—importantly, a woman in this case—but also with the gendering of sexual relations in general, for he was receiving and a woman was giving.

Sometimes musicians, especially women musicians, collapse the distinction between a musician and someone who is attracted to, has sex with, or develops intimate relationships with musicians. One night I was talking with a local musician in Chicago about a recent article she had read in a fanzine about groupies.

She said, "I always worried about being called a groupie because I've always dated musicians. But you know, that's who I'm around. I admire them and what they do. And I wanted to do what they were doing. I'm a group*er*, not a groupie."

Her use of the word *grouper* rather than *groupie* signified a conscious rejection of the false dichotomy between those interested in the music and people interested in who is playing the music. There was still an attraction to and, as this woman said, an admiration for, musicians. However, at the same time she was a professional musician. The word *grouper* changes the word *groupie* into someone who acts. The grouper acts as both musician and someone who dates musicians. Also, the word *grouper* is not a diminutive derivation of the word "group," as in "rock group." Like "708ers," "teenagers," and "yuppies from the suburbs," "grouper" does not have a straightforward gender valence.

Jennifer Finch also talked about being a young woman interested in rock music and being attracted to musicians. She said, "When I was young I remember seeing Mick Jagger and thinking 'I want to be his girlfriend.' I saw Jerri Hall and how glamorous she was. I wanted to be her. I wanted to be Mick Jagger's wife. Then I got into punk music, and I started wanting to be Mick Jagger, not his girlfriend. It became an option to be Mick Jagger."

One of the most interesting cultural gender maneuvers to destabilize the groupie/musician dichotomy was the transformation of *groupie* into rock performer. One evening the opening act at Lounge Ax was Cynthia Plastercaster, reading excerpts from her diaries. Plastercaster is a world-famous groupie who gained acclaim not only by having sexual relations with rock stars such as Jimi Hendrix and Mick Jagger, but also for having made plaster casts of her conquests' penises. Rather than a band playing music for the opening act, Plastercaster described in detail not only her sexual experiences with and the sexual adequacy of various "rock guys," but also anecdotes about the casting of their genitalia in plaster.

Although Plastercaster brandishes the identity label *groupie* with pride, the practices that led to that identity label were transformed into rock performance. By making groupie practices rock performance, the groupie/musician dichotomy was disrupted. Plastercaster's sexual activities did not cast her onto one side of the binary or the other. Not only did this maneuver dissolve the gender line between rock performer and groupie, but it also transformed the subject/object binary that is mapped onto the musician/ groupie dichotomy as well. The groupie was publicly constructed as subject acting on her sexual desire for male musicians. The musicians she had sex with became the sexual objects of that desire.

That her performance was a description of making plaster casts of penises quite literally objectified masculine sexuality attached to the position of musician and took it almost to the point of parody.

In only one report of sexual relations between a woman and a rock musician was the woman's behavior cast as groupie behavior. In this case, Maddie was telling me about how she was not on speaking terms with Janet, who, according to Maddie, had recently had sex with a famous rock star.

"God, I can't stand her. She's such a groupie. Not that I care who she sleeps with. But I think she's just interested in Paul because he's in a band."

Paul was Maddie's boyfriend at the time. Maddie rationalized the identity label by arguing that if Janet was not only after her boyfriend, but also having sex with other musicians, she must be some sort of groupie. What was significant about this was that Maddie used the label *groupie* to put Janet down. The insult worked because Maddie was implying that Janet willingly put herself in the objectified, disempowered position of groupie, and within this subculture that is demeaning and unacceptable.

There is really no way for me to empirically identify whether or not individual musicians actually have sexual relations with fans on a regular basis. It is entirely possible that, while in their talk and public performance they construct a normative framework that challenges hegemonic gender relations, individually they might reproduce it. However, it is still the case that, in interviews and in their interactions with others, alternative hard rockers construct a set of subcultural norms and meanings for doing rock that depart from mainstream rock ways of doing and thinking about the relationship between musicians and groupies, and male fans and female fans. Constructing a sexualized public persona has been part of doing rock musician from the beginning. Alternative hard rock musicians use this practice to construct their own identity as musicians and their relationship to fans in a way that disrupts the gendered subject/object relations in mainstream rock.

As the Wesley Willis Fiasco takes the stage, a woman next to me does the alternative real fan and says, "Check out the drummer. He's so cute. Best fucking drummer in the city."

When the band starts, a rather large man pushes Maddie and steps right in front of her. Maddie, with a disgusted look on her face, turns and makes eye contact with both me and Colleen. As the bodies begin to move with the music, the man becomes very aggressive, pushing others and bumping into Maddie. Maddie and Colleen begin to casually, but very pointedly, bump back into the him. Eventually, tired of elbows in the ribs, the man moves to a different spot and Maddie and Colleen look at each other and smile, acknowledging a job well done. I keep my eyes on the man as he moves through the crowd. Both men and women work together to move him out of their space or to get him to curtail his aggression. Eventually the collective effort of the crowd gets him to the side. After a minute or two, he disappears toward the front of the bar, I assume giving up on the idea of getting a mosh pit going.

A *mosh pit* is a mass of bodies, sometimes slam dancing, sometimes just moving together, and "floating," which is when the crowd lifts one person up above their heads and passes him along in the air. Although moshing is a central component to alternative hard rock, it does not happen at Lounge Ax probably because the ceiling is very low and the space in front of the stage is very narrow. Whether at Lounge Ax or at a club where moshing is likely, the crowd and the bands consistently work together to curtail aggression and to make the space relatively safe.

When I first started going to the shows where moshing did occur, from the outside it looked to me like an aggressive free-for-all; actually going into the pit was more than a bit scary to me. Once I mustered the courage and dove in, however, I soon realized that it wasn't as chaotic and competitive as it appeared from the perimeter. Whenever someone lost her footing and fell, a circle immediately opened up and hands reached to get her back up onto her feet. That people were aware of others falling indicated that they were very much aware of what was going on around them. One night I was in the middle of the pit as the whole crowd was undulating to the music of Poster Children. Suddenly, as if some unseen force gently guided people, a hole opened up to my left. People around me stopped moving. I watched as one guy pulled out a pen flashlight while another guy dropped to his knees and began groping the ground. The others who had stopped now formed a buffer zone to keep the other moshers from pushing through. To my absolute amazement, the guy groping the ground suddenly stood up and held up a pair of eyeglasses that were perfectly intact. The human buffer zone cheered, the hole closed up, and we started moving again to the music. While this is an extreme example, it was not uncommon for people to demonstrate that they were concerned about the well-being of others. I had people accidentally elbow me or slam exceedingly hard into me and stop to ask if I was alright.

Of course there were times when individuals would violate the rules, but others felt justified in enforcing the norms and would work together to get that person back in line.

At a Veruca Salt show, I watched the crowd rally in order to get one particularly aggressive man to calm down. I was standing just on the edge of the pit. There were two women directly in front of me who were not moshing, but just beyond them bodies were moving. A man behind me sort of pushed and began slamming against me. Losing my footing, I bumped the women in front of me. They both turned around angrily and shot me a dirty look. I immediately turned around to the man.

"Hey, get in the pit if you want to do that!" I screamed over the music.

"Move to the back if you don't like it!"

They must have been watching, because the two women stepped up and started yelling at him and pointing, "The pit is over there, asshole!"

Others around us started yelling at him. Eventually he shook his head and stepped up in front of us and disappeared into the crowd. Everybody around me shook their heads in disapproval. A few people smiled at each other or laughed.

It is not uncommon for the members of bands to encourage the crowd to maintain this norm by saying such things as "Let's not be too rough out there. Don't hurt anybody"; "Hey, watch out for each other and be careful"; or, "There are people up here getting crushed. Everybody move back and stop pushing." When violence does break out in the audience, often the bands stop and refuse to play until the violence ends.

At a Hole show, Courtney Love decided that the crowd had gotten a little out of control, so she said, "You're getting too rough! Everybody step back. People are getting smashed up here." She took her hands off of her guitar and looked at the crowd as if to say, "Well?"

After a few seconds she continued, "I said step back! Step Back! If you don't step back, I'm leaving."

I did not see anybody step back, though everybody had stopped moving. This wasn't good enough for Love.

"Fine! I'm outta here!"

She dropped her guitar and walked off the stage. The rest of the band stood there a moment looking at each other. They too left the stage. After about a minute, they returned. Love stepped up to the microphone and said as if she were speaking to a kindergarten class, "Now I want you to all step back. When I say *three*, everybody take one step back. One—two—three."

The entire crowd took one step back. Without saying anything, the band slammed into their next song and the mosh pit came back to life. Fugazi, Pearl Jam, and L7 have all done the same sort of crowd control. At one Fugazi show I attended, Ian MacKaye chastised the audience for floating, and a man in the audience yelled back. I interviewed MacKaye after this show, and he had much to say about violence in the audience.

"I try to interact [with the audience]," he explained. "If I see something I don't like I say it, if I see something I like, I try to acknowledge it."

I asked him what kind of impact this might have on the audience, and he responded,

> Some people get mad, apparently, and some people like it. . . . Have you ever been to a party and there's a band playing, and everyone's having a good time? That's all. It's sort of the same thing. I'm just trying to be at the party. I want to be there too. I don't want to be just the hired entertainment. I want to be at the party . . . I must say that bands who don't interact with their audience are highly responsible for the behavior of the audience. The audience will lose perspective. They don't know what it means anymore. So they treat each other like shit. I think if bands responded to situations, people might think about them. Why is it so hard to realize, hey, you're crushing everybody. You're kicking

people in the face. But most bands don't say anything, partly because they just don't want to be bothered. They're comfortable in their position. We just play, that's it. But for me, if I'm gonna play music, I don't want to see people hurting each other. I want everybody to feel comfortable. I want everybody to feel safe when they come to see us. To be comfortable and to get off. Not just a few people, and I guess I'm willing to make a lot of noise about that.

In a later interview, he tied this to gender by saying, "I don't know what to make of [aggression in the audience] myself. It's boring to me. It's just really a drag. Because ultimately it really does get to the point where it drives women away from the front of the stage. That is a clear result of that kind of behavior."

This is another way in which alternative hard rock musicians have redefined their position as musicians. MacKaye, and most of the other musicians I interviewed and watched, seemed to define the position as including responsibility for the crowd's behavior and the safety of everybody involved.

For instance, when I asked Kat Bjelland if she feels responsible for what happens in the audience, she responded, "Yeah. You're putting out a lot of energy there." Similarly, Donita Sparks said, "You know, like we hate violence, but the crowd [tonight] seemed a little more violent. We stop whenever we see shit like that and won't start until it stops." Rather than being set apart from or above the audience,[5] MacKaye and others saw themselves as simply one part of the social scene. Musicians would usually hang out in the bar, not backstage. As MacKaye suggests, it was one big party, and all who were there were invited, including the band.

It is understood that any hierarchy of authority conferred to musicians should be used to ensure safety for everyone there and allow everyone, including the musicians themselves, to openly participate in the music. This not only allows women to participate as equals in the audience but also disrupts the hierarchical relationship between musician and fan. By reducing this hierarchy, it encourages the men and women in the audience to not only see themselves as like the people in the bands (virtually every audience member I was familiar with played an instrument or was starting a band), but also to understand themselves as part of a community or subculture. Part of that social bond is to know, as

MacKaye suggested, what the music "means." What it means, among other things, is that physical aggression is taken out as a lever of power.

Jennifer Finch summed this up when she said, "You know, we kind of watch out for people. We're not gonna let some asshole ruin it for everybody else. It's the new pit of the nineties. There's more women. It's just not as violent."

Like Maddie and Colleen in Chicago tonight, people work together to force others to go along with these subcultural norms. This collective effort to eliminate physical aggression seems an odd contrast to other Chicago alternative hard rockers' tolerance for Jack's interpersonal violence outside the rock club. I watch the people in the crowd. Some have their eyes closed, concentrating on the music and the physical pounding in their bodies. Others are watching the band, especially focusing on Wesley Willis, who is the only African American in the whole bar. All are moving some part of their body at least a little, and most are head-banging. Maddie, while slightly gyrating her hips, moving her head back and forth to the rhythm of the music, says to nobody in particular, and probably to the music itself, "Just fuck me now!"

This, strangely, does not surprise me because the atmosphere is really all about sex and power. The music, like all alternative hard rock, is very loud, so not only is it a visual and auditory experience, but it is also a bodily experience. You can feel the vibrations in your body, and this kind of music gives the physical experience a particular valence. It is very rhythmic, and through the use of power chords and instrument syncopation, the music brings power into the body and fuses it with sexual arousal. The sexual component to experiencing the music is clear in the way people move their bodies—gyrating, closing their eyes, and expressing sexual pleasure on their faces with furrowed brows and pursed lips. To my right, standing on the bench that lines the area in front of the stage, there are two women holding onto each other, moving together to the music. To my left there are three women head-banging and gyrating, looking at each other, smiling and laughing. The men will sometimes look at each other and nod or smile their approval, but for the most part focus on the stage. The sex in the music is clear when the band finishes and Colleen sighs and says, "Shit, I need a cigarette after that!" Maddie pulls a cigarette out and offers it to Colleen. "I was speaking figuratively, smartass." Maddie shrugs her shoulders, pops the cigarette in her mouth and lights it.

After saying goodbye to a handful of people and chatting for a few minutes about the show, Maddie and I once again step out onto Lincoln Avenue. A crowd of people has spilled out onto the street in front of the bar. People from the sports and singles bars pass by, looking almost frightened as they quicken their step and direct their gaze to the pavement. As Maddie and I walk back up Lincoln Avenue toward her car, we are once again "different" and drawing attention. It becomes apparent to me that, although we left the space of the bar and the affirmation from other alternative rockers, Maddie carries the same air of humor, toughness, and sexual assertiveness with her. It is carried in her body out of the physical and social space of alternative hard rock and back into the mainstream, just as she had carried it at the beginning of the evening. She meets hostility and harassment, but she does not abandon her alternative gender and sexual practices. In the world outside the club, she brandishes these in resistance, forcing men off the sidewalk and, for a brief moment, out of their privileged position of occupying a disproportionate amount of physical space.

4

GENDER MANEUVERING IN FACE-TO-FACE INTERACTION

Have you ever stopped to wonder what it means when a man walks up to a group of women and asks, "Are you alone?" I'm not talking about just in that instance. Everybody knows the man is asking, "Are you accompanied by other men?" What I am asking is, have you ever wondered what it means in the larger scheme of things? How could it possibly make sense to anybody that women talking with each other could be alone? Yet, we go along. Men ask, and women respond as if there could be any other answer besides "No, I'm with her."

By looking at gender and sexuality as features of structuration—that is, as both organizing structures and resulting outcomes of everyday activities—the "alone" question and why we tend to go along begins to make sense. This and other sorts of gendered interactions are part of and reproduce the larger sexual and gender orders. By way of examples taken from my observations of alternative hard rock, in this chapter I will demonstrate and discuss how the gender and sexual orders are not simply reproduced, but are contested and negotiated through the ongoing process of face-to-face interaction.

Once we look at sexuality and gender as contested terrain in everyday interaction, a few important questions emerge. What sorts of talk and activities provide grist for the hegemonic gender and sexual mill, and what might strip the gears? For instance, what sorts of interactive responses to the question "Are you alone?" keep the gender and sexual order in place, and what sorts of responses throw it off course? What happens to the power relations within the interaction itself when one or more individuals refuse to go along with the gender or sexual rules? To start addressing this question, let me begin with a brief story of interactive gender maneuvering.

A STORY ABOUT NOT GOING ALONG

One night well into my research, I was with a group of four other women taking advantage of the between-band space for chatting. The women were discussing the autoerotic benefits of thigh-high tights, when a man who none of us knew approached our group. After taking a brief moment to visually consume us, he smiled and said, "Hi girls. Are you alone?" I could feel the blood rush to my limbs preparing for flight or fight. Having been raised with five brothers, I was leaning toward the latter when the rest of the women burst into hysterical laughter. While completely ignoring this man who was simply trying to strike up a conversation, the women dove into a humorous performance of gender that would put RuPaul to shame.

"Where's my big, strong man?" Nancy asked in a Southern, damsel-in-distress drawl.

In a husky, Midwestern antidrawl, Jane piped in, "Right here, honey. Me and my balls will take care of you."

"Damn" lamented Susan.""And I thought girls were people. Now who am I going to date?"

The man, looking somewhat frightened and more than a little confused, chuckled in discomfort, and without much notice from the women around me, who were now thoroughly enjoying each other's performances, slipped away to another part of the bar.

We were at Cabaret Metro, which is a relatively large venue that draws people from all over the city. We were there to see the Wesley Willis Fiasco open for a somewhat more popular "manly band," as Bryan put it.

Earlier in the evening Bryan had told me that he was talking with one of the men in the band and asked him what kind of music they play. The man responded, "Let's put it this way. We're a manly band." According to Bryan, this was code for, "Not only will the music be loud and aggressive, but there will also be a lot of aggressive posturing on stage, probably some cracks about women from the guys in the band, and therefore, obnoxious guys walking around looking for some action." "Action" could mean fights, sex, or both. This was how it was at these clubs. The band set the tone for how people in the audience would behave. You could bet that if there were manly men on stage, there would be manly men milling about in the audience. It wasn't long before another manly man sauntered up to the group.

"Hi, girls."

While this guy didn't make the fatal mistake of asking if we were alone, calling these twenty-something women "girls" didn't score him any points. He was also a stranger, and among alternative hard rockers, men who approach women they don't know were considered out of line and intrusive, especially if they interrupted a conversation. The women were not going to bite. They sort of glanced at him and continued the conversation. I don't know if his line was meant to flatter or to insult us, but the stranger awkwardly inserted himself into the conversation by blurting out, "You all look like the band in that Robert Palmer video."

The infamous Robert Palmer music video deserves a brief description. It depicts Palmer singing his song "Addicted to Love" with an all-woman backup band. The women in the band are all dressed in black minidresses, high-heeled pumps, and heavy, mannequin-like makeup. They are, like most mannequins, difficult to distinguish from each other and hauntingly semihuman. The camera eye shifts from a close-up of Palmer's lip-synching face to the women's breasts, legs, and deadpan expressions swaying or bouncing—depending, of course, on the specific part of the body. I had heard many conversations among alternative hard rockers, including women and men, about how insulting and sexist the video was. They had come to a collective understanding of this particular depiction of women rockers.

It was as if someone had run fingernails down a chalkboard. The stranger might as well have said, "You are brainless, mildly titillating objects." The conversation stopped, eyes widened, and everybody looked to see what Maddie was going to say. Maddie is a master at verbal slam-dunking, and the severity of the situation called for drastic measures. Never allowing herself to walk away from a challenge, she said,""Yeah? That's cool 'cause you remind me of someone." Buying herself time to think of the perfect match in kind to the Robert Palmer women, she continued, "Someone on TV or in the movies."

The man puffed up his chest and said, "Oh yeah? Who?"

Maddie very slowly looked to each of us drawing us in to fully participate in the fun, turned to the man, leaned her face in close and said, "Paulie Shore."

The women roared with laughter, "Oh my God! You're right! He does!"

The man, desperately trying to maintain his footing, stammered, "Oh yeah, he's pretty funny."

Paulie Shore is a comedian whose media personae is a parody of the uncool, geeky guy trying desperately to be the suave, hip, ladies' man. The joke is that everybody but Shore's character is aware of how ridiculous his attempts are. The character always thinks he's the coolest dude around, while the audience is simultaneously embarrassed for him and entertained by his confidence, which is born out of ignorance.

There was no way the stranger could continue any attempt to "schmooze" us, as alternative hard rockers call it. By invoking Paulie Shore, Maddie situated any move that was intended to be smooth or sexy as completely ridiculous. Once Maddie slammed this guy into the Paulie Shore pigeonhole, he had two choices. He could remain and provide entertainment at his own expense, or he could leave us alone. He chose the latter.

Maddie successfully accomplished several goals with the one blow. First, she managed to shift the attention away from us as sexually objectified women and place it squarely on the man as a pathetic geek. The man's statement drew attention to our appearance, and while the women in the Palmer video represent a hyperreal image of dominant standards of beauty, they are at the same time completely dehumanized. The man's comment was not only an evaluation of the way we look, but also implied something about our femininity, who we were, and/or what we were like as women. The man's statement placed us in a particular social role as sex objects or bimbos. However, when Maddie suggested he was similar to Paulie Shore, his masculinity came under scrutiny, and he was not measuring up.

In both interactions, the women decided not to play along with the men. They laughed, they mocked, and they maneuvered out of typically feminine positions, either by asserting a different position for themselves, as when Susan suggested that she dates girls, or by situating the men into a specific role, as when Maddie said the man was similar to Paulie Shore. With Maddie's comment and the other women's willingness to follow her characterization, the man was transformed from suave "player" to desperate loser. At the same time, and in direct relation to his transformation, the women were maneuvered out of the position of sex objects and into that of discerning subjects. It is difficult to imagine the women in Palmer's video having the temerity or savvy to come back with such a brilliant maneuver. While paired with Robert Palmer, the women in the video work as sexually objectified eye candy. Throw in Paulie Shore, however, and suddenly it's possible that they could come to life as discerning, powerful women who can decide to reject or accept his advances. It was almost a tangible, visible transformation for Maddie. With one statement, she went from being the evaluated object of the man's sexual desire to being, in relation to the desperate geek, the sexually powerful bombshell who decides who is worthy or unworthy of her attention.

By doing so, Maddie accomplished her most important goal: she got rid of the man. Once it became clear that the women were not going to be playing a particular feminine part in either of these interactions, the men no longer wanted to participate; both slipped into the mass of bodies around us, never to be seen again.

These interactions were struggles over what W. I. Thomas has called the *definition of the situation*.[1] When we are in the presence of others, we assess our surroundings to decide what kind of situation we are in. We do this so that we know how to behave and can make some predictions about how others will act. We use all kinds of cues to define a situation. We look at the social setting (a rock club, in this case), our position within that setting (part of the audience and patrons of the club), the positions of other people around us (other audience members and patrons), and individual characteristics of others (how they are dressed, their ages, genders, races, and so on). When the strangers approached us, we all assessed the situation to search for some sort of guidelines for the interaction. The strangers were men, and the people I was with were women. We were all white and around the same age. The women in my group were dressed in tight, black dresses and skirts; the first stranger was wearing jeans and a plaid, short-sleeved, button-down shirt, and the second was in khakis and a white T-shirt. The men probably defined the situation based on what they already knew about bars: scantily clad women not in the company of men, race and age homogeneity in sexual relations, and a variety of other cues caught their attention. These were signs for what the situation was, and therefore how the men should proceed with the interaction and how the women might act in response. Likewise, the women defined and made their own assessment of the situation and predictions for how the men would act.

The reason we feel comfortable defining the situation and predicting how others will act is because our ideas about what the situation is and how we should act are not simply a matter of choice or individual interpretation. Before I or any of the women I was with that evening had even entered the club, there already existed what Erving Goffman calls a *frame*—a network of meanings and rules for interaction that intersect in a particular social setting and frame the range of possible interpretations and actions.[2] The frame provides the pattern for how to act out particular roles; included in the frame are networks of rules specific to one's own and others' positions. In this instance, our interaction was framed by the rock club, but also by the meaning of gender and by sexuality.

GENDER AS A FRAME FOR AND EMERGENT FEATURE OF SOCIAL INTERACTION

There are socially defined rules for how women and men interact among and between each other within this kind of social setting. This is where the broader gender order comes in. Doing gender while doing all other social activities is expected and often defines the meaning of not only our activities but also the social position we hold while doing them. For instance, both women and men raise children. However, the meaning of and role expectations for "mother" are different than those for "father." Depending on the gender of the parent, the meaning of being a parent and how to "do" parent differs. Also, as people interact with each other, not only do they create meanings for gender, but they also create the meaning of the relationship between masculinity and femininity. For instance, as women and men parent, they create meanings for the relationship between the identity labels *mother* and *father*, including hierarchies of power and legitimacy. This hierarchical relationship between masculinity and femininity, when acted out in day-to-day life, translates into material hierarchies of power, prestige and resources.[3]

The hierarchical relationship between masculinity and femininity as complements/opposites frames all interactions, including those at rock clubs. For instance, in straight bars, the normative patterns and therefore expectation is that men actively pursue women as potential sexual partners, and unless a woman is with another man, she is a potential sexual partner. The men in Cabaret Metro that night were acting out and further creating this gender frame for interaction. They approached us and situated us in feminine positions that complemented their masculine positions. For instance, saying "Are you alone?" both reflects and recreates the hegemonic gender order. It is an insistence on femininity having a particular relationship to masculinity, and it reflects an assumption that women only make sense in their relationship to men, not other women. The feminine, in other words, is seen as needing a masculine counterpart. The women I was with could be "alone" while in the company of other women only if there was some symbolic meaning frame that excluded the possibility that women can be simultaneously not in a sexual relationship with a man and not be alone. This meaning frame then came to life or emerged through the words and actions of the stranger as he approached us. In a sense, he transformed the symbolic structure of gender into concrete action by asking us, "Are you alone?" The gender order goes from being a frame for the interaction to becoming an outcome of the interaction. The relationship between masculinity and femininity is as much created as it is reflected.

When the second man said we looked like the Robert Palmer models, his understanding of our femininity was framed by preexisting assumptions about women and women's sexuality. At the same time, however, he placed us in the subordinated, sexual object position in relation to his and other men's sexual subject position. Thus, our gender positions resulted or emerged from his statement. His actions created the meaning of our positions while at the same time reflected the preexisting gender structure of masculine subject (Robert Palmer) and feminine object (his makeshift video "band"). In other words, the gender positions emerged out of this situated interaction as much as the symbolic meaning of gender difference framed the interaction.

Candace West and Don Zimmerman suggest that gender is not only produced by our performance of it in everyday activities, but is also "a routine, methodical, and recurring accomplishment" produced in social interaction.[4] As we interact with others, we give them constant feedback or cues about how well they are following the rules for their gender while simultaneously looking for feedback about how well we are performing ourselves. As we provide cues and monitor the cues of others, we encourage appropriate practices and discourage inappropriate displays of gender. The rules reflect the preexisting pattern and frame for gendered performance in the setting, and these patterns are always inextricably tied to the symbolic meaning of gender defined more broadly. Through this constant feedback loop within interaction, the existing gender structure not only provides the rules for gender display but is itself constantly being re-created. Thus, we don't simply perform gender, but interactively call out gender performances from each other. In this sense, gender is an *interactive process*. As we all enact those performances or *do gender*, gender hierarchies are further created. For instance, West and Zimmerman point out that if doing femininity means doing subservience and doing masculinity translates into doing dominance, within face-to-face interaction this sets up male dominant relations of power. For this reason, West and Zimmerman conclude that gender and unequal power relations are as much an outcome of social interaction as it is a normative framework for interaction.

Barrie Thorne builds on West and Zimmerman, and develops a theoretical framework for how gender difference itself is produced through social interaction.[5] According to Thorne, everyday interactions and activities not only enforce rules for how to do gender, but they also produce gender difference as an organizing feature of social life. In her book *Gender Play: Girls and Boys in School* Thorne uses data collected through participant observation in schools to demonstrate how the everyday activities of teachers and students produce "boys" and "girls" as important, salient, dichotomous groups. For instance, when teachers split classes into gender groups for the purposes of games, when children enforce or violate gender segregation on the playground, and when children tease each other for crossing gender boundaries, gender difference becomes salient, while in other settings gender difference recedes and becomes relatively less important. By focusing on *how* gender difference and gender segregation are created and enforced, Thorne empirically demonstrates that gender difference and its meanings not only guide social interaction, but are also constructed within an ongoing process of social interaction as well as being an outcome of such interaction.

A similar process was operating in the interactions I described between the women and men at Cabaret Metro. Interactively, the women and men were situating each other into particular social positions in a struggle over the meaning of their interaction. As I described above, when one said, "Are you alone?" and the other made the comment about the women in the Robert Palmer video, they were simultaneously following a gender frame for the interaction, and reproducing the heterosexual matrix by situating us into particular feminine positions. Importantly, the emergent gender structure for the interaction and resulting insult were in the relationship between masculinity and femininity as the men constructed it. Judith Butler's model for the symbolic gender order points out how negotiated social interaction not only reproduces and maintains gender difference and enforces the rules for doing and thinking about masculinity and femininity, but also that it reflects and further creates a coherent relationship or matrix between masculinity and femininity.

An emphasis on the relationship between rather than the creation and performance of masculinity and femininity brings into focus the negotiated aspect of gender as an emergent feature of social interaction. As an interactive process, gender can be negotiated through the manipulation of the relationship between masculinity and femininity. For instance, when a man does masculinity in a way that reproduces already existing patterns of gender structuration, Butler's theory, in combination with West and Zimmerman's, would predict that there is not only positive feedback from other people, but also a corresponding "call to performance" attached to femininity. That is, it is not simply doing masculinity or doing femininity that reproduces the gender order; it is the resulting and corresponding relationship between the two that is established by that performance.

Because this process is a continuous feature of all social interaction, most of the time it goes unnoticed by everybody involved. It is so much a part of everyday life that most people do not think about it while they do it. It is similar to tying shoes: you do not have to think about how you are manipulating the laces; your body just does it. Even though we do not have to think about tying our shoes, this does not mean that we did not, at some point in our life, learn how to do it. It is similar with producing gender. Enacting masculinity and femininity, providing cues to others, and monitoring others' feedback goes without much notice, unless of course we encounter something out of the ordinary or unexpected. Like tying your shoe, only when you encounter a knot or broken lace do you recognize what you are doing.

The knots or broken laces of interaction can occur when someone does not follow the rules or does gender in an unpredictable way. The interaction is disrupted. Doing gender is no longer seamless for others because they do not know what appropriate responses would be. West and Zimmerman suggest that others will try to get the outlier back in line or will end the interaction. If the outlier continues to break the rules, her character, motives, or predispositions will be questioned. In the end, according to West and

Zimmerman, when someone breaks gender rules, because others marginalize her, the preexisting patterns and rules remain unquestioned and unchanged, and the gender order remains in tact.

However, if the gender order is negotiated, produced, and recreated through social interaction, there must be room for gender relations to change through social interaction. Is it not possible for individuals to consciously refuse to follow the rules, not bend to the pressure to do so, and through their persistence, have some effect on others or even on the rules themselves? If the relationship between masculinity and femininity in localized settings is created and maintained through the activities of individuals, couldn't that relationship be manipulated by the activities of individuals? Also, if the meaning of the relationship is partially constructed within any interaction, couldn't individuals actively resist or try to manipulate their own or others' positions to transform the meaning of their relationship and of the significance of gender difference? If we take Butler's suggestion that we focus on the matrix or relationship between masculinity and femininity created through gender performance, then it becomes possible that refusing to go along with a call to performance is not simply a rejection of one's own expected gender display. By not going along, or by performing an alternative gender display, we can also situate others into gender positions. This is a transformation of not only the meaning of the positions of individuals, but also of the actual structure of the interaction itself. Thorne provides some evidence that this happens among grammar school children. Thorne observed that boys reproduced male dominant power relations by talking about girls as "polluted" or as contaminated with "cooties." (*Cooties* originated as a slang term for body lice.) This reflects, but also *constructs*, girls as defective simply by being girls. Thorne also observed, however, that the girls actively resisted this by shifting the meaning of the word *cooties*. Girls would sometimes define and use their cooties as a weapon, threatening boys with contamination, which thus transforms the significance of cooties from that of inadequacy to that of a tool of power. This move shifts the meaning of not just the cooties, but also of being a girl. It is an effective strategy not just because the girls refuse to remain in the "contaminated" position, but also because it transforms the boys' position as well. The boys become victims who are vulnerable to cooties rather than being superior for not having them. The hierarchy established by the re-lationship between masculinity and femininity is flattened, if not inverted. On other occasions, the girls would unite to define a boy or girl who is a social outsider as polluted, thus distinguishing them-selves from the those who are contaminated. This destabilizes the power of contamination to signify gender difference and feminine subordination. That is, it transforms the meaning of gender differ-ence and thus the hierarchical relationship between masculinity and femininity, for both girls and boys are in the uncontaminated group. Through negotiated social interaction, the boys established one meaning for the term *cooties* and thus for gender difference, while the girls sometimes volleyed back alternative meanings. The girls were not simply determined by the term's already existing gendered meaning, but actively negotiated the meanings with the boys and among themselves. As those negotiations took shape, the meaning of gender difference, and thus the relationship between masculinity and femininity, shifted.

This negotiated aspect of the gender organization of interac-tion becomes clear when we take a look at the range of possible responses the women could have chosen that night at Cabaret Metro. There are a range of lines women might adopt in this sort of situation. The women could have smiled coyly and said, "Why yes, we are alone," or "Thank you; I've never been told I look like someone on television" and then given each man their undivided attention. They could have politely asked, "Would you mind? We would rather be alone." Each of these lines would have probably made sense to the men because they would be consistent with the gender frame for the setting and the men's corresponding defini-tion of the situation. By saying "thank you" and giving the men their undivided attention, the women would have been enacting the male dominant expectations for women to direct their atten-tion to the needs and desires of men and to play the heterosexual counterpart to men's sexual advances. The relationship between masculinity and femininity would remain in tact, and thus, the hegemonic gender frame or structure for interaction in this setting would have been sustained. The second option of politely asking the men to leave them alone would have also reflected and maintained the hegemonic frame for the interaction. Being polite and taking care of the feelings of others is expected of women; it is also a normal part of heterosexual scripts for women to be somewhat hesitant in response to men's sexual advances. In both scenarios, the man would have maintained his masculine position as sexual subject acting on desire in relation to the women as the objects of that desire. That is, the relationship between their masculine and feminine positions would have remained in tact and the gender structure of the interaction would have reflected and maintained the larger gender order.

Still another answer might have been, "You sexist asshole. Get lost!" While perhaps less predictable and socially acceptable than the lines above, this line probably would not have caught these men completely off guard. They probably would have acted quite differently than if faced with something less abrasive, but they would have had some idea about how to respond.[6] "You sexist asshole. Get lost!" is not, like the first two answers, a simple acceptance of the man's definition of the situation. It would instead be an overt naming of the meaning of his statement and, as West and Zimmerman describe, an attempt to exit the interaction altogether. In this situation, the man's position would not be so much supported and maintained as it would be named and rejected. He would walk away rejected, but would still occupy the masculine position of sexual subject. While sexist assholes might lose face in certain contexts by being banished from interaction, they do not lose face in terms of masculinity. Sexist assholes are, after all, as masculine as the next guy. Thus, with this response the meaning of the positions would be unchanged, though made explicit and rejected.

The women refused to go along with any of these options. Instead, they did something that was unpredictable. They *gender maneuvered.*

INTERACTIVE GENDER MANEUVERING

The women acted in a way that violated the rules, and they manipulated and shifted their own and the men's positions midstream. While part of the women's maneuvering was to expose the men's sexism, they did so by mocking it, not explicitly naming it. Nancy overplayed the feminine, making the performative and optional character of femininity explicit and ridiculous. Jane claimed the masculine position by referring to her "balls," and performed it through her style of speech and by claiming the masculine protector role. This reproduced a hegemonic gender frame for the inter-action—masculine protector of feminine virtue. However, their maneuver disconnected the identity label *man* from the role of masculine protector and replaced him with a woman. This, and the women's hysterical laughter, exposed the posturing as a ridiculous facade and challenged gender coherence. The man who approached us was cast out of the interaction, not by explicitly rejecting the hegemonic gender frame, but by manipulating the relationships among his masculinity, Nancy's femininity, and Jane's femininity *and* masculinity.[7] While Nancy's feminine position perhaps stayed the same (and the parody makes this questionable), both the man's and Jane's positions took on different meanings and became some-thing different as Nancy and Jane acted out their positions. In the second interaction, Maddie's Paulie Shore maneuver was also a re-jection of the stranger's definition of the situation. Through nego-tiated social interaction, Maddie dislodged the man from his comfortable position in hegemonic masculinity.

In both situations, the relationship between masculinity and femininity shifted and thus the symbolic meaning of the interac-tion changed. Gender was an emergent feature of the interactive process, not simply a set of rules that framed the interaction. Fur-ther, the gender structure was not simply a microtranslation of the hegemonic gender order. It was actively negotiated and volleyed back and forth. The women asserted an alternative gender struc-ture for the interaction, and a different set of gender relations emerged. The interactive process was a negotiation characterized by individual maneuvers to respond to the actions of others and to ultimately manipulate the meaning of the interaction as it hap-pened. Because we expect others to follow rules and to act in pre-dictable ways, the men lost their footing; they did not know how to respond. As Goffman would describe it, they lost face, and the women did nothing to help them regain a positive standing. The men had little choice but to exit the interaction.

Losing face is often accompanied by a loss of esteem in the eyes of others and therefore a loss of power or influence in the interaction.[8] However, these interactions suggest that it was not simply the loss of face that shifted the power relations; power dynamics emerged along with the relationship between masculinity and femininity.

INTERACTIVE GENDER MANEUVERING AND POWER

Michel Foucault suggests that commonsense understandings of power include only one part of power relations and ignore one of the most important ways in which power operates.[9] According to Foucault, power is not simply something possessed and used by one person to suppress or force others to do things against their will, as is commonly thought. Instead, power is a force field created by the relationship between positions; it mutually situates and affects both parties. Because it is such a force field, power then can be manipulated through changes in the relationship between the positions. Power within social interaction, then, is not possessed by individuals, nor is it simply conferred by structural position;[10] it is instead a dynamic, organizing feature and outcome of social relations.

Adopting this model of power, Butler's theory would suggest that it is not simply acting out femininity and masculinity that produces unequal power relations (as West and Zimmerman assert), but that power operates through the meanings and concrete workings of the *relationship* between the two. The relationship between masculinity and femininity in any situated social interaction will set up a field of power; manipulating that relationship can potentially affect the field of power—at least within that interaction.[11] It is possible, then, that even if subservience and deference are part of doing femininity the play of power will depend on how others in the interaction are situated in relation to the person doing femininity; it will also depend on the meaning of the relation for those involved. If gender is viewed as relational rather than as a performance, this opens the possibility that doing femininity might, in some circumstances, shift power relations to the advantage of the individual doing so.

For instance, Maddie was relying on both the relationship between masculinity and femininity and on the hierarchical relationship between different masculinities to shift the power relations. As discussed in chapter 1, R. W. Connell suggests that the social organization of gender is not simply based on distinctions made between masculinity and femininity, but also among different masculinities: hegemonic masculinity, subordinate masculinity, complicit masculinity, and marginalized masculinity. When Maddie invoked Paulie Shore, she slammed the man into a subordinate masculinity. Because subordinate masculinity is defined as inferior, this shift in positioning constituted a loss of status for the man, at least in comparison to the position he attempted to establish and in relation to other men.

This shift in the man's position not only situated his masculinity, it also situated and defined Maddie's feminine position. As the man's social position shifted from player to geek, Maddie transformed from sexually objectified bimbo to bombshell despite both Maddie and the stranger doing gender in roughly the same way. While the bombshell is not far from the sexual object, given the masculine position of the man in this particular context, the distinction between the two became quite important in terms of power. The bombshell has agency and some power to reject or accept the advances of men. The desire created by being sexually attractive, when combined with subjective agency, transforms the implications of being a geek. The geek can, with the same cache of masculine privilege as any other man, visually consume and thus possess the feminine sexual object. However, when the object comes to life as a thinking, feeling, desiring subject, he cannot sexually possess her. For this reason, when the geek is situated in relation to the bombshell, and the bombshell in relation to the geek, it is arguable that sexualized femininity actually worked to Maddie's advantage. Through an interactive fixing of the definition of the situation, the meaning of the relationship between masculinity and femininity changed. It was through this shift in meaning that the power relations were altered. Much like the girls in Thorne's research turning cooties into weapons of power, these women's maneuvers did not put them in some objective "power position" but instead manipulated the force field so that power shifted in their direction. Importantly, this was a shift brought about through the manipulation of the symbolic meaning of masculine and feminine positions, and not by the exchanging of positions with men. As well, the symbolic meaning of the positions was produced, not only by individuals enacting or doing gender, but by individuals interactively situating others in a particular relationship to their own performances. The gender maneuvering, then, was a struggle over the relationship between masculinity and femininity, because it is that relationship that partially determines how power operates in face-to-face interaction. The *interpersonal* power relations had as much to do with the transformation of Maddie's femininity as did the symbolic relationship between masculinities. This was, in other words, a maneuver that played upon the relationship between multiple femininities as much as it was on the relationship between multiple masculinities.

ESTABLISHING SUBCULTURAL NORMS THROUGH INTERACTIVE GENDER MANEUVERING

Manipulating power relations is not the only reason individuals in alternative hard rock interactively gender maneuver. They also gender maneuver in order to establish or reinforce subcultural norms. By manipulating the meaning of masculinity and femininity within particular interactions, they remind themselves and others of what are and are not legitimate ways of doing rock. For instance, one evening a local musician, Dan, was telling a group of us about a time when his band showed up at a bar to unload their equipment, and they had to wait for over an hour in windy Chicago's February temperatures for the manager of the bar to unlock the door.

"Man, we were so pissed. The guy was just like, 'Uh, sorry.' Here's a bunch of bald-headed, scary lookin' guys and he wasn't worried."

Dan paused and finished the story,""If we were girls, we would have kicked his ass."

Dan initially situated himself as tough, scary, and potentially capable of physical aggression. However, he immediately defined that toughness into a relationship to femininity by suggesting girls would be even more scary. Even though Dan suggested that the manager should be afraid of the men, he quickly inverted the gender coherence of physical aggression and masculinity by suggesting that only if there were women around would the manager really be in danger. This reinforces the subcultural norms against men's use of physical aggression and the construction of women as tough and able to kick ass.

Shifting the relationship between masculinity and femininity in midconversation was also a strategy for fortifying the subcultural rejection of the mainstream groupie culture. One evening, I was talking with Bryan, Maddie, and Colleen about a local band. Bryan was a big fan of the band until they switched lead guitarists.

"They had this girl who played guitar," he said. "She was so awesome. She played like Angus Young (of AC/DC), you know on stage and stuff. She was so cool. I went up to her once after a show, and she was like 'I'm married.' I just wanted to talk about music."

Maddie and Colleen burst into laughter.

Poking fun at Bryan, Colleen smirked, "You should have put your dick back in your pants before you went up to talk to her."

Bryan laughed. "I should have taken my coat off my dick and put it back on."

Colleen added, "Hide it behind a newspaper or something."

When Bryan talked about approaching the musician after a show, the women jumped at the opportunity to interactively establish an alternative gender structure for the musician/groupie relationship. By suggesting Bryan had an erection, they constructed him as primarily interested in the woman because he was sexually attracted to her. This put Bryan in the position of groupie and the woman in the position of musician. The meaning of his interaction with the woman was created by all of the people hearing his story, and through a set of common understandings they worked together to expose and challenge the gendering of the groupie/musician dichotomy.

Musicians also construct the meaning of their position in relation to women fans to maintain this normative structure. During my conversation with Kim Thayil, he talked about how difficult it was to maintain the subcultural meaning for the identity label *musician* as his band Soundgarden moved into the mainstream.

"What I've found in the experience of touring is that there are a lot of dumb guys out there. But I also came away thinking, God, chicks suck. They're just as dumb."

"Do you mean in the audience?" I asked.

He sort of snickered and replied, "Just the ones you sometimes run into. And I started using that. Chicks suck. It was so disappointing. I think it's because of the types of bands we've always dealt with. Generally pretty decent guys. We weren't hanging around the glam-rock stars of the mid-eighties or whatever. It's just a different thing. . . . [We] just didn't want to be stupid idiots. They hated rock and roll. They hated the way it was characterized. They didn't like popular music. They just innately knew what was cool and what wasn't. . . . "

I was still interested in his feelings about "chicks," so I pushed him further: "And there were dumb chicks hanging out?"

"Yeah. It doesn't matter. You can characterize yourself as a certain type of person and there are still going to be idiots showing their tits in the audience. What are they getting out of that? Do they think 'Oh gee I think I'll play my guitar 'cause she showed me her tits'? You know, it never happened to us and it's happened the last four or five shows. Like, come on. . . . "

Surprised, I asked, "Women lift their shirts?"

"Yeah."

"Wow!"

"Well it didn't happen to us because we weren't that kind of band. I know those kind of bands, I've seen their shows. I've seen that kind of behavior."

When women lifted their shirts, they were doing groupie. They were situating themselves as sexual objects in relation to Kim Thayil the musician. However, in his telling of this story Thayil wiggled out of that position by explicitly focusing on his ability to play guitar as the only real important thing about doing musician. Thayil's perspective, at least within the context of this interview, was that this kind of behavior was characteristic of mainstream rock, and he did not want to play the part. Within the context of my interaction with him, he was establishing and maintaining the normative structure of the subculture by shifting the meaning of his position as musician and its relationship to the groupie.

One night I watched a woman walk up to a man who was in

the band that had just finished a set. She grabbed his arm and kind of jumped up and down, and in a shrill voice said, "Are you in a band?" He laughed, and then she said in a lower, matter-of-fact voice, "Me too."

This woman collapsed the distinction between musician and groupie by simultaneously occupying both positions within this interaction. The structure of the interaction itself could in no way be interpreted as that between musician and groupie. She not only constructed herself and her relationship to the man, but she also fortified the subcultural structure for relationships between fans and musicians.

There were often times like these when alternative hard rockers established alternative hierarchies between different masculinities and femininities—not so much to manipulate power relations, as Maddie had, but instead to bolster subcultural norms. For instance, at the Hole show mentioned in chapter 3, Courtney Love had left the stage because the crowd refused to obey her request to move back and stop pushing each other. When she returned to the stage, she said, "Aren't I bitch?"

A few men in the audience yelled "Yeah!" and one yelled back "Fucking bitch! Go home!" Not from the area and thus not knowing her audience, Courtney Love decided she needed to teach the audience a little lesson about the word *bitch*:

"Okay, yeah. That's nice. When I say *three* I want you to scream *bitch* as loud as you can. One—two—three—"

The audience took great pleasure in screaming, "BITCH!"

"Nice. Very good. Again. One—two—three—"

"BITCH!"

"Okay. Now, on the count of three, I want you to all yell *nigger*. One—two—three—"

The audience was silent. People around me were visibly uncomfortable and appeared to be confused, saying things like, "What the fuck, man?"

Love proceeded, "How 'bout *kike*? Wouldn't you guys just love to be able to scream *kike* at the top of your lungs? One—two—three—"

Again, the audience was quiet. With that, Love sort of whispered, "Fucking idiots," and the band launched into its next song.

The subcultural critique and reclamation of language used to keep women in line came through loud and clear in this interaction between Love and the audience. She initially called herself a bitch, like many women in the subculture do, as a sort of badge of honor. When the handful of men in the audience volleyed back the hegemonic meaning of the word, Love responded with her own maneuver. She redefined *bitch* not so much as a positive label but as an equivalent to straightforwardly offensive words like *nigger* and *kike*. Perhaps because she was not sure if her audience shared her subcultural sensibilities, Love quickly moved back to square one. The first step to reclaiming a derogatory label is to understand the way it is used to maintain relations of subordination. Love was, within the ongoing process of her interaction with the audience, constructing the word *bitch* as an offensive label used to dehumanize and keep women in their place, much as *nigger* and *kike* have been deployed to dehumanize and legitimate the subordinate position of African Americans and Jews, respectively. An initial maneuver to redefine *bitch* as a favorable femininity turned into a maneuver to simply politicize the word.

These sorts of maneuvers to establish subcultural norms became even more apparent after attending different kinds of shows. Alternative hard rockers are relatively choosy in terms of which bands they are or are not willing to see perform live. In order to get a handle on their subcultural norms, I attended a handful of shows explicitly avoided by the people with whom I was spending time.

On one occasion when I planned to attend one of these shows, I stopped by Bryan's on my way to the club. Colleen and Carrie were hanging out with Bryan when I arrived. After a few minutes, I told them that I was on my way to Lounge Ax to see the Dazzling Killmen and Shorty.

Colleen sort of scoffed, "I can't fucking stand Shorty. The lead singer is so fucking obnoxious."

Bryan stood up and started doing his own impersonation of the lead singer. He strutted around with an aggressive, angry look on his face and then said, "Okay, so here's what he does when the band is just playing."

Pretending to shove the microphone in his front pocket, Bryan thrust out his hips and just stood there motionless with his head tilted slightly back.

Carrie chimed in, "We saw them, right? I think they made me really angry. Why are you going to that show?"

"Well, I'd heard a lot about them and I kind of wanted to check it out for myself."

Colleen laughed and said, "Oh, it will be really interesting for you."

Bryan added, "Yeah. It will be a bunch of men."

All three laughed. Colleen continued, this time with a disgusted look on her face. "Some people just love Shorty. There will be a bunch of manly scensters there. I hate them. It will be full of men who are really into it."

While their interactive effort to distance themselves from Shorty and the "manly men" who were really into the band was an interesting example of interactive gender maneuvering, it left me just a tad apprehensive. When I arrived, I immediately sensed a different sort of crowd than had been at other shows I had attended. The men outnumbered the women by at least ten to one. The area in front of the stage was for the most part occupied only by men. There were one or two women who were sort of leaning into or holding onto men. The rest of the women were in the front by the door. I was acutely self-conscious and the head-to-toe stares from men as I made my way through the crowd didn't alleviate my discomfort. I wished I had dressed differently.

There was some action on stage and the audience got relatively quiet, so I tried to move closer to see what was happening. One person dressed in a gorilla suit and another in a mummy suit walked onto the stage. The mummy handed the gorilla a banana and walked off stage. The crowd cheered. Then a man dressed as Darth Vader came out with the guys in the Dazzling Killmen. As the band picked up their instruments, Darth approached the microphone.

Addressing the audience, he said, "I really like you guys. I really do, you fucking idiots. Are you having a good time?"

A few people clapped and yelled, "Yeah!"

"Are you drinking?"

More applause, and more aggressively than before, "Yeah!"

"Are you tipping? You know you can't get an abortion on good looks."

The audience erupted in laughter.

"We've got some hillbillies from St. Louis here tonight. Give it up for the Dazzling Killmen!"

The band launched into a hard, aggressive riff. It didn't sound all that different from what I had been hearing at other shows, but the band's interactions with the audience were very different. They seemed to be taunting the audience; the bass player leaned over the crowd, snarling and spitting. The crowd responded by getting more aggressive and more agitated. People were slamming into me with elbows, heads, and fists. I managed to move farther away, where people were a little less aggressive. Still, I was continuously bumped or shoved around.

Unlike other shows where being in the mosh pit was actually a pleasurable group experience, I didn't feel I could hold my own and decided to give up "participating" in that aspect of the show. I walked to the front of the club and bummed a cigarette from a woman sitting at the bar. As I was making my way to search for a spot where I could watch without getting pummeled, a man tapped me on the shoulder. At first I couldn't make out what he was saying, but it seemed he was saying something about my cigarette. I assumed he was asking me for one, so I yelled, "I just bummed it off someone else."

He leaned close to me face, held eye contact, and said back, "No. I asked you if you would burn me with your cigarette. I want you to burn my hand with your cigarette."

I was startled. It was something I never would have expected, and it took me completely off guard. He smiled at what must have been a confused look of horror on my face.

All I could come up with was a very stern, "No!"

I quickly turned and moved away from him. Suddenly I didn't feel at all safe. I thought about where I had parked my car. Even when I first started going to shows in Chicago by myself I never worried about my safety. Now I was wishing I hadn't come to this show alone.

I found an out-of-the-way spot, pulled my body into myself

trying desperately to disappear, and watched the mayhem. As the band got progressively more aggressive and more belligerent, the men in front of the stage got more aggressive and physical.

When the Killmen finished their set, I felt it was safe to leave my little space and go to the bar for some water. I was in the corner, at the end of the bar and close to the wall. While I was standing there, a man came up and stood between me and the wall. He looked me over.

"Damn, you're tall."

There was a small wood box next to the wall, and he stood on it.

"I'm not standing on this because you're taller than me. I just want to get the bartender's attention."

"Whatever," I said flatly, turning away.

"You don't have to get snippy about it."

One of the servers came up. She set her tray down on the bar, let out a huge sigh, and waited for the bartender. The man next to me stepped off the wooden block, walked around me, and tapped her on the shoulder.

"Can I order my drink from you?"

"Order from the bartender. I'm the waitress. You're at the bar."

"But I'd much rather have you serve me."

"Order from the bartender."

"If I move away from the bar, can I order my drink from you?"

"You can do whatever the fuck you want. Just get out of my way. I'm trying to work."

As the man walked away, the woman turned and with a look of exhaustion said to herself, "Fucking assholes."

After the bartender filled her order, he gave me a glass of water. I moved out into the crowd once again. Within five minutes, the man who stood next to me at the bar walked up to me.

"Hey, I know you. I talked to you earlier."

Tersely, and without looking at him, I responded, "Yeah, you did."

"Yeah, I asked you to burn my hand with your cigarette."

Confused because he was not the man who had approached me earlier, I was again completely taken off guard. All I could muster was, "Get out of my face right now!"

He laughed and said, "Well, it was nice meeting you. Maybe we'll talk later."

"Get out of my face right fucking now."

"Maybe next year."

Out of the corner of my eye I watched him walk over to the man who actually had asked me to burn him with his cigarette. They high-fived each other with laughter. It was apparently great fun to work together in shocking and frightening women.

I seriously feared for my safety by this point and decided I had seen enough. As I left the bar, I was thankful I had found a parking spot on Lincoln Avenue instead of a side street. I now understood why the other women that evening were either accompanied by men or remained at the front of the bar. I also understood why I couldn't find anyone with whom I had attended other shows to go with me to this one. There were different rules operating here, and the way people interacted was intolerable to alternative hard rockers. Unlike the bands I had been seeing, bands that took responsibility to interact with the audience to establish norms against aggression and violence, these bands mocked their audience and whipped them into a frenzy of aggression. The alternative hard rockers I knew would have had no part of it.

Interactive gender maneuvering among alternative hard rockers was sometimes both about power and about establishing subcultural norms. This was evident the first time I met Jim. After a few minutes of group discussion, Jim addressed me specifically.

"So what do you do?"

"Oh, I'm in school. Part of why I'm here is because I'm trying to do this research project on rock music."

Jim raised his eyebrows and slowly nodded, "Wow. You must be really smart."

Not yet fully understanding the subcultural dynamic of men adopting a somewhat deferent masculinity in relation to women, I got flustered and embarrassed, and awkwardly stammered, "Well, you don't have to be that smart to go to school. You just have to know how to do it."

"Well, I'm pretty stupid, so I don't think it would matter."

I looked at him with a puzzled expression and uncomfortably blurted out, "Oh, I'm sure you're not *that* stupid."

He smiled and said, "It's okay. You can be stupid and still be in a band."

This interaction was not just a struggle over the subcultural norms for a somewhat deferent masculinity, but also a negotiation of interpersonal power. Jim, in a sense, rejected my quite inadvertent and accidental construction of our interaction as one between a smart woman and a stupid man by reconfiguring it as one between a smart woman and a guy in a rock band. By doing so, the power relations shifted between us. Even though outside the club—and particularly in certain institutional settings that I was accustomed to—being intelligent would trump being in a rock band, in the club that night, it put him much higher in any status hierarchy, gendered or otherwise. He was reminding or telling me that intelligence is fine, but in the end, what gets you status in this subculture is the music.

This points to the importance of context. The relationship between an academic and a rock musician is going to depend on the context in which they are situated in relation to each other. In a classroom, for instance, the power dynamics of this interaction might have operated differently than they did in a rock club, and the maneuver would not have made much sense.

Context becomes particularly important when we introduce racial, class, ethnic, age, and sexuality differences. How would power operate in similar or different kinds of exchanges—for instance, between an African-American man and a white woman, an economically privileged African-American man and a working-class white woman, or a working-class white man and an economically privileged Latina? How would the negotiation differ if among African Americans, or among Chinese Americans? These questions point to the importance of context in any negotiation of interpersonal power, and defining context must include not only the institutional setting and the social positions of people involved,[12] but also the meaning of the relationship between the masculinities and femininities operating within the setting. Within face-to-face interaction, the hierarchies set up by Connell's theory for the social organization of masculinity might not hold up in terms of interpersonal power. Connell suggests that subordinate and marginal masculinities function as comparisons to define and legitimate hegemonic masculinity as the ideal, and therefore do not challenge but instead maintain the gender order of male dominance.[13] According to Connell, both the meanings and the practices associated with subordinate masculinity maintain male dominance because their existence reifies hegemonic masculinity as the ideal. However, if we shift our analysis from a macro understanding of male dominance—from looking at the overarching structure of masculinity and how it confers power to men as a group—and instead redirect our gaze to the micro relations of face-to-face interaction between women and men rather than among men, subordinate and marginal masculinities result in different power dynamics. Deploying a set of marginalized masculine practices is going to be perceived, responded to, and negotiated differently in different contexts. For instance, doing rural, working-class, white masculinity at a country music concert is going to mean something quite different and produce different gender and power structures of interaction than if done at a hip-hop concert. The status of an individual man in relation to other women and men, and his place in the field of power, will likely vary depending on the setting.

In order to get a handle on the workings of power in everyday life, then, we must pay close attention to the gender, racial, class, ethnic, and sexual organization of localized settings as much as the identities of individuals and where they are situated in the larger, macro gender, racial, class, ethnic, and sexual orders. Connell is right when he suggests that our everyday practices reflect and maintain macro relations of male dominance. Depending on the organization of race, class, ethnicity and sexuality within a specific context, and depending on the femininities and masculinities adopted by others in any situation, subordinate or marginal masculinities can serve to maintain male dominant power relations; they might, however, also undermine male dominance depending on the context and depending on how they are situated in relation to femininities operating in the same context.

Further, at the level of social interaction, the relationship between subordinate masculinities and some forms of femininity can shift power relations to the advantage of women while still perhaps maintaining the overarching gender order that values particular characteristics that benefit men in general. In the story of not going along that began this chapter, there is no doubt that Maddie was relying on the hierarchical relationships among masculinities. However, within this interaction it worked to shift power to her advantage. At the level of interpersonal negotiations of power, her deployment of that hierarchy undermined one man's dominant position. This suggests that different masculinities *and femininities* are implicated in the larger gender order,[14] and that these multiple genders can be bandied about to manipulate the relationship between and among the gender positions of individuals in any given interaction and to manipulate power relations.[15] While the interactive gender maneuvers of alternative hard rockers does not change nor transform the dominant cultural hierarchies among and between masculinities and femininities, individuals do utilize that structure in order to undermine male dominant power relations within their own subculture and in their interpersonal interactions.

In conclusion, it can be said that there are different levels of social organization at which gender structures social life. At the broadest level, there are dominant constructions of gender that organize the social structure overall: the structure of our major institutions; the global, national, and local production and distribution of resources; and the structure of overarching power relations. Gender also organizes smaller subcultures and interactions within specific contexts. Finally, gender structures our identities, our understanding of who and what we are, and our bodies. We have looked at alternative hard rock at the level of subcultural norms and interactive practices. In chapter 5 I will focus on alternative hard rockers' use of the body to gender maneuver.

5

THE BODY IN ALTERNATIVE
HARD ROCK

Jennifer Finch of the band L7 had her back propped up against the wall and her legs stretched out and crossed. She was wearing faded jeans, combat boots, and a black bra. We were in O'Cayz Coral in Madison, Wisconsin, and because of the noise of the crowd still buzzing from L7's raucous set, it was difficult for us to hear each other. We had moved behind the drum kit on the small stage at the front of the bar.

As we began talking, a young man sheepishly approached her and asked her for her autograph. She obliged, he thanked her, and she turned back to me to continue her thought. The man remained standing over us. Finch sort of glanced at him suspiciously and then back at me. The man began talking.

"I really liked the show. You guys rock. . . . "

First glancing down to her breasts and then looking up with her eyebrows raised and a look of irritation on her face, Finch posed the rhetorical question, "We 'guys'?"

"Well, you women," the man stammered and sort of shuffled his feet.

"Look, I'm doing an interview right now. I can't talk with you."

She looked back toward me, rolled her eyes, and began talking again.

"That's cool. I just wanted to say that, you know, if you guys . . . I mean women . . . didn't have a place to stay, I've got plenty of room."

Finch placed her hand on my knee, looked me in the eye, and said loudly and pointedly, "I'm sorry. Apparently he doesn't get it. I apologize for this."

She then turned, leaned toward the man and tersely said, "Read my fucking lips. What part of this do you not understand? I said, I am doing an interview. I can't talk with you right now."

Laughing nervously, the man retreated, "Hey, no problem. I'll catch up with you later."

As he stepped off the stage and disappeared into the crowd, Finch turned back to me and said, with sarcastic laughter in her voice, "Maybe I'm sending the wrong message having my tits hangin' out like this."

Somewhat incongruently, she continued, "I just think people are more aware of sexism these days. You know, the old, tired bullshit doesn't work anymore. Like, you know that decal that truckers have on their mud flaps? You know, the naked woman with the Barbie tits, leaning back?"

I nodded and scoffed, "Oh yeah. I fucking hate that."

"Well I bought one. On our last tour I bought that decal at a truck stop. The rest of the band gave me a lot of shit because it was offensive. I wasn't thinking that when I bought it. It's not offensive. It's a cheesy piece of Americana. Someday it will be seen as ridiculous. People are tuned into sexism more. People aren't buying it anymore. If I buy the decal, it's not the same as some fucking truck driver buying it. It's already making it sort of stupid."

At the one 7 Year Bitch show I attended, not only were they selling T-shirts with this image and their band name on them, but it was also painted on the drum kit. The image clearly has some significant meaning to at least some of the women in this subculture, as it pops up repeatedly on women's bodies, on instruments, and in conversations. Why would a woman conclude that owning the image herself, having it tattooed on her body, or painting it on her drum kit was somehow different from "some fucking truck driver" owning it?

As truckers scream down the highway, they flash to other

motorists the image, painted on the cab of their trucks or embossed on their tires' mud flaps. It is meant to convey to others something about the trucker himself, and what it conveys is heteromasculinity. The image itself is a silhouette, which means it could be any woman. Like the groupie, she is a nameless, faceless, sexually alluring body—the feminine sexual object. The image symbolizes not only feminine sexuality objectified, but also masculine sexual subjectivity. It says, "I am a real man" as much as a bumper sticker that reads MEAT IS MURDER says "I am a vegetarian" or JESUS SAVES says "I am a Christian." The image constructs the trucker's masculinity and sexuality by publicly claiming the masculine subject position in relation to the feminine sexual object. It works as a marker of masculinity because heterosexual masculinity only makes sense in its relationship to heterosexual femininity. As defined through the gender order, the feminine sexual object is heterosexual femininity, so the image works as a badge of manhood as well as of heterosexuality.[1]

What might it mean, then, when a woman buys or wears a T-shirt displaying the image? Finch said, "If I buy the decal, it's not the same as some fucking truck driver buying it. It's already making it sort of stupid." That she viewed this as "making it sort of stupid" suggests that there is some way in which a woman can appropriate the symbol to give it a different meaning. By displaying it on her own body, the relationship between herself as a woman and the symbol of objectified femininity changes. The real woman is no longer encompassed by the image as sexual object, but instead possesses it herself. By shifting the relationship between real women and the image, the image comes to mean something else. It breaks down the dichotomy between subject and object because the woman is both the object and the person who possesses it.

By dissolving the subject/object split, the woman possessing the feminine sexual object also destabilizes the relationship between masculinity and femininity. First, if the woman is situating herself as desiring subject in relation to the feminine sexual object, this disrupts the gender coherence and heterosexual requirement for desire.[2] It takes the man out of the position of desiring subject and replaces him with a woman. However, when a woman puts the image on her own body, such as on a T-shirt or tattoo, she, unlike the truck driver, is not in the position to look at the image. Others are encouraged to look at it, but when they do so, they are also confronted with a real-life, individual woman. This shifts the meaning of the relationship between the one who displays the image and the image itself so that a straightforward gender reading becomes more difficult. When a woman buys or displays the symbol on her own body, it opens the possibility for other meanings or relationships to the decal—namely, from the perspective of a woman. Once an alternative option is exposed, the seemingly natural or inevitable relationship to the symbol is neither natural nor inevitable. Truckers' use of the symbol is exposed as a strategy of masculinity, not a natural expression of maleness or manhood, and the women saw this as ridiculous and mocked them by appropriating the sexualized, feminine body.

I do not think that it is a coincidence that it is this image that keeps popping up all over alternative hard rock. Popular culture is central in the lives of most participants. When Finch said that the decal was "a cheesy piece of Americana" she was suggesting that this sort of sexism is outdated or passé. She ridiculed men who are not with the times and haven't realized that we've moved beyond the sexual objectification of women, at least in this particular form. You could almost hear her saying to truckers, "Haven't you even seen *Thelma and Louise*? You're a joke!" The film *Thelma and Louise* first introduced a critical perspective of the image by explicitly tying it to the character of an obnoxious trucker who is a cinematic caricature of masculine sexuality on the highway. The image had become an outdated "cheesy piece of Americana" in these women's view because the film had made it so. Their investment in popular culture as a measure of what is hip and what is not comes through in their cultural gender maneuvering. From their perspective, everybody who's anybody knows that the mud flap image was obliterated by the film, and anybody who doesn't is a loser. When women in the scene appropriated the image, they were pointing out just how uncool the men who take it seriously are.

The belief among alternative hard rockers that truckers who still buy into this symbol are losers did not change the fact that I still saw the image flashing by on Interstate 94 as I traveled between Madison and Chicago. No matter how many women in alternative hard rock wear the shirts, or buy the decals, or laugh at men who take it seriously, truckers still display their heteromasculinity and continue to encourage other motorists to go along and look at feminine sexuality objectified. It is difficult to say whether other motorists have more critical consciousness of the decal. I think it would be safe to say that if they do, it has more to do with the film *Thelma and Louise* than the purchasing practices and stylistic choices of alternative hard rockers. At the same time, however, people who participate in alternative hard rock or who have gone to a 7 Year Bitch show probably experience the truck mud flaps with at least some dissonance. It can no longer simply refer to the trucker's sexuality, but can probably also bring to mind women as thinking, feeling, singing and playing human beings. The hegemonic construction of the female body as sexual object was, at least within the context of the rock club, disrupted.

While an individual woman might appropriate a symbol of feminine objectification by constructing her own transgressive meaning for it, this alone does not change anything in the gender order of social relations. However, when bodies and bodily practices are placed within the ongoing process of gender structuration in situated social relations, they become rather significant in the gender order. Doing masculinity and femininity includes gender display, or the way we present ourselves to others as men or as women. One of the most obvious ways in which we present ourselves as gendered is with our bodies—that is, through the clothing we wear, our hairstyles, and whether or not we wear makeup, as well as through our body comportment and how we move.[3]

Not only do our bodies display our gender, but the gender order gets reproduced and depends upon how the embodied identity labels *woman* and *man* set up a relationship between masculinity and femininity. For example, the clothing women are expected to wear emphasizes their sexual attractiveness by revealing the body, by highlighting and sexualizing facial features through makeup, and by donning hairstyles that emphasize youth and reproduce mainstream standards of attractiveness. That is, the physical appearance of women reflects or mirrors the hegemonic construction of femininity as sexual object. While men are also encouraged to wear clothing and hairstyles that will make them sexually appealing, the styles themselves do not sexualize the body as an object of desire in the same way that women's styles do. Style is one of the main signifiers of gender identity and a central mechanism of what Judith Butler calls *the myth of gender coherence*. As people who identify as men put on masculinity and others who identify as women put on femininity, the gender order is reconstructed. Thus, style and other bodily practices are part of the process of gender structuration.

Because the matrix between masculinity and femininity is partially constructed and maintained through embodied gender, this opens the possibility for disrupting that relationship through bodily practice. That is, what is worn, how it is worn, how what we're wearing relates to what others are wearing, the way we move our bodies in relation to other bodies, and the meaning of the gendered body could be manipulated to gender maneuver. In previous chapters, I discussed how alternative hard rockers gender maneuver to create a subculture and how they gender maneuver within face-to-face interaction. In this chapter, I will focus on how alternative hard rockers bring gender maneuvering down to the body to construct an alternative gender order for rock culture.

Like most subcultures, clothing and style play an important role in the lives of alternative hard rockers and are part of the drawing of boundaries around the subculture. There are patterns in what women wear and what men wear. In general, the word that comes to mind to describe the women is *slutty*. The men, in a strange, asymmetrical way, did not look the complement to the slut. There were two styles worn by men in alternative hard rock. The first was the "'grunge" look; the other produced an image more akin to a self-conscious geek.

The grunge look became popular in the early to mid-1990s and is most associated with nationally recognized alternative hard rock bands like Pearl Jam and Nirvana. The main point of this style is to meticulously put together seemingly discoordinate, secondhand clothing and appear as if style and economic success were unimportant. The look is comprised of army fatigue pants raggedly cut off just below or above the knees and sometimes worn over leggings or long underwear; it also includes combat boots, leather motorcycle jackets or army jackets, and faded flannel shirts worn unbuttoned over threadbare T-shirts displaying the names and logos of bands like Black Sabbath and Led Zeppelin. Once in awhile I might see a shirt that read THIS IS NOT A FUGAZI T-SHIRT.[4] Facial hair, such as sideburns, goatees, or chin tufts is common, and most men either wear their hair very long or shave their heads. These general standards of grooming cast an interesting light on the military fatigues: there would be no mistaking these guys for ROTC students.

The grunge style is not all that different from other rock styles; army surplus clothing was a staple in hippie and rock culture in the 1960s and early 1970s. The flannel shirts perhaps suggest an interesting look toward poor, rural white culture,[5] but for the most part, the look itself is quite masculine and, unlike mainstream rock, does not include any form of gender-bending. Because gender-bending through style has always been the "gender" story of men in rock, the mainstream media immediately picked up on and criticized "Seattle grunge" for replacing feminine styles with masculine. In fact, largely because of the styles and sound of the music, grunge was billed by the mainstream media as a renaissance and celebration of masculine adolescence. It was assumed that grunge bands threw off the feminine styles used by the rockers of the 1970s and '80s, fully embracing aggressive, hard music, and therefore that grunge must represent a movement backward in terms of gender rebellion.

However, characterizing the music as masculine because it sounds hard and aggressive simply reproduces the old gender bifurcation of musical sound described earlier. More importantly, to characterize this subculture as simply a renaissance and celebration of male adolescence because the men no longer wear spandex and makeup is to miss the layers of gender going on within all cultures, including alternative hard rock. This criticism of grunge ignores the ways in which gender is not simply an individual-level identity we put on through clothing or style; it is a *social* relationship among and between masculinities and femininities that gets produced, sustained, and contested through social practice and interaction. While these men look masculine in their gender display, their embedded social practices and relations with others, including other men and women, are far from a straightforward reproduction of adolescent masculinity.

Within the context of rock culture, adopting masculine styles actually makes a lot of sense. Alternative hard rockers consciously rejected the gender-bending, glam-metal bands of the 1980s, acutely aware that the same men who were wearing makeup and spandex were also the ones who fully embraced the sexualized masculine position in relation to women. In their efforts to create something new, they not only threw out the sexual norms of glam metal, but also rejected the gender display.

For instance, when I was talking with Kim Thayil of Soundgarden, we were discussing differences between Soundgarden and glam metal. He said of those kinds of bands, "Ahh . . . fucking idiots . . . get a girl to blow the whole crew. . . ."

"What's interesting is the whole kind of grunge thing," I suggested. "The mainstream media is casting that as hypermasculine because they don't wear makeup."

Thayil rolled his eyes. "No. They're normal people. They're not playing some kind of rock dream of dressing up and getting girls or whatever."

One interesting twist on this rejection was adopted by the Wesley Willis Fiasco, one of the most popular Chicago bands at the time. For a short period of time, the staple attire for their gigs looked a lot like the glam-metal bands of the 1980s—skintight, sequined bell-bottoms, spandex tights, a bright pink, fur-trimmed tank top, and sometimes, bright, almost carnivalesque makeup. Along with the glam garb, they would all have some ridiculously large, phallic-shaped object strapped to their legs under their pants. As they moved about the audience or while they performed on stage, they would thrust their hips out to ensure the audience took notice of their super pseudophalluses. The most common response from others was laughter. They and their audience were mocking the masculinity of glam-metal musicians who, quite often, wore very tight pants that accentuated their penis, a sausage, or some other tube-shaped object extending down one leg. For glam rockers, and not unlike many men, their penises were their badges of embodied sexual prowess and power. Displaying a ridiculously large penis was much like displaying the truckers' mud flap image; the exposed phallus, especially combined with incessant talk about "getting girls," was a declaration of heteromasculinity. It is not a coincidence that in this subculture, the men in the Fiasco chose that aspect of mainstream rock to tip others to their parody.

On some occasions, individual male musicians do adopt feminine styles, not as parody, but as a stylistic maneuver. Kurt Cobain would sometimes, for instance, wear a skirt on stage and/or rouge, lipstick, and eyeshadow. Unlike the glam rockers however, there was nothing outlandish or carnivalesque about the skirt or the makeup. They were worn as if the skirt was simply one possible choice among many others hanging in the closet and the makeup was meant to enhance his natural features.

However, despite the fact that these individual men may wear femininity as a sort of natural expression of themselves rather than an explicit performance, many women I spoke to articulated strong reservations about Kurt Cobain or any other rocker wearing women's clothing.

For instance, during my conversation with Jennifer Finch of L7 she said, "Supposedly they do it to express their feminine side. That's sexist bullshit. It's not about a feminine side or masculine side; it's about human traits."

For Finch and others, the tired old cliché of men dressing up like women reproduces the idea that there is a natural divide between masculinity and femininity and that the clothing we wear somehow expresses an internal femininity or masculinity. This sort of gender display is, however, an aberration and certainly not the boundary-defining style for the subculture that the grunge look was. It is true that most alternative hard rock men are most often certainly not embracing femininity in their gender display. However, at the same time that they have rejected femininity, in a sense, they embrace feminism. If we extend gender to include not only individual gender display, but also the relationships between masculinity and femininity produced through talk and practices, it becomes clear that these men are not simply reproducing the old gender order. They certainly look the part of the manly man, and their music is aggressive and loud, but when you listen to what they say on stage and watch how they interact with each other and with women, the layers of their gender performance are revealed as discoordinate. The image of their bodies does not cohere with their talk nor with their interpersonal styles. That is, these men occupy a sort of no-man's-land in terms of gender coherence.

For instance, I spent some time backstage after Pearl Jam played at Cabaret Metro. The men in the band, Eddie Vedder, Stone Gossard, Mike McCready, Jeff Ament, and Dave Abbruzzese, were mingling among the crowd. To be honest, they each looked like a cross between a lumberjack and a punk rocker—both fairly masculine social positions. However, I watched as these lumberjack punks politely talked with and listened to women and men. Eddie Vedder approached me to check to make sure everything was okay. During our conversation, he spoke in a soft, quiet tone. Mike McCready and Jeff Ament both did the same sort of checking in, and were very polite and soft-spoken. In other words, the visual impression of their bodies cloaked in flannel, army fatigues, concert T-shirts, and combat boots struck a discordant relationship to how they talked and interacted with me and with others. The lumberjack punk was, not only a rather nice guy, but if you took the time to listen to what he had to say and paid attention to how he said it, it became clear that he was also committed to challenging sexism, racism, and heterosexism; not quite what you would expect from a lumberjack. In other words, it is simply inaccurate to conclude that alternative hard rock is a renaissance of hegemonic masculinity in rock music.

The second main look, as I've mentioned, can only be described as "geeky." These men wear their pants too short (referred to in my high school as Harry High-waters, flood pants, or simply floods), and the short pants reveal white tube socks and some form of loafers or sneakers. It seems they all wear glasses, which makes me wonder whether they are actually visually impaired or if this is simply a fashion statement, and invariably the glasses have excessively thick lenses and thick, black frames. To finish the look, the men button their shirts all the way up to the top button. This style reproduces the stereotypical image of the kid in high school who was perhaps good at math and science, but never asked for, let alone had, a date in his life. He was the "brain" who would drop his books in nervous intimidation when an attractive girl would talk to him— hardly the picture of a suave, confident, sexually assertive man. Like the grunge look, there was absolutely nothing feminine about this style.

While the men are either grunge or geek, the women look the part of the stereotypical slut. Very tight, revealing clothes are common. Miniskirts, hot pants, halter tops, fishnet stockings, or thigh-high stockings that don't quite reach the hem of the skirt or dress are all common staples of the women's wardrobes. The women dye their hair platinum blond, red, or dark black. There is some variation in whether or not makeup is worn, but when it is, it is heavy. A tube of bright red lipstick was one of the first things I bought in my efforts to enter the subculture as a legitimate participant.

It is a common practice for women to purchase conservative dresses at the thrift store and alter them by bringing in the bodice and skirt for a snug fit on the body. They remove sleeves and backs, and lower the bustline: the 1950s or '70s debutante and housewife are transformed into the bombshell. Because the body is a central terrain upon which men and women in alternative hard rock gender maneuver, having the skill to sew and alter clothing is greatly valued and considered art. When I first talked with Carrie, one of the first things she revealed about herself was that she is an artist and that her medium was thrift-store dresses and other clothing. Women on the scene constantly talk about and comment upon each others' clothing. If a woman has made or altered what she is wearing, all the better. While one might expect that such a traditionally feminine, domestic activity would be rejected by young women trying to forge a new way of doing gender, the women in this subculture reclaim the activity as empowering. Within a mainstream fashion culture characterized by limited choices and a continuously boxed-in range of possibilities for embodied gender, having the skill to transform what is offered is a necessary part of cultural maneuvers and therefore highly valued.

Despite there being distinctive feminine and masculine styles, there are some ways in which the gender divide is blurred. Like most rock cultures, women and men share certain kinds of clothing and style. For instance, many of the women also wear the same sorts of flannel shirts, concert T-shirts, army fatigue pants, combat boots, and leggings that the men wear. However, they do so usually in combination with the miniskirts, hot pants, and low-cut tops and dresses. For instance, a woman might wear hot pants, a flannel shirt worn over a Jimi Hendrix T-shirt, and combat boots. While the "slut wear" of women creates a stylistic gender divide between masculinity and femininity, the articles of clothing that most signify hegemonic masculinity (combat boots, flannel shirts, army fatigue pants) are worn by both men and women. The specific way in which women appropriate masculine styles—by combining them with rather extreme markers of feminine sexuality—undermine their power to articulate a straightforward masculine sexual subjectivity for the men. While combat boots and flannel shirts masculinize the look, the hot pants and miniskirts scream feminine sexuality, and do so just loud enough to pull the masculine clothing into the realm of sexual objectification. That is, flannel, boots, and army surplus become sexualized. The balance between feminine sexual objectification and military or rocker drag simultaneously masculinizes the miniskirts and feminizes the flannel shirts. As is the case with most gender-bending styles, once feminized in this way, the boots and the shirts can no longer straightforwardly signify masculinity.

Women's slut wear is always combined with something that disrupts seamless sexual objectification, and not always simply by adopting masculine signifiers. The markers of feminine sexual objectification never stand alone: fishnet stockings are worn over leggings, and heavy makeup is accompanied by a shaved head, tattoos, and/or any variety of facial piercings. Hair that was dyed platinum blond is grown out to expose one- to two-inch darker roots, making the cosmetic facade explicit. Other hair colors are just a tad off any natural hue or in some cases completely unnatural: pink, green, purple, or orange. A low-cut tank top often reveals not only cleavage, but also unshaven armpits. As discussed above, miniskirts, dresses and hot pants are worn with heavy combat boots or with a flannel shirt, but also, more often than not, reveal unshaven legs. This bricolage of sexualized femininity, white working-class masculinity and/or butch dyke (flannel shirts, combat boots, army fatigues), punk (piercings; pink, green, purple, or orange hair; shaved heads) and feminism (unshaven legs and armpits) signifies that the masculine items are not simply cute, sexy, or more diminutive expressions of masculinity (as is usually the case when women wear certain kinds of men's clothing—remember Marlene Dietrich in *Morocco*, or Diane Keaton in *Annie Hall?*).

When you first catch a glimpse of these women, you are immediately drawn in to consume them visually. They invite what Laura Mulvey calls the scopophilic view,[6] which refers to deriving sexual pleasure simply by looking at a sexual object. However, once inside, you are smacked in the head by the inconsistency, expecting and wanting these women to be feminine sexual objects, but denied that conclusion at the last moment. It's like the Three Stooges staple gag in which Mo affectionately beckons Curly. When Curly is within reach, Mo's attitude changes to anger, and he scissor-pokes Curly in the eyes. The women's style coyly beckons, and when it has you pulled in, pokes you in the eyes with gender disruption.

The feminine strategy of using beauty and sexual attractiveness to manipulate gender power relations is not new. One angle, for instance, is to do sexualized femininity in order to gain power in relation to men. Beautiful women get all kinds of "doors opened" for them, and there is no denying that sexual attractiveness can work to women's advantage in many social settings.[7] In this case, a woman situates men in the position of "looker," creates a desire, and then uses her control over access to the object of desire (which is herself) to manipulate the man. While constituting hegemonic gender structuration, this can be a relatively effective way for sexually attractive women to manipulate interpersonal power relations between themselves and others.

Another strategy might be to obliterate the relationship between masculine sexual subjectivity and the feminine sexual object by refusing to do sexualized heterofemininity. By not shaving, not wearing makeup, cutting off her hair, gaining weight, and so on, a woman can refuse to play the game of heterosexual gender, or, as Luce Irigaray says, "refuse to go to market."[8] This is a gender maneuver that manipulates the relationship between masculinity and femininity by refusing to embody the feminine sexual object. Without a feminine sexual object, one cannot adopt the hegemonic masculine sexual subject position, which necessarily needs an object to look at and desire. This is one of the rationales for many feminists' refusal to shave or wear makeup.

Alternative hard rockers suggest yet a third strategy, which is to stylistically collapse the line that divides the sexually desirable from the sexually undesirable. In this case, the sex object meets the feminist, the butch lesbian, the punk rocker, and the boy. This combination works so well because it plays on the socially acceptable and largely unconscious practice of visually consuming women. The meaning of bleach-blond hair, miniskirts, and hot pants is so transparent that, upon first glance, it instantly situates others into the position of "looker." However, the dark roots, piercings, and boots make that position extremely uncomfortable, or at least perhaps for many, not very pleasurable. The discomfort comes from thoroughly expecting the sexual object and a confirmation of all the meanings attached to her, but instead being confronted with a feminist; a punk rocker; a white, rural, working-class boy; and a butch lesbian. This makes it very difficult for the looker to fix any straightforward meaning on to the style and therefore he finds it extremely difficult to understand how to relate to her or to predict how she will act. The looker does not know if the woman is articulating a sexual invitation or a warning that she will kick your ass, spit on you, make you confront your sexist attitudes, or make a move on your girlfriend. This combination of styles situates feminine sexuality in relation to the looker but then by manipulating the image of the feminine position disrupts the masculine position of looker at the same time; that is, the relationship between the masculine sexual subject/looker and the feminine sexual object of the gaze is disrupted. The inconsistency in the image shifts the looker's desire for the sexual object to a desire to get out of the position of scopophile entirely. This would not work without the initial invitation to look produced with the revealing clothing, makeup, and dyed hair. The traditional slut wear is, in this sense, a central, strategic component of the embodied gender maneuver.

While the women's styles combine femininity and masculinity, the men's styles are straightforwardly masculine; when taken alone, it might be difficult to see how they are anything but a straightforward reproduction of the gender order. Men have been dressing this way for a long time. Instead of adopting femininity, as many hard rockers had previously, these men embrace a subordinate masculinity—the uncool, sexually inept and unconfident but brainy high school nerd. R. W. Connell's model for the relationships between masculinities would suggest that these men are simply doing a form of subordinate, or perhaps marginal, masculinities. Because such masculinities are defined through their difference from and inferiority to hegemonic masculinity, Connell suggests they maintain male dominance by keeping hegemonic practices in the center as the ideal masculinity. However, if we look at style within the process of structuration as not simply gender display but also as articulating a relationship between masculinities and femininities, we must focus not simply on one style, but on how a style is situated within a specific context, and how a style situates or is situated by other styles in the same context.

While there has been much written about how clothing and style reinforce or challenge hegemonic masculinity and femininity,[9] most of this work focuses on either women's styles or men's styles and on style as a form of gender display or an articulation of gender identity. Through the theoretical lens of Butler's heterosexual matrix, however, I began to view women's and men's styles as a whole—as an articulation and production of a relationship between masculinity and femininity. Instead of seeing them as separate and both as gender display, I focused on them as *gendered dress*,[10] which meant taking style as a mechanism for producing a relationship between masculinity and femininity. My analytic focus on gendered dress rather than dress as gender display brought my attention to how the clothing women wear derives meaning from and articulates meaning for men's clothing. That is, an analysis of gendered dress brings the relationship between women's styles and men's styles to the surface. A different picture thus emerges than would have if I had only focused on women's styles as articulating femininity and men's styles as articulating masculinity.

The women of alternative hard rock, as I have stated above, articulate the identity label *slut* through style. In mainstream rock, the slut is collapsed with groupie, and she is defined by her relationship to the rock musician, who enacts hegemonic sexualized masculinity as sexually assertive, confident, and exploitive. The styles associated with hegemonic masculinity in mainstream rock include makeup, big hair, spandex, and high-heeled boots. In alternative hard rock, the slut is not situated in relation to the main-

stream rock musician, but is instead paired with the geek. This subordinate masculinity, when paired with this particular femininity,
disrupts the relationship between hegemonic masculine sexual desire and feminine sexual availability. If it does not flatten or invert
the hierarchical relationship between masculinity and femininity,
situating the slut in relation to the geek instead of the assertive,
confident, exploitative masculine sexual subject at least complicates
gender power relations.

We might think of the slut as occupying a marginalized femininity. To reiterate Connell's conceptualization of marginalized
masculinities, there are practices associated with marginalized class
and race groups that are not feminine, but are defined as different
from and in most cases inferior to hegemonic masculinity. The slut
is still within the boundaries of femininity, but is marginalized as
a less legitimate and/or inferior form of femininity. Hegemonic constructions of the slut still situate her as a sexual object, and this is
particularly clear in mainstream rock culture. She is, however, outside the bounds of legitimate femininity, which requires sexual restraint. She is the sexual object for too many men and is inferior
to the woman who is the sexual object to only one man. As suggested by Connell, this relationship between femininities works to
maintain male dominance in that it ensures men's exclusive access to individual women's bodies, labor, and resources.[11]

However, when we move our analytic gaze from the overarching gender order to the level of interpersonal, face-to-face
interaction, gender power relations become somewhat more complicated. Connell theorizes the relationship between masculinities
and how power operates between men through these relationships.
But what happens when we introduce multiple femininities and
their variant relationships to the multiple masculinities? While both
the hegemonic construction of the slut as a marginalized femininity and the geek as a subordinate or marginalized masculinity work
to uphold male dominance ideologically, when the slut and the
geek get together in face-to-face interaction, it is not completely
clear how the interpersonal power relations might operate. It is
conceivable that doing slut in relation to the geek could be an
effective gender maneuver to manipulate power relations within
the context of the interaction. One might predict that the slut

might have more interpersonal power in relations to the geek than to the sexually assertive man. Within alternative hard rock, this cultural gender maneuver is not simply about gender bending or blurring the lines between masculine and feminine dress, but is also about manipulating the relationship between masculinity and femininity as it is articulated visually through style.

Another way in which women gender maneuver is through their embodied stage performances. They may often refer to their bodies—especially the parts of their bodies that distinguish them from men, such as their breasts or their genitalia. However, they might do so in ways that emphasize simultaneously being a woman *and* a musician *and* a desiring sexual subject *and* a person with a woman's body.

For instance, at one L7 show, the lead singer and guitarist, Donita Sparks, said to the audience, "There's a roadie gettin' slapped in the face by three women's bosoms in the front row. It's makin' me moist."

It was not exactly clear whether it was the thought of being slapped in the face by three women's bosoms, the idea of slapping the roadie in the face with her own bosoms, simply observing it, or perhaps something else altogether that was making Sparks "moist." Whatever the reason, by making such an explicit reference, Sparks maneuvered out of being the sexual object of desire and publicly expressed not only her subjective desire but her embodied response to that desire. Her comment made it impossible to construct the roadie as the active subject. This was in stark contrast to the roadie getting to "have" the groupie fan in his role as gatekeeper. Rather than being "one of the boys" by comfortably occupying hegemonic masculinity, this roadie was getting slapped in the face by women. In fact, he was getting slapped by the quintessential marker of feminine sexuality objectified—breasts. Any hint that the roadie's subjective sexual desire was at issue was obliterated when Sparks claimed her own subjective sexual desire and response. In this instance, the musician is occupying the position of sexual subject, as is the case in mainstream rock; however, masculinity no longer matches up with the identity label *musician* because the musician is getting "moist." The ambiguity of what, exactly, was titillating to Sparks also destabilized any gender structure for the relationship between subjective sexual desire and the object of desire.

During the same show, Jennifer Finch took off her T-shirt so that she was just wearing a black lace bra and jeans. Unlike other contexts in which women take off their clothes on a stage in front of hundreds of people, as in a strip club, the women in the band were explicit about having sexual desire, which disrupted a straight-forward objectification of themselves as women. More importantly, at this show and others like it, the meaning of their nudity was constructed in the way the women removed their clothing. When women musicians took off their shirts, they used the shirt to wipe sweat from their brow, their upper lip, or sometimes from under their arms. They would also comment on the heat or ask for water for the band. During this show, Jennifer Finch had been working hard at her task of pounding out bass rhythms before she slipped her T-shirt over her head, used it to wipe her hands and face, quickly picked up her bass, and got back to work.

Removing their shirts is a relatively common practice for women musicians in this subculture, and sometimes for women in the audience. Public displays of women's seminudity as sexual ob-jectification is thus transformed into a nonsexualized effort to be-come comfortable. The result is an audience watching half-naked women onstage, and not only being constantly confronted with the women's subjective sexual desire but also respecting their skill as musicians. By choosing to remove their shirts, these musicians quite literally expose women's sexuality not as some object sepa-rate from subjective desire but as one part of a human being who not only experiences subjective desire, but who plays her music bet-ter than anybody else in the club could and works up a sweat while doing so.

As with any sort of gender maneuvering, these kinds of stylis-tic strategies and their effectiveness are context-specific. *Gender maneuvering* refers to taking the existing gender order and twisting or changing it so as to not reproduce the patterns of structuration that keep the hierarchical relationship between masculinity and femi-ninity in tact. Though the overarching gender order is characterized by the heterosexual matrix more generally, the specific form it takes in terms of gender display, practices, and rules for interaction will vary depending on the specific context. This means that the particular styles, practices, and rules for interaction that are established through gender maneuvering will completely depend on the preexisting rules for what is appropriate or inappropriate within a setting or among a group of people. Gender maneuvering will be most effective when articulated toward, and also in opposition to, the specific rules for gender operating in a localized setting or among a group of people, as well as in the larger social structure.

For instance, alternative hard rockers' strategy of combining masculine styles, feminine styles, and a punk aesthetic makes a lot of sense within the context of rock culture. These stylistic maneuvers are developed in opposition to a mainstream rock culture, which constructs *groupie* as the quintessential feminine position and where gender-bending has a long, illustrious history. The women's styles are a fusion of the punk rocker, the feminist, and the groupie, making the oppositional relationship explicit. Punk rock was a cultural rejection of all that could be construed as mainstream, including arena or glam rock, and punk styles are a "cold shower" for hegemonic masculine sexual desire, especially when combined with a feminist aesthetic. Within this subculture, where the women and men were trying to use feminism and punk sentiments to forge a new path, most rockers in this subculture responded to the smack upside the head produced through women's styles with "Cooooool!" It worked as rock culture by simultaneously being sexy and subversive. However, unlike in other rock strategies, to be sexy and subversive alternative hard rockers added a feminist twist and created a way to do rock'n' roll style without straightforwardly reproducing the mainstream gender order.

Being a good participant-observer, I was committed to adopting the subculture's styles even though miniskirts and hot pants were not my normal attire when I started this research. The first time I went out to buy a miniskirt as part of my movement into the scene, I spent an embarrassingly long time in front of dressing room mirrors trying to find a skirt that didn't scream *duped, male-identified ditz*. I went home empty-handed, thinking I just hadn't found the right one.

The next time I went shopping, I took Maddie with me. I put on the first skirt, which was a cotton and lycra, black tube skirt that was skintight and barely covered my ass—not unlike the dozens of skirts I had tried on my previous shopping excursion. I sheepishly walked out of the dressing room and, much to my surprise, Maddie smiled and said, "Yeah, baby."

"I don't know," I answered squeamishly. My women's studies training kicked in. "I don't think I'd be able to run in this."

Flatly, as if to convey "Don't you get it?" Maddie said, "Put your boots on." Despite being completely alone in the dressing room, I self-consciously pulled the skirt down as far as I could as I sat down on the built-in corner ledge. I was certain that, as I reached for the boots, the skirt would snap up around my waist, or worse, my neck and cut off the oxygen. I sort of leaned forward, trying desperately to keep my legs together and the skirt somewhere in the vicinity of my pelvis. It was, to say the least, very uncomfortable. In retrospect, the discomfort was less from the actual feel of the material on my body—for, despite my spastic body contortions, it remained snug on my legs and hips—and more about the meaning of the skirt. It was about sexual objectification, which meant sexual access, which felt a lot like having my sexuality exposed, which in turn felt like having my body exposed.

Shaking my head and considering moving my research topic to bowling leagues or a winter sport, I managed to get the boots onto my feet. I stood and, once again, walked out. The boots were heavy, sturdy, and felt powerful. The skirt was tight, but had somehow become remarkably comfortable. It hadn't snapped up to reveal my body, my sexuality. I stepped in front of the mirror, and without much thought or self-awareness, struck a rather sassy pose, saying, "Yeah, baby."

Maddie smiled and said, "I wanna fuck you, but I'm afraid you'd kick my ass." Not only did I feel like I could run; I felt like I could kick *anybody's* ass. Putting on those boots transformed not only how the skirt looked, but how it felt. And while I had worn the boots before, they felt different once I combined them with a miniskirt. There was something about the transgression of combining or collapsing the two images and embodied feelings that changed my miniskirt consciousness—including my embodied, feminist consciousness.

I want to suggest that in addition to being an important

component to cultural gender maneuvering and subcultural boundary construction, these styles are an embodied experience as well. That is, putting on a skintight miniskirt and big, clunky combat boots is not simply a visual contradiction; it is an embodied contradiction as well. My own experience of this corporeal contradiction necessitated a reassessment of my feminist consciousness. How could a sexually objectifying miniskirt, when combined with combat boots, feel more powerful than jeans? I had assumed that wearing a miniskirt was incapacitating and objectifying. It would limit mobility and would reduce my body to the status of sexual object. But feeling sexy *does* sometimes feel powerful; and the boots also added power, mobility, and stability. Unlike mainstream feminine couture, alternative hard-rock's hybrid did not sacrifice mobility, stability, and strength; they were instead now combined with sexual power, and the combination created a potent embodied and visual whole that increased the *overall* feeling of power in general. I really did feel like I could kick anybody's ass.

While I still think the world would be a much better place without miniskirts (unless, of course, men as well as women wore them), I no longer look at a woman in a miniskirt and think that she is a duped, male-identified ditz. (Okay, if she's also wearing pink pumps, the thought crosses by mind; but if she's wearing "sensible" shoes— and all girls know what I mean— I cut her a break. If she's wearing boots of any kind I think, "Right on sister. I'm all on top of that action.")

It is, however, also true that feeling powerful is not the same thing as being on the advantageous side of interpersonal or structural power relations. No matter how a person feels, she is still situated in relation to others interpersonally and structurally, and the distribution of power, prestige and resources stems from our place in the social structure, not our feelings. No matter how much I feel like I'm the millionaire CEO of a multinational corporation, my structural position does not allow me to reap the material and social benefits of being a CEO. Likewise, no matter how powerful I feel in my miniskirt and combat boots, I am still perceived as and occupy the social position of *woman*, which situates me in relation to others interpersonally and structurally. It is my structural location, not my feelings, that largely determine my relative power, resources, and prestige. Thus, while the embodied feeling of power and its impact on my feminist consciousness is important, this is an individual experience and does little to transform the gender order in any direct way. It feels great, but that feeling must be translated into some form of social action, whether it is a more traditional form of political activism or gender maneuvering. A *feeling* does not change the gender order; *action* does. While my own experience suggests some interesting implications for embodied gender experience, this is not the same as gender maneuvering to disrupt the hegemonic relationship between masculinity and femininity as it manifests in social relations.

In her book *Unbearable Weight: Feminism, Western Culture and the Body*, Susan Bordo convincingly argues that representations of the body in popular culture increasingly construct it as both malleable and a source of political empowerment. According to Bordo, this sends the dangerous message that one can become empowered and/or change her social position by changing the outward appearance of the body. The body, rather than social relations of inequality, becomes the political battleground and solution. Bordo notes that "subversion is contextual, historical, and, above all, social. No matter how exciting the destabilizing potential of texts, bodily or otherwise, whether those texts are subversive or recuperative or both or neither cannot be determined in abstraction from actual social practice."[12]

When we situate the body and embodied gender in the ongoing process of social structuration, how the body is presented and used is always in relation to other bodies within the localized context. In this way, alternative hard rockers' bodies do matter in their gender politics; they were not simply images or feelings of gender transgression. Their bodies are situated within, and an inextricable part of, their interactions with each other and the production of their subculture. In the ongoing process of negotiating the relationship between masculinities and femininities, what they do with their bodies disrupts, to some degree, the heterosexual matrix that depends upon masculine sexual subjectivity and feminine sexual objectification. Importantly, the disruption does not result from an individual feeling of empowerment in the body nor from simply the image of the body. It resulted from manipulating the relationship between gendered, raced, and classed bodies in the ongoing process of social relations.

Bordo provides an insightful analysis of Madonna's shifting identities as implicated in the pop culture message that we can put on and take off identities and destabilize sexual objectification. When I spoke with one local musician in Chicago, she invoked Madonna as an example of someone who can use sexuality as a mechanism of empowerment. She said, "There are very few strong images. It's new when women are sexually strong and manipulative. Look at Madonna. She's manipulated sexually and called a bitch. But I see her as being strong, and manipulating sexuality for her own gain. That erotica shit and her book is just to advance herself. I think I'm on the same terms as men. I don't think I'm any different from any other woman. We all have it in us."

As Bordo suggests, the image of Madonna using sexuality to manipulate for personal gain is, in some ways, conflated with structural or interpersonal empowerment. I watched this woman in Chicago onstage. I, along with the rest of the audience, saw her being both sexy and a powerful, talented musician. She was not simply an image, but a woman that we were all interacting with as her audience in the rock club.

During the show, she told the audience, "I've been told I'm not feminine enough. All that did was make me wear bigger fucking boots."

The audience erupted in cheers.

The image of her on the stage in a tight black tank top, cut-off shorts, and "bigger fucking boots" was part of the message. When I spoke with her, she told me a story about a show she played in another city.

"This asshole came on stage and started thrusting his crotch at me," she said. "It was the only way he could think to disempower me. Sexually. So I threw him off the stage and had him kicked out."

This is a body politics that cannot be reduced to media images nor to individual gender display. This woman looked the part of the sexual object, but she spoke of rejecting femininity, throwing men off the stage, and having them ejected; only through this combination did the sexual object come to life as a subject. While I cannot make claims about how each individual at these shows

read the women's embodied performances, their collective practices—including their talk about musicians and their ways of interacting with each other—suggest that women in this subculture
do come to life as sexual subjects. This is an embodied politics embedded in social life and fucking with gender (if only in the localized setting of the rock show) in a way that Madonna on a TV
screen, an individual in drag, or someone dressed to feel empowered never could. During the time I spent with them, I witnessed
how women in alternative hard rock related to others on the street,
in the clubs, and in all-night diners. There is little doubt in my
mind that the powerful feeling and their strategies for interactive
gender maneuvering translated into interpersonal action in these
contexts. I never had an opportunity, however, to witness how
these women related to others in different contexts—at school, on
the job, or with their families. How does alternative gender maneuvering in one context impact the gender performance of participants and gender relations in other contexts? This is an
important question that I can't answer here, but that other researchers might pick up and explore themselves.

Finally, the form of embodied gender maneuvering is also inextricable from the race and class positions of most alternative hard
rockers. Because feminine and masculine sexualities are mediated
by race and by class, playing the slut would probably mean something quite different and have different outcomes if adopted as a
gender maneuver by working-class or poor white women, or by
women of color. Such women have historically been stereotyped
as sexually promiscuous, and the stereotype works to construct
white, middle-class womanhood as chaste, pure, and asexual. This
race and class hierarchy for feminine sexualities works not only to
uphold the gender order but also keeps the white supremacist racial order in tact. Thus, women's power-slut attire and men's subordinate masculinity, if adopted by working-class, poor, or
nonwhite women and men, could reinscribe both the gender and
racial orders. Rather than subverting hegemonic constructions of
masculinity and femininity, sexualized styles among these groups
of women might not challenge hegemonic femininity but instead
reinscribe it as white, economically privileged, and sexually
restrained. As bell hooks suggests, the deployment of *slut* as

transgression is limited to women with race and class privilege. In her analysis of Madonna's film *Truth or Dare*, hooks compellingly argues that Madonna can pull off the role of sexually powerful slut only because she is white and rich. She notes that "we have always known that the socially constructed image of innocent white womanhood relies on the continued production of the racist/sexist sexual myth that black women are not innocent and never can be. Since we are coded always as 'fallen' women in the racist cultural iconography we can never, as can Madonna, publicly 'work' the image of ourselves as innocent female daring to be bad."[13] Both race and class privilege buffer Madonna from simply reproducing hegemonic constructions of femininity by doing slut.

The women in alternative hard rock that I met were, without exception, white and, with only a few exceptions, college-educated and from middle- to upper-middle-class suburban backgrounds. Their race and class positions were inextricable from their stylistic maneuver to reclaim the label *slut* through appearance. Only because of their race and class privilege as white, middle-class women could they do slut as a transgression and power move in relation to the white, middle-class geek.

Likewise, the geek is buffered from completely losing social status by his class and racial privilege despite his gender marginality. In fact, "brain" is arguably one of the safest subordinate masculinities for white, middle-class, college-educated men to adopt. Unlike being queer or poor or brown, being smart is still valued (though perhaps not as much as being athletic or wealthy, or getting laid all the time).

It is because of their class and racial privilege that alternative hard rockers are relatively safe to gender maneuver by "slumming" in marginal and subordinate gender styles.[14] While they are relatively successful at gender maneuvering in order to reconfigure the gender order of rock culture, their maneuvers are simultaneously embedded within race, class, and sexual relations. In this way, gender maneuvering is never simply about gender, but is also always about negotiating race, class, ethnicity, and sexuality.

Any one interaction is going to include multiple levels of social organization. Further, any one interaction is going to be structured by not only gender, but also by race, class, sexuality, and so on. Gender maneuvering, then, is always embedded within the broader social structure, the localized setting, and within race, class, and sexual relations. When we introduce these multiple levels of social organization and multiple systems of inequality, it becomes difficult to distill which sorts of cultural practices and interactions challenge relations of domination and which ones reinscribe them. If we take seriously hooks's assertion that any attempt to challenge male domination is only useful if it does not reinforce race, class, and sexual domination, then we must look closely at the ways in which gender maneuvering within any given context challenges or reinforces race, class, and sexual structures as well. I have identified only a few ways in which the maneuvers deployed by alternative hard rockers relate to race and class hierarchies. For instance, using labels like *white trash* and adopting a thick southern accent to put down people who do not subscribe to their alternative sensibility reinscribe class and race hierarchies. While it works as a gender maneuver, it fully supports class domination that relies on stereotypes of rural, poor whites as stupid and incompetent. Their uncritical use of *white trash* also perpetuates the racist assumption, implied by that label, that nonwhite people are always already trash (and thus the "necessity" of stipulating *white* trash). Similarly, their use of marginalized and subordinate genders such as *slut* and *geek* are far from transgressive within the racial order. In the next chapter, I will further explore the relationships among different systems of inequality as they operate at different levels of social organization by focusing specifically on the intersection of sexuality and gender.

6

SEXUALITY AND GENDER MANEUVERING

It was just after midnight as Maddie and I approached The Empty Bottle. Maddie hated the first band scheduled to play, so we had hung out at Bryan's until she was confident they had finished their set. There were several people standing outside the bar in the door-way and on the sidewalk. As she scanned the faces, Maddie said, "Either they're still playing . . . and sucking . . . or we timed this per-fectly. There's Colleen. She loves Munch.* She wouldn't be out-side if they were still playing."

As we came up to her, Colleen feigned a whisper to the man she was talking with, but said loudly enough so that we could hear, "Did you know she's a lesbian?" with a nod toward Maddie. She laughed and then said, "Not only that, but she's a bitch, too."

Maddie laughed and spat back, "And don't you wish you could be?"

"Hey, I'm a bigger bitch than you could ever dream of being."

Both Maddie and Colleen laughed, hugged, and continued a playful banter about who deserved membership in the "lesbian club" and "bitch club." By the tone of their exchange, it was clear

---

* This is a fictitious name for the opening band.

that there was something admirable about being a lesbian and a bitch.

After chatting for a few minutes, Maddie said, "Well, we're going in. See you in there."

"Now be careful, she's a lesbian," Colleen said to me as we walked away.

Maddie quickly responded, "She knows. She's my girlfriend. Jealous?"

Colleen laughed and said, "Yeah, but I have my own girlfriend," and with a small gesture toward the man she was standing with triumphantly yelled, "*He* is really a *she*!" Everybody, including the man, laughed.

In this politicized, antiestablishment rock world, it is uncool to be a bigot, and alternative hard rockers include heterosexism as bigotry; being able to talk freely and openly about homosexuality is part of being cool. This cool pose translates into challenging, chastising, and making ridiculous derogatory talk about gay and lesbian people when it occasionally comes up. It also manifests as ironic performance, as when Colleen performed heterosexism and then, in the interactive process of face-to-face interaction, dismantled it. Alternative hard rockers engage in a lot of this kind of sexual play and sexual contact. There is a set of subcultural beliefs and practices about sexuality, just as there is about gender. The subculture has a gender order and a sexual order, and as alternative hard rockers go about the business of rocking, they construct and maintain that sexual order.

Sexuality, like gender, is a system of beliefs and patterns of practice that structure or shape social life. We might call these patterns the *sexual order*.[1] As conceptualized in queer theory, the contemporary, Western sexual order is partially based on the symbolic construction of sexuality as a hierarchical, binary relationship between heterosexuality and homosexuality.[2] Like gender, sexuality is defined in terms of fixed identities, so there are assumed to be homosexual or heterosexual persons. These identities are believed to represent some internal, fixed characteristic of the individual person. There is an assumption that everybody has a sexual orientation, and that it is a central, defining feature of not simply a person's sexual desires and practices but also her personality. It is this understanding of sexuality that made the label *lesbian* significant in Maddie and Colleen's interaction. Within the meaning structure of sexuality, to call someone a lesbian is to identify what kind of person she is.

Further, within the dominant sexual order, heterosexuality is constructed as preferable, superior, and normal, while homosexuality is considered undesirable, inferior, and marginal or deviant. It was this assumption that homosexuality is inferior that gave Colleen's whisper meaning. Only within a larger cultural context that defines homosexuality in terms of a shameful secret would Colleen's actions make any sense.[3]

Finally, sexuality not only defines and organizes identities, but is also an organizing feature of face-to-face interaction and of larger institutional and cultural settings. Like the gender order, the sexual order does not simply translate into assumptions about identities, but is also an organizing feature of social interaction and institutional relations more generally.[4] At all levels of social organization— identities, practices, the structure of face-to-face interactions, and institutional structure—the norm is heterosexuality and there is an underlying assumption that everybody is heterosexual unless proven otherwise.

If we look at the interaction between Maddie and Colleen, we can identify the ways in which sexuality organizes the interaction and the subculture. While Colleen's whisper about Maddie being a lesbian reproduced the identity hierarchy by suggesting there is something shameful about being a lesbian, in the ongoing process of this interaction, the meaning of that whisper as a parody of heterosexism was established. Meanings emerged from the interaction, and importantly, the sexual organization of the interaction itself emerged through the play of meanings. Colleen performed the role of homophobe, and through that performance set up a hierarchical relationship between herself and Maddie that reproduced the broader sexual order. With her own performance of sexuality Colleen set up and reproduced a heterosexist sexual organization for the interaction.[5] However, rather than leaving heterosexism as the frame for the interaction, Colleen reconfigured the interaction as one that is critical of heterosexism. First, she overplayed her part by making sure the whisper was actually a public statement. It was clear that the meaning of the whisper was to expose and reject the secret of lesbian sexuality. Then Colleen said that Maddie was "a bitch, too." The women often called each other and themselves "bitch"; while sometimes it was used to put down particular other women, it was most often worn as a badge of honor, and like the label *slut* it was only used positively or affectionately in women's interpersonal exchanges with each other. Within this exchange, Maddie's and Colleen's insider knowledge about and understanding of the meaning of *bitch* shifted the meaning of *lesbian* to something positive through the fluid process of interaction. Maddie went along as they competed with each other over who was more lesbian and who was more bitchy, driving the antiheterosexist meaning and structure of the interaction home. Colleen and Maddie turned what first appeared to be heterosexism into a fairly scathing critique of heterosexism through a process of interactive moves or maneuvers. Further, they challenged compulsory heterosexuality by validating lesbianism through their competitive, interactive volley for the lesbian badge.

Through their interactive maneuvers they not only challenged the hierarchy that places heterosexuality above homosexuality, but also disrupted the hegemonic insistence on stable sexual identities. That is, they "queered" sexuality. Because the sexual order depends upon the construction of homosexuality and heterosexuality as stable identities, some queer theorists and activists suggest that one strategy for undermining heterosexism is to challenge the hegemonic construction of sexuality as consisting of two hierarchical fixed identities defined by the biological sex of one's object of desire.[6] One way to destabilize the sexual order, then, would be to queer sexuality. To queer sexuality is to in some way step out of, blur, or challenge hierarchical, sexual identities that define individuals as homosexual or heterosexual.[7] Sexuality can be queered through sexual practice and discourse about desire, identities, or sexual practices. I want to suggest that sexuality can also be queered through sexual maneuvering or by manipulating the meaning and performance of desire within any given interaction. Maddie and Colleen engaged sexual maneuvers in their interaction about being lesbians.

First, they disrupted the notion of stable sexual identities through their specific use of the identity label *lesbian*. As the two women engaged in their banter about who was more lesbian, they were reproducing the general belief that lesbians have a set of personality characteristics. While those characteristics were constructed as positive by Maddie and Colleen, there was still the underlying assumption that a lesbian is a particular kind of woman. This is very much characteristic of the sexual organization of the larger social structure. However, within the confines of this particular interaction, by invoking a language (and self-made claims) of being more lesbian, they suggested that lesbianism is a continuum, not a fixed category, and that one can move along this continuum through a set of behaviors, styles, and actions. This challenges the assumption that one either is or is not a lesbian, that *lesbian* is a fixed identity.

Likewise, Maddie and Colleen queered the sexual organization of the interaction as they manipulated the positions of everybody involved. When Maddie claimed that I was her girlfriend, Colleen responded by saying "I have my own girlfriend. . . . *He* is really a *she*!" Of course, the dominant sexual order has no room for women to have men as girlfriends. With an interactive maneuver to situate herself in a relation of erotic desire with her male companion, Colleen constructed herself as having a lesbian relationship with a man—very queer indeed. Also, Colleen's on-the-fly shift from the role of homophobe to that of lesbian within the same interaction challenges the sexual order's insistence on stable sexual identities. In other words, the sexual organization of the interaction, as it emerged, was queer to the extent that it disrupted or challenged the insistence on stable sexual identities that neatly match up with desire and practices. In the middle of the interaction, the sexual organization shifted and a different set of sexual arrangements emerged. That is, the sexuality of all involved emerged from negotiated social interaction as much as it framed the interaction.[8]

Despite Colleen's move to mock this sort of heterosexism, and Maddie's and Colleen's collaborative construction of a rather queer structure for this interaction, within the context of the larger sexual structure of the subculture overall this interaction reflects the dominant sexual order more than it challenges it. Colleen had to have assumed Maddie was heterosexual for the banter about lesbians and bitches to have been not only funny but also effective as a cool, antiheterosexist pose. If Maddie was indeed a lesbian, this interaction probably would have backfired on Colleen, and she would have been chastised for being both heterosexist and sexist. Colleen would never have risked "outing" Maddie if there was any remote possibility that Maddie was a lesbian. Colleen must have safely assumed that people are heterosexual unless proven otherwise and, depending on that assumption, could construct herself, Maddie, and the meaning of the interaction as countercultural.

This interaction between Maddie and Colleen captures the sexual order of alternative hard rock. The women's subcultural practices and beliefs were grounded in a collective desire to not reproduce the old patterns of inequality in mainstream rock, including heterosexism and homophobia. While they were relatively successful at challenging compulsory heterosexuality and heterosexism in their talk and practices, there was still a rather heterosexist normative structure for the subculture overall.

THE SEXUAL ORDER OF MAINSTREAM ROCK

Mainstream rock is organized by sexuality. To reiterate, with the term *sexual organization* I mean that there are agreed-upon rules for thinking about, expressing, and acting on erotic desire. These collective beliefs about sex, sexual desire, and sexual identities, and expected patterns of sexual behavior structure or frame the activities, interactions, and expectations of people as they go about doing rock culture. For instance, as I've outlined in previous chapters, the relationship between musician and groupie is sexualized as well as gendered, and this relationship is heterosexual. At the same time, there is much work done to mask or eliminate any homoeroticism in the relationship between musician and real fan. There have been very few rockers who have come out as gay or lesbian, and many rockers overtly express hostility toward homosexuality. No mainstream rocker, let alone a genre within mainstream rock,[9] has publicly enacted intragender erotic desire as a central way of doing *rock musician*. While there have been some notable exceptions, the sexual meanings attached to the identity labels *rock musician*, *groupie*, *teenybopper*, and *real fan* set up a heterosexual structure for mainstream rock as an institutionalized cultural form. Within the world of mainstream rock, especially the mainstream rock of the 1980s that alternative hard rockers have more recently rejected, everyone is presumed straight until proven otherwise. As people performed rock in concert, on recordings, in videos, and in interviews, they simultaneously performed heterosexuality either by not explicitly situating their sexual desire or, more commonly, by compulsively expressing heterosexual desire.[10]

THE SEXUAL ORDER OF ALTERNATIVE HARD ROCK

The sexual structure of mainstream rock parallels and reproduces the dominant sexual structure that both constructs sexuality as consisting of stable identities and defines homosexuality as inferior or, at best, marginal. While alternative hard rockers have rejected homophobic and heterosexist attitudes or behaviors in order to create a different form of rock, there are aspects of alternative hard rock that, like mainstream rock, parallel the dominant sexual order. For instance, the implicit assumption that everybody is heterosexual unless proved otherwise is a central feature of the organization of sexuality within alternative hard rock.[11] This becomes apparent in the ways in which alternative hard rockers talk about gay people. As I discussed earlier, being comfortable talking about gay and lesbian people is considered "cool." The most common adaptation of this comfort with homosexuality manifests itself in talk about their gay, lesbian, or bisexual friends, roommates, family members, work colleagues, and so on. For example, in the first real conversation I had with Colleen, I asked her about her background. She told me about how strong her Catholic roots were. She even had two nuns in her family. Though we were not discussing sexuality, it came up in a story she told me about her aunts.

"Oh my god. This is hilarious. My roommate is gay. I'm like 'whatever' and don't really think about it. Well, when my aunts found out I had a man for a roommate, they sort of freaked out. I told them there was no way anything 'romantic' is going to happen. They were like, you know . . . "—here Colleen adopted an Irish accent—"'Oh Colleen, my dear sweet child, you can never predict a man's behavior.' So I say, 'Don't worry. He's gay.' They covered their mouths and giggled. One of 'em said, 'Oh, do you mean he's happy?' I just rolled my eyes and said, 'Yeah. That's exactly what I mean. He's really happy.' They just can't wrap their heads around the fact that there are gay people. It's like, get over it."

Colleen was conveying her comfort with homosexuality as much as she was telling me something about her family background. Like Colleen, it seemed everybody had gay friends, relatives, or, in the case of Nancy, a work colleague. One evening Nancy was telling me about how frustrated she was with her job and that her manager was a large part of her frustration.

"I hate him. He'll come up and talk to me, and I won't even look at him. With everybody else I'm like 'Hi, how's it goin'?' He's gay but he won't admit it. It's like so obvious. Anyone who is so worried about letting everybody know that he's not gay probably is. Closets are for clothes, asshole."

While much of Nancy's hatred for her manager was expressed in terms of his structural position and his authority over her, she also included not being "out" as part of the reason she couldn't stand him. She was doing the "cool pose" around sexuality by acting as if being gay is no big deal. However, the only way Nancy could claim that her manager's gay sexual identity was so "obvious" was if she assumed first that *gay* is a stable sexual identity, and second, that the identity has corresponding character and personality traits—both assumptions constructed within the dominant sexual order. Looking at Nancy's claims about her manager through the lens of queer theory, it becomes clear that, despite her comfort with talking about her manager's sexuality, the dominant sexual order was being filtered through and reproduced in the assumptions she made about her manager. Not really knowing with whom her manager had sex or developed romantic relationships, she was certain he was gay by how he acted at work. For Nancy, his personality and his mannerisms were consistent with her notions of what a gay person acts like. More importantly, Nancy fused her hatred for her manager to his alleged sexuality. Even though she claimed it was being closeted that really angered her, it certainly was not clear that her anger did not also spring from an underlying homophobia or heterosexism. And because of the negative stereotypes of gay men and lesbians as more secretive, shameful, and distrustful, Nancy's efforts to demonstrate her sexual tolerance ended up supporting the sexual order.

Despite alternative hard rockers' comfort in talking about the gay and lesbian people they know, I never heard anyone I spent time with in the subculture truly self-identify as gay, lesbian, homosexual, or bisexual. On a few isolated occasions people did talk about one woman in the subculture being a lesbian. Interestingly, I rarely saw this woman really interact with others, and I never saw her in the clubs unless her band was playing. I never heard of a man in the subculture being gay. For the most part, gay and lesbian people were constructed as people outside the subculture. And while they were deemed as deserving of all the rights, respect, and happiness of everyone else, homosexual people were nonetheless a marginalized "other." In this way, the overarching sexual organization of the subculture itself is very much in line with the dominant sexual order in that sexualities are assumed to be stable, identifiable personality traits, and it is heterosexist to the extent that nonheterosexual people were marginalized as outsiders.

Nonetheless, this overarching sexual organization for the subculture does not translate into straightforward heterosexual behavior, nor a simplistic heterosexual microorganization of face-to-face interaction. Like the gender order, the sexual order is not a fixed determinant of how people act and interact, but is instead a general set of rules. Those rules get reproduced and challenged as people go about their everyday lives. Through a process of *sexual structuration*, the sexual order simultaneously frames or guides behavior and interaction and is also an emergent feature of social interaction. For instance, Nancy's talk about her manager simultaneously reflected and produced derogatory beliefs about homosexuality.

Despite the construction of homosexual people as outsiders, often talk about gay and lesbian people reveals a conceptualization of sexuality that is somewhat more complex than the one offered by the dominant sexual order. For example, I was at an alternative hard rocker's house with several other people, including four men from a local band. These four were talking about whether or not it would be a good idea for them to take a gig opening for Tribe 8, a band out of San Francisco that consists of five women who are all very much out about their sexual desire for women and who make their sexual desire a central part of their performance. Joe, the singer and guitarist for the local band, was dubious about the whole thing.

"Man, I don't know if it would be such a good idea," he said. "It's going to be a bunch of lesbians who probably would not appreciate a bunch of aggressive guys up there." Egged on by everybody's laughter, Joe continued, "Shit, I don't want to get my ass kicked! There's no way they'd put up with us if they're waiting to see Tribe 8. I don't think we should."

Susan agreed: "And they *will* kick your ass!"

"And not because you're guys," Bryan added. "Because you fucking suck!"

Everybody except Joe laughed. While getting his ass kicked by lesbians for being a guy was pretty funny, someone kicking his ass for not being a good musician, even if it was a bunch of women, was serious business. Perhaps this was an expression of an underlying heterosexism, but the way he phrased this expression revealed at least some ambiguity. For instance, Joe did not say that he didn't want to open for Tribe 8 because *he* had something against lesbians. Instead, he expressed his concern in terms of what lesbians might expect. The problem was their legitimate rejection of him and his all-male band. Further, when he said he did not want to get his ass kicked, he was laying a fairly positive evaluation on the audience. Remember that, for alternative hard rockers, the notion of "kicking ass" has a positive connotation, especially when referring to women. As discussed earlier, this meant that a woman was exceptionally cool because she transgressed the requirements of femininity. Joe was implying that the women at the show would be tough, but also cool. In characteristic form for the subcultural norms, Joe constructed lesbians as deserving of respect, but also as outsiders. The combination of the sexual and gender display of Tribe 8 and the resulting gender and sexual dynamics of the audience would create a scene in which the presence of an all-male band would either not make sense or would possibly become a rallying point around which the women could express their feminism. Either way, the audience would be less than receptive. This was quite a daunting prospect for a group of guys whose self-worth is inextricable from their audience's adoration.

For our purposes, what is particularly interesting about Joe's characterization of the Tribe 8 show was that he said it was "going to be a bunch of lesbians." Later, attending the Tribe 8 show, I concluded that Joe's concerns about being aggressively rejected were well-founded, but the audience, even though it consisted mostly of women, could hardly be characterized as "a bunch of lesbians." There was more overt physical contact among women than I had seen at other shows, and many of the women were quite aggressive about keeping men out of the space in front of the stage. But I also noticed that—though there were some women there I did not know and who might self-identify as lesbians—there were also many women there who had regularly attended shows that Joe's band and other local bands had played, and these women did not self-identify as such. The women I had been spending time with in the alternative hard rock scene in Chicago were indistinguishable in their behavior from most of the women I did not recognize. These women did not become lesbians in the identity sense by attending nor by having sexual contact with other women at this show. They worked with other women to create a counter-hegemonic structure for sexual and gender display and interaction, but there is no reason to conclude that their sexual identities were or became lesbian. Joe did not have a language to identify the transformation of the normative structure, so he simply said that the audience would be "a bunch of lesbians"—including Maddie, Colleen, and others. It was the practices, interactions, and normative structure that differed at the Tribe 8 show, not the identities of the individuals who participated.[12] When a group of women become "a bunch of lesbians" because of how they act and express desire, especially if there is an implicit assumption that these women do not limit their romantic and sexual relationships to women, the word *lesbian* gets somewhat dislodged from its hegemonic meaning.

This tension between sexual identity labels and sexual practices came through at a Hole show, when Courtney Love decided to reveal who her current sexual partner was.

"Guess who I'm fucking. If you can guess, I'll tell you. Come on, try to guess."

Several people in the audience, including both men and women, raised their hands. Someone from the crowd yelled,

"Drew!" Eric Erlandson, the guitarist for Hole, was dating the actress Drew Barrymore at the time.

Love laughed and said, referring to Erlandson, "No. *He's* fucking Drew; I'm not. I'm not a lesbian. I'm only a part-time muff-muncher." Gesturing first to drummer Patty Schemel and then to bass player Melissa Auf der Maur, she continued, "She's a full-time muff-muncher, and she's a virgin." Schemel pounded out a quick power-thump while Auf der Maur looked down, shaking her head and smiling shyly.

When someone in the audience suggested Love was "fucking" Drew Barrymore, she responded by saying "I'm not a lesbian." What did that mean to Love? It meant that she is only a "part-time muff-muncher," referring to the act of cunnilingus. Although Love first used an identity label, and by doing so supported the dominant sexual order, she quickly shifted the emphasis to what one does in practice to define sexuality. That the bass player was a "virgin" in comparison to herself (a "part-time muff-muncher") and the drummer (a "full-time muff-muncher") meant that *not doing anything* defined one's sexuality. Sexuality was thus constructed as *what one did* and not so much as *who one was*: Love's immediate shift to who was a "muff-muncher" and who was not transformed sexuality from an identity to a set of practices. This is precisely what queer activists call for in their efforts to dismantle the heterosexist, sexual order—for sexuality to be defined as erotic desire and practices, not kinds of people. Through her talk, Love constructed the notion of lesbian not as some ontological state of being, but instead as a sort of becoming through sexual behavior: one *becomes* a lesbian when one limits her sexual practices to muff-munching full-time. There was still an underlying assumption that there *are* lesbians in the identity sense, but in her banter on stage, Love complicated or queered lesbianism's definition.

Love did not simply queer the definition of *lesbian*, but also the sexual organization of her interaction with the audience itself. Through the ongoing process of this stage performance and interaction with the audience, Love constructed her own and other band members' positions in the matrix of sexual desire. She situated herself as one who practices cunnilingus (albeit on a part-time basis), yet rejects the label *lesbian*. This disrupted the coherence between identity and practices built into the dominant sexual order. She also situated the bass player as a "virgin." In the dominant sexual order there are *homosexuals* and *heterosexuals*; there is no room for *virgins* in this construction. However, by suggesting that *virgin* is somehow a point of difference from *lesbian*, Love constructed virginity as a sexuality. Within the context of this interaction, the audience could no longer simply box everybody into either heterosexual or homosexual. How does one, within the scheme of sexualities, interact with a virgin? There is no longer the possibility for using the identity labels *homosexual* and *heterosexual* as cues for defining the situation and thus predicting the other's—in this case the bass player's—erotic desire. The sexual organization of the interaction itself fell outside of the rules for hegemonic sexuality by blowing apart the heterosexual/homosexual binary and was thus queer. Though I can't say—nor do I want to suggest—that Love had an explicit agenda for queering sexuality, the organization of sexuality nonetheless emerged in a queer formation as sexual positions were established and the meanings of those positions developed in the ongoing process of interaction.

Though there are not "out" gay and lesbian people in the subculture, and alternative hard rockers only infrequently speak about sexual identities and gay and lesbian people as subcultural outsiders, this does not mean that intragender sexuality is not often present in their interactions. While there is an underlying assumption of heterosexuality in terms of sexual identities, their expressions of sexual desire and their sexual interactions and actions as they do rock music are not always heterosexual. For instance, while there are strong subcultural norms against heterosexual contact between women and men, there is a great deal of sexual contact among women and overt expressions of sexual desire by women. It is very common at rock shows for women to have eroticized or sexual contact with each other: women rub their bodies together and gyrate against each other as they listen to the music. On rare occasions, I observed women kissing, and all of the women I knew expressed sexual desire for women musicians.

Women would often engage in playful, sexualized interaction with each other. One evening, Maddie had a cigarette hanging from her lips and asked Carrie for a light. Carrie leaned in and put her mouth over Maddie's cigarette and pretended to bite it. When she pulled away, Carrie said, "Oh, I thought you said, "Can I have a bite?' I suppose I could give you a light, but I'd rather give you a bite."

Another time Maddie and Carrie were sitting a few seats away from each other at the bar. Carrie was looking at Maddie, winking and licking her lips. After ten or fifteen minutes, Carrie yelled to Maddie, "I'm leaving for a little while, will you miss me?" Maddie responded, "Of course, darling. But we're leaving anyway." Carrie exaggerated a pout and said, "Well then, there's no reason for me to come back." Though neither Carrie nor Maddie self-identified as lesbians, they often situated each other in an intragender erotic interaction.

Sometimes alternative hard rockers situate themselves as those who engage in intragender erotic behavior through storytelling. For instance, one time Maddie told me she had an especially fine time at a concert the night before because she "made out" with Colleen all night.

When I asked her what she meant, she said, "You know. I had my tongue down her throat. She had her tongue down my throat."

This story was told in the presence of other alternative hard rockers. Whether or not the story was true, when others went along and did not marginalize Maddie, they accepted and validated her position as a woman who "makes out" with other women. It is important to note that Carrie, Colleen, and Maddie had steady boyfriends. Though this sort of sexual play was a common feature of their relationships with each other at the rock shows, their steadypartnerships were with men.

Interestingly, women's sexual desire is not in this instance limited to women and men but is extended to the sound of singers' voices, the sound of guitars, the syncopation of instruments, and other tonal or musical experiences. I heard women talk about wanting to "fuck the music" or about a singer's voice as "totally fuckable." When women particularly enjoy live or recorded music, a common expression they use to convey this is, "Just fuck me now"; sometimes they say "I need a cigarette" or "I'm spent" after a live performance. The sexual references are not addressed to any particular person or people, but instead are made toward and about the music as an object of desire and as sexually gratifying. As Lawrence Grossberg suggests,[13] rock music, especially live rock music, is simultaneously an auditory and bodily experience. At these shows, the music is not only heard but also felt in the body. The rhythm and syncopation among the bass, drums, and guitars gives the bodily experience a sexual valence, which is thus expressed by the women. While this experience of the music is not limited to alternative hard rock, in this subculture it was common and expected for women to verbally express that feeling. It is entirely possible that women's "dirty dancing" together could be as much about sexualizing the music as it is about their sexual desire for each other.[14] In other words, sexual desire, as expressed by the women in talk and through their actions, is far more diffused and fluid than the dominant sexual order would have it. This more diffused, fluid sexuality breaks down the relevance of sexual identity labels that reduce sexual desire to the biological sex of one's sexual object. For this reason, women's sexual desire cannot be simplified as bisexual or lesbian, but instead can be characterized as *queer* because it is opened up to include more than other women or even other individuals so that the sex category of the object of desire becomes irrelevant.[15]

At the same time, it is uncommon at most of these shows to see men moving their bodies to the music, except for head-banging or playing "air guitar"; dancing is not something men in this subculture usually do. The men most often keep their eyes on the stage or each other while conversing between bands, so overtly "checking women out" is relatively uncommon. At least in the company of women at these shows, men do not usually express sexual desire for or attraction to a woman unless she is a musician and the attraction is couched in musical appreciation. On the rare occasions when men do appear to be expressing an overt sexual desire for women, others invariably make fun of them to keep the normative structure intact.

Though men in the audience do not engage in any sort of dirty dancing, some of the men on stage participate in some forms of intragender sexual contact. For instance, as part of their performances, men musicians sometimes publicly express sexual desire for other men. At one show the lead singer (a man) was wearing chaps with only a thong underneath. The drummer (also a man) had a microphone for backup vocals. At one point, the singer introduced the rest of the band. When he got to the drummer, the drummer then introduced the singer, saying, "Ass—I mean *voice*—of the gods." The singer then shook his ass toward the drummer. The drummer, expressing his admiration for the singer's voice, conflated that with a reference to the singer's body. That it was a reference to his ass put a fairly straightforward sexual valence on the compliment to the singer's vocal ability. This is an expression of the field of appreciation I outlined in chapter 3. The drummer combined musical appreciation with sexual attraction.

The field of appreciation is not the limit to men's intragender erotic contact. Men on stage sometimes gyrate their hips against each other, kiss each other on the lips, roll around on the floor in a sexualized embrace, lick each other, and engage in various other overtly sexual behaviors. Interestingly, the only time I saw a woman and man doing anything close to dirty dancing, they were not reproducing anything like heteronormativity. It was at a Babes in Toyland show at Lounge Ax, and the man and woman were standing on a wooden ledge along the wall. The man was in front of the woman ,who was holding on to the pipes that hung from the ceiling and grinding her hips into his ass. It looked like fucking, but if it was, *she* was fucking *him*.

On rare occasions, male musicians explicitly refer to having had sex with men. One singer talked about a journalist's evaluation of the band that suggested they were homophobic because the band had a song that included the word "faggot" in the lyrics. The singer had read and was referring to that article when he said, "So I guess I'm a homophobe. It's scary when some fucking critic can't tell his head from his ass and mixes up metaphor and reality. It's kind of hard to imagine how someone like me, someone who's given men head on several occasions, could be a homophobe. You know what I gotta say to that guy? Fuck you! Then again, no thank you."

Not only does this reflect the subcultural norm for confronting homophobia or heterosexism, but it also reveals something else about what was going on in this subculture. While people do not take on sexual identity labels for themselves but instead reserve them for people outside the subculture, people inside often talk

about having sexual contact with others of the same gender, or actually do so as they rock. Like other alternative hard rockers, this
singer did not say, "I'm gay" or "I'm bisexual"; he said he had
"given men head on several occasions." In response to a charge of
homophobia, this man responded by talking about his sexual experiences and behavior, not his identity. Rather than an expression of a sexual identity, sexual practices become an expression of
a political stand in relation to heterosexism. Intragender sexual contact no longer reflects an internal essence or identity; it is a way to
be "cool" and countercultural. In other words, the bodacious heterosexuality of mainstream rock is transformed in alternative hard
rock into an audacious queer sexuality.[16]

It is queer on several levels. First, despite claiming to know gay
and lesbian people "out there," alternative hard rockers engage in
an impressive amount of intragender sexual activity and the expression of intragender sexual desire. These self-identified straight
people fully embrace homoeroticism without claiming to be bisexual or homosexual. The marginalizing of gay- and lesbian-
identified people while also doing homoerotic desire means that
sexual desire is, in a sense, dislodged from sexual identity labels.

The sexual organization of face-to-face interaction is queered
as well. As people in this subculture interact with each other, there
are subcultural norms against men hitting on women and against
women hitting on men; that is, heterosexual interaction is not a
patterned feature of face-to-face interaction at the clubs. But because the men do not shift their sexual desire from women to men,
the sexual organization of interaction can neither be construed as
homosexual in any way. What is important here is that men's
sexual desire is, for the most part, taken out of the equation, making social interaction something other than heterosexuality, or bisexuality. Sexuality is also queered in face-to-face interactions in
that the men's sexual desire is not an explicit nor a central component to doing masculinity, so the women's sexuality is no longer
articulated in relation to hegemonic masculine sexuality. (This is
in sharp contrast with woman-on-woman "freak dancing," where,
in the context of a fraternity party, for instance, the men are expected to hit on women or gain access to potential sexual partners.)
Thus, the patterned organization of interactions is neither hetero-

sexual nor bisexual.[17] At the same time, women's desire is not simply directed toward other women, but is opened up to include more than other women or even other individuals. Thus, as women move about the club engaging in face-to-face interactions with each other and with men, there is no straightforward sexual identity structure to the interaction. The sexual positions of women shift constantly, setting up fleeting and unstable relations among themselves and other women, men, and the music itself. While sometimes the practices women engage in could be construed as straight or lesbian in isolated occurrences, the constantly shifting valence of sexual desire queers the patterned organization of face-to-face interactions.

At two Tribe 8 shows, the lead singer, like female musicians at other shows, removed her shirt. Unlike most other such musicians, however, she was not wearing a bra. She also, at one point in the show, slowly unzipped her leather pants and pulled out a harnessed dildo. She stroked it for awhile and then asked if anybody would like to give her a blow job. At one show, nobody from the audience volunteered, so the bass player kneeled down in front of her and sucked on the dildo to the rhythm of the music. At the second show, a woman from the audience volunteered, and when she was finished, a man stepped up and took over. At both shows, after the blow jobs, she removed a large knife from her pocket and cut the dildo off at the bass near the harness. A woman topless and getting a blow job from a woman and then from a man tears open any straightforward, conventional gender or sexual meaning of these practices. She shifts from performing woman to performing far more slippery gender and sexuality. Is she a woman when she takes out the dildo? Is she a lesbian when she gets a blow job from a woman or does she become a man, in the gender sense, getting a blow job from a woman, and therefore performing heterosexuality? Is she a lesbian when she gets a blow job from a man? Is she a woman? Where in the current gender and sexual order is there room for women to get blow jobs from women? Certainly there is no room for men to give women or lesbians blow jobs. And when the singer cuts off the dildo, what has (s)he become? Any one moment in this series of acts and interactions cannot easily be fixed as neatly heterosexual or straight, but taking the sequence of events as a whole, it becomes virtually impossible to comfortably identify the singer as gay, lesbian, bisexual, or straight. It falls completely outside of, and therefore challenges, the hegemonic gender and sexual order. It is, simultaneously, gender and sexual maneuvering.

The explicit use of queer sexuality is a fairly central strategy for gender maneuvering among alternative hard rockers, and becomes an important vehicle with which to challenge the gender order. Cultural gender maneuvering in this case means setting up a normative framework for rock culture that does not reproduce the sexism of mainstream rock. As discussed in previous chapters, these rockers have done so through style and by setting up subcultural norms for behavior that disrupt both the gender framework for social identities and the relationship between those identities.

Sexuality as an organizing feature of the subculture cross-cuts their strategies of cultural gender maneuvering. For instance, the women's styles combine clothing that signifiy sexuality as much as they do gender. Masculine clothing (such as combat boots and flannel shirts) and extremely short hair or shaved heads are often stylistic markers of lesbian sexuality. The lesbian is not the sexual complement/opposite to masculine subjectivity, so stylistically combining lesbian with punk, slut, and feminist makes the gender maneuver that much more effective.

The subcultural field of appreciation plays with sexuality as well. There is a cultural expectation for people to express sexual attraction to musicians regardless of gender. By introducing homoeroticism, they are able to disrupt the gender framework for rock fandom. When musicians express or enact intragender sexual desire, they are able to construct a different sexualized location for the identity label *rock musician* that works to undo the gender relationship between musician and groupie or musician and teenybopper. The ways in which alternative hard rockers queer sexuality and focus on sexual practices rather than identities also opens up space for cultural gender maneuvering. Sexual desire is articulated and enacted by women in a way that is different from the set of practices that undergird the identity label *woman* and hegemonic femininity as constructed by the heterosexual matrix. That is, queering sexualities opens the space for the development of alternative femininities, or of femininities that do not reproduce the hierarchical relationship between masculinity and femininity.

It is more difficult for me to draw conclusions about the range of masculinities. Because my observations were limited to mixed-gender interactions—I am, after all, a woman—I cannot make any claims about the forms of masculinity adopted by men when they were not in the immediate presence of women. For instance, while women's expression of sexual desire for women, men, and the sounds of voices and instruments queered sexuality in the interactions I overheard or participated in, it is entirely possible that individual men, or men as they interact with each other, could construct women's desire in relation to men's sexuality in ways that create an old pattern of hegemonic gendered sexuality. Depictions of so-called lesbian sexuality are a staple of heterosexual pornography marketed to men. Women having sexual contact with each other is constructed in dominant masculinist discourse as a heterosexual turn-on for men, and thus androcentric and male dominant. Although there are in the alternative hard-rock world rigid subcultural norms against men expressing and acting on sexual desire in the presence of women, it is entirely possible that men's collective understanding of women's sexual activities reflects and reproduces this aspect of the sexual and gender order. Despite this possibility, however, queering sexuality does, nonetheless, open space for women to challenge the gender order.

For instance, the subcultural emphasis on behavior rather than identity works to open public space for women who might identify as heterosexual, or who have been or are presently in sexual relationships with men in order to express sexual desire for or engage in sexual play with women without "becoming" something else. This transforms the public space of the bar into a place where women can overtly express sexual attraction for and have playful sexual contact with other women. As Adrienne Rich suggests, compulsory heterosexuality forces or encourages women to focus all of their attention on men.[18] This not only reinforces male identification, or the belief that men's interests are more important than women's, but also compromises women's solidarity. Because women are set up to compete for the attention of men, they are also set up to see each other as adversaries rather than allies. Within the context of this subculture, the combination of the sexual and gender organization of the rock show does not situate women in competition with each other for the attention of men. Introducing queer sexuality into the overall normative structure of the rock show is central to opening this space in which women can focus their attention on each other. As women move about the space of the rock show, they experience the power of the music in their bodies; the power has a sexual valence, and this most often is directed toward other women. Both power and sexuality become the glue that bonds women to each other. This is possible among women who do not define themselves as lesbian precisely because sexual identities are not a central feature of the sexual organization of the subculture. Doing intragender sexuality does not mean becoming or being a sexuality, and thus it is relatively safe.[19]

This is also true for the men, most of whom have intergender romantic partnerships like the women—and in some cases, *with* the women—in the subculture. Despite their relationships, some of these men overtly express and enact erotic desire toward other men. R. W. Connell, in his theory of masculinities, identifies gay men as exemplars of a subordinate masculinity.[20] Heterosexual desire is a central, perhaps even pivotal, component to hegemonic masculinity. Being a man necessarily means expressing desire for the feminine object and always being ready and willing to act on that desire. Being gay is often deemed the antithesis of being masculine. Within the context of alternative hard rock however, the men could engage in quite a bit of intragender erotic play without "becoming gay."

This works particularly well as a gender maneuver within rock culture. In fact, in alternative hard rockers' efforts to do rock differently from the mainstream without being sexist, queering sexuality becomes the perfect form of a countercultural rock 'n' roll sexuality. While retaining a central, cultural feature of rock music—a countercultural, in-your-face, public sexuality—alternative hard rockers are able to reduce sexism by queering sexuality in their performances. Not having been done before, this audacious public sexuality is thus "perfect" rock authenticity.

And yet, are alternative hard rockers successful in their efforts to reject heterosexism? Within mainstream rock there is an underlying assumption that rockers, fans and musicians alike, are straight, and the relationship between positions within rock sets up a heterosexual structure that marginalizes homosexuality. While alternative hard rockers manage to disrupt the heterosexual structure of social positions within rock, they are unsuccessful at dislodging the overall assumption of *heterosexual until proven otherwise*. This aspect of sexual organization is very much a part of alternative hard rock, as it has been since the beginning of rock culture. In fact, I would argue that, in the end, there needs in this case to be a subcultural norm that marginalizes gay and lesbian people precisely so that participants can gender maneuver by queering sexuality and not "become" gay or lesbian; that is, maintaining the heterosexist ideology that gay people are "out there" and not "in here" is as much a part of opening the space for gender maneuvering as is embracing feminist ideology. This points to the complicated organization of sexuality within alternative hard rock. Hegemonic and counterhegemonic sexual relations are operating all at the same time. Depending on the levels of social organization on which one focuses—the overarching normative structure, face-to-face interaction, or the behavior of individuals—any event might reproduce the sexual order, disrupt the sexual order, or both.

More importantly, this points to the importance of looking at sexuality and gender as separate but intersecting systems of social organization. Gender is one system that orders *gender identities* and the relationship between masculinity and femininity, while sexuality is another system that orders *sexual identities* such as the relationship between heterosexuality and homosexuality.[21] As queer theorists suggest, sexuality and gender are separate organizing features of social relations but intersect by mutually constituting, reinforcing, and naturalizing each other.[22] Gender relations—which include how masculinity and femininity are mapped onto identities, how gender is displayed, enacted, and understood, and also how it organizes social relations—naturalizes, reinforces, and supports sexuality, and this includes the display, enactment, meanings, and institutionalization of erotic desire and sexual identities. Likewise, sexuality simultaneously naturalizes, reinforces, and supports gender. For instance, the identity labels *musician* and *groupie* as complements/opposites situate masculinity and femininity in a particular relationship to each other and thus support the gender order. However, the relationship is sexualized in a way that normalizes and naturalizes heterosexuality and marginalizes homosexuality. At the same time, marginalizing homosexuality and homosexual desire keeps the musician/groupie relationship in tact; heterosexism normalizes and fortifies the matrix that holds together the relationship, while gender naturalizes it.

Conceptualizing the relationship between sexuality and gender in this way encourages us to think about gender and sexuality as separate but mutually reinforcing—much in the way that race, class, and gender intersect.[23] In any one interaction or behavior, both gender and sexuality will be operating. That is, in any one social encounter we can look at how the relationship between masculinity and femininity is being produced, challenged, or undermined, and then look separately at how the relationship between heterosexuality and homosexuality and other relationships of erotic desire are being produced or challenged. For instance, when we look closely at the interaction between Maddie and Colleen described at the beginning of this chapter, it becomes clear why a lens of intersectionality is so important. Maddie and Colleen were relatively successful in challenging the requirements for femininity, and for disrupting gender coherence. When Colleen said that Maddie was "a bitch, too," she brought gender to the surface. *Bitch*, like *lesbian*, is a derogatory label hurled at women who step out of the bounds of acceptable femininity and is used to get women back "in line." Both bitches and lesbians do femininity in ways that disrupt the relationship between masculinity and femininity and therefore break the rules of the gender order. By validating both bitchdom and lesbianism, Colleen and Maddie challenge the expectations for femininity as passive, insecure, and other-centered. Further, there is no straightforward masculine counterpart to the identity label *bitch*, so this works not only to challenge gender expectations but also to disconnect the women's gender position from masculinity. In other words, when Colleen re-created her position into "lesbian" and "bitch" and Maddie went along, they negotiated a new gender organization as much as a new sexual organization for the interaction by shifting their positions and the meaning of those positions.

The gender organization of the interaction is further constructed through Colleen's reference to the man as her "girlfriend" because he "is really a *she.*" First, this challenges gender coherence.

The man suddenly becomes a "girlfriend." Also, the pronoun *she* constructs his gender identity as feminine. This is interactive gender maneuvering in that Maddie and Colleen disrupt the hierarchical relationship between masculinity and femininity as stable gender identities that neatly match up with biological sex, gender display, and sexual desire. They do so by cooperatively negotiating their own and the man's gender positions and the meaning of those positions. They also challenge the gender order by suggesting a man could be a "she" and a "girlfriend," the notion of which subverts the sexualized, complementary relationship between masculinity and femininity.

Colleen and Maddie were in the middle of a playful, but at the same time very serious, creation of their own gender identities, the gender and sexual organization of the interaction, and importantly, a re-creation and fixing of the subcultural norms against heterosexism and sexism. While relatively successful in disrupting the gender order on all levels of social organization, they were, however, less successful at disrupting the *sexual* order. First, their assumptions that lesbians are assertive, bold, tough, and so on parallel the hegemonic sexual order. Colleen actually used the word *lesbian* to tease or test Maddie and then to claim some sort of gender outlaw status. This can only work if both Maddie and Colleen have a common understanding of *lesbian* as a stable sexual identity with a whole set of corresponding characteristics. Most importantly, as I suggested earlier, Colleen has assumed that Maddie is heterosexual, reproducing the hegemonic assumption that everybody is heterosexual until proven otherwise. In other words, their gender resistance is enacted by deploying sexual identity labels which, though effective within the interaction to disrupt both the gender and sexual order, fully reinscribed the broader, dominant sexual order. In the end, their gender maneuvering is quite effective. However, through their gender maneuvering, they ultimately rely upon and fortify the sexual order.

Once again, bell hooks insists that those engaging in feminist practice must always consider the ways in which their efforts to challenge male dominance end up reproducing relations of domination along the lines of race and class.[24] The interaction between Maddie and Colleen suggests that efforts to challenge male dominance could reproduce relations of domination along the lines of sexuality. While this chapter focuses explicitly on the intersection of sexuality and gender, it is suggestive of the ways in which other systems of social organization such as ethnicity, race, class, and age will always be implicated in gender maneuvering. For instance, as I've argued throughout this book, both the meaning of and power relations operating in interpersonal relations will be constituted by the overall, dominant systems of inequality, the ways in which those systems manifest within the immediate context of specific social settings, and the group membership and social identities of individuals who are present and interacting. Gender and sexuality are just two systems of inequality. One could just as easily focus on racial structuration and racial maneuvering in face-to-face interaction, or class structuration and maneuvering, or age, or ethnicity, and so on. In other words, future research might address the ways in which the meaning of social positions and the interpersonal power relations between people are negotiated through the manipulation of the relationships among racial, class, age, and/ or ethnic positions. Similarly, an analysis of intersectionality might focus explicitly on the ways in which gender meanings and power are negotiated through a manipulation of the relationships among race, ethnic, class, and/or age positions, or how racial meanings and power are negotiated through a manipulation of the relationship between masculinity and femininity. In other words, *maneuvering*, as I've defined it, is not limited to negotiating gender, but might also apply to other systems of inequality as well. While my analytic interest and focus for this project is on resistive efforts to negotiate the gender and sexual order, it would have been equally possible to focus on class and race; sexuality and age; class, ethnicity, and sexuality; or any other configuration of intersecting systems of inequality in alternative hard rock. My hope is that the concept *gender maneuvering* provides enough analytic substance for other researchers to pick up and use for projects on racial, ethnic, class, and/or age maneuvering in rock and elsewhere. I also hope that people who are interested in challenging these systems of inequality might begin thinking about strategies of maneuvering more generally. What would it mean to *race maneuver*? In what ways can an individual or group disrupt the hierarchical relationships between racial identities through processes of interaction or by developing subcultural spaces that reconfigure the relationship between whiteness and blackness? What about class positions? Ethnicity?

Perhaps the most important question is, What is the relationship between maneuvering and larger systems of inequality? If our goal is to dismantle these systems of subordination, we must always keep an eye on not just the actions of individuals, groups, or subcultures but also on the broader political implications of those actions. For instance, alternative hard rockers seem committed to challenging homophobia and heterosexism. However, as I have demonstrated, they limit their understanding of heterosexism to individual attitudes and behaviors. There is no explicit subcultural awareness of nor efforts to transform heterosexism as a structural feature of rock or of social relations more generally. Sexual inequality is defined in terms of individual acts of homophobia, discrimination or bigotry, not as a characteristic of the social structure. So while participating in the play of gender and sexuality at a Tribe 8 show, they simultaneously marginalized Tribe 8 and their audience as outsiders and a "bunch of lesbians."

As I will discuss in the final chapter, this individualistic approach to sexual politics is characteristic of alternative hard rockers' approach to politics more generally, including feminist politics. In the end, gender maneuvering is the limit to feminist politics in alternative hard rock, and while this is quite effective in transforming the gender structure of the rock clubs in Chicago, the alternative hard rockers reproduce the sexual order. And, importantly, there are significant limits on their ability to impact gender relations more broadly.

7

FEMINIST POLITICS

As the band Hole ripped through their first song of their encore set, the mosh pit surged toward the stage, receded, and surged again. It was rougher than usual. Hole had been getting a lot of mainstream media attention because of the death of Courtney Love's husband Kurt Cobain and the simple fact that their record *Live through This* was one of the best recordings of the year and getting much attention and airplay. This mainstream attention meant that the crowd had grown to include people who did not share alternative hard rockers' sensibilities, and the alternative hard rockers in the audience were unable to establish, let alone maintain, any kind of collective responsibility for safety. The front was dominated by very large men who had bullied everyone else to the side.

Between songs, someone in the audience must have called for Courtney Love to jump in to the mosh pit. Love sort of laughed and spat back,'"Yeah, right. You're all a bunch of fucking idiots. Like I'm going to jump into that? It's all a bunch of fucking linebackers up here. Why don't you girls get them the fuck out of here. I'd jump in and they'd try to stick their finger up my ass. Donita [Donita Sparks of L7] jumped in and got anally penetrated. And you girls won't do anything to protect me. Fuck all of you. Fuck you, you fucking assholes."

The band launched into their next song and the mosh pit erupted again. After three or four minutes, Courtney Love moved to the edge of the stage and began leaning into the hands outstretched to touch her. Slowly she leaned over farther and farther until the hands lifted her and her guitar up and over the crowd.

It all happened so quickly from there. The crowd energy grew to a frenzy as people tried to lay their hands on her. Love disappeared as the crowd swallowed her up like lions on a fresh kill. The men who lined the stage to keep people off plunged into the crowd trying to get to the spot where she had disappeared. There was a lot of commotion as the band continued to play.

After a few moments, I could see Love being escorted back to the stage by the burly bouncer-bodyguards. With only a black bra, black underwear, and black platform-heeled sandals remaining on her body, Love was lifted back up onto the stage. Her baby doll dress had apparently been ripped off and retained by the crowd. She remained at the edge of the stage screaming something to the bouncers and pointing into the audience. Someone brought a towel from back stage and handed it to Love. She held it to her chest, but was more concerned with what was happening in the crowd than the exposure of her body. Two of the men moved through the crowd as Love continued to point and scream. Nobody really knew what was happening because the band continued to play.

I watched with horror and a sick pleasure as the men dragged a young man from the crowd up and on to the stage. When the young man was presented before her, she let the towel fall completely as she grabbed him. Again, clad only in black lace undergarments and heels, she dragged him to the microphone. The band finally stopped.

Love pushed the man in the chest and screamed into the microphone, "Tell them why you ripped my dress off! Tell them! Tell them!"

The young man stood expressionless and silent. Love pulled back and delivered a fisted punch to the man's face. The crowd, which had been silently watching up until the blow, erupted. Most people, like an angry mob or the crowd at the Roman Coliseum, raised their fists and cheered. The bouncers dived on top of both Love and the man. While two escorted Love off the stage, the rest dragged the man back to the front of the stage and tossed him to the lions. There was a commotion, but bar staff immediately intervened and pulled people toward the door.

I was stunned. The next morning, as I relayed the story to a friend, her response shocked me even more than what had transpired the night before.

"Oh, I've heard she does that at all her shows. Some guy in L.A. is suing her. It's part of their show."

With my mouth hanging open, my mind reeled, trying to come up with some way to understand this. I had already written my fieldnotes and had interpreted the event as a woman publicly naming sexual violence and fighting back. This was, I thought, a fantastic example of interactive gender maneuvering. The woman musician jumped into the crowd. The audience resituated her as an object to possess, as sexual prey. The musician was forced back into the position of woman. The woman reasserted her position as musician by climbing back on the stage, blurred the lines between woman and musician by remaining on stage in heels and black lingerie, and then kicked the perpetrator's ass in front of the whole crowd. Woman/musician/sex object/aggressor/victor all wrapped up in one neat package through a series of events and interactions.

However, when I learned that this was a routine occurrence at Hole shows, my neatly constructed analytic bubble burst. This was not the ongoing process of everyday interaction; this was a carnivalesque performance, staged, planned, and arranged. Yet it was a performance that critically examined sexual assault. Courtney Love constructed the audience as dominated by a certain kind of man—"linebackers" in this case—and therefore potentially sexually aggressive. She chastised women for not taking control of the mosh pit and for not protecting her. According to Love, the entire audience, including the women and men, was initially culpable and responsible for making sexual assault likely and possible. When the assault happened, she publicly named it and fought back. This was rock performance, but it appeared to be rock performance with a feminist political agenda.

Putting aside gender maneuvering for a moment, I came up with two possible interpretations. On the one hand, I could leave sociology for the time being and conclude that this was simply a manifestation of Courtney Love's personality, tastes, and/or personal experiences and traumas. She was an angry woman who needed to get it out in some form or another, so she beat up on young men in the audience. This, in fact, was what most of the press was concluding about Courtney Love. On the other hand, I could use my sociological imagination and examine how Love's performance might be exemplary of some aspect of the subculture, and/or, perhaps of the larger sociocultural context in which she was constructing her performance.[1]

Fortunately, with the ongoing process of ethnographic data collection, I had two strategies with which to begin searching for answers. With a fresh eye and a new focus, I could go back to my fieldnotes, or I could go back into the field. I decided to focus my questions on the relationship between a feminist political agenda and rock performance. I paid particular attention to how alternative hard rockers explicitly talked about feminism, feminist politics, and the relationship between feminism and rock music. I discovered three things. First, alternative hard rockers generally didn't talk about feminism unless I brought it up. They talked about sexism and gender inequality, but the words *feminist* or *feminism* did not seem to be part of their vocabulary. Second, when I did bring it up, all said that they support feminism, that feminism has had a positive impact on their lives, and that they used feminism as a guiding set of principles for how to do the right thing. Third, they all said that they do not consciously politicize their music with feminist messages, but instead use feminism as a guide for how to do rock culture differently, and by example, encourage others to go along.

"IT'S NOT GIRLS AGAINST BOYS": ALTERNATIVE HARD ROCKERS TALK ABOUT FEMINISM, MALE DOMINANCE, AND ROCK 'N' ROLL

Among alternative hard rockers, feminism is a set of principles and ideas that is useful for evaluating one's own and others' behavior. All agree that sexism exists and that it is a problem in need of change; the main problem is that individuals continue to behave and interact in ways that are sexist. There are behaviors and ways of interacting with others that reproduce the gender order, and there are behaviors and attitudes that do not. Any person, man or woman, who did gender in a way that those I spoke to identified as sexist is labeled an "asshole." For instance, when a man "schmoozes," when a woman lifts her shirt to expose her breasts to a band, when someone makes a derogatory remark about gay men or lesbians, when a musician encourages "a bunch of group-ies" to collect backstage, they are "assholes." Those who do things differently, do not reproduce old patterns, are labeled "cool." For instance, when a man makes an antirape statement on stage, when a woman can or does "kick ass," when a woman openly expresses her sexual desire, when a man consciously avoids invading the personal space of people around him in the audience, they are "cool."

While alternative hard rockers use these labels to identify and then repudiate or encourage certain behaviors, at the same time they work very hard to deemphasize gender identity as having any importance in their challenges to male dominance. It does not matter if one is a man or a woman; what matters is how one acts. A woman can just as easily reproduce male dominant gender relations as could a man, and a man can just as easily undermine male dominance as could a woman. Men and women are equally culpable, and there is no real difference between a man who reproduces old patterns of masculinity and a woman who enacts complacent forms of femininity.

In my discussion with Kat Bjelland of Babes in Toyland, we discussed the problem of sexism. She explained that "you can do whatever you want if you put your mind to it. If you choose to be oppressed . . . I mean in the past . . . I mean some people are born into oppression, which is bad, but I've never been in a situation where I felt oppressed by males. I feel like I can take care of myself." Later in our discussion she came back to this theme saying, "as far as I know, like racism and sexism . . . it seems like someone is not open-minded or not brought up right or something. It's not oppressive. They're just idiots; dumb; closed-minded or uneducated or scared and they need to bug other people. . . . I just think it's bad people who are like that."

Sexism and racism are characteristics of "bad people" and they manifest as efforts to "bug people." Sexism is an individual action of someone who is somehow deficient or ignorant and challenging sexism means not letting it bother you and doing what you want. In my interview with Kim Thayil of Soundgarden, we talked about feminism. He said that his perspective had changed over the years. "In my young twenties, when I was a college student, I used to have this position like men are assholes, and they're jerks, and they're rapists, and women are victims, and they're nice and they're angels, and I realized that's the position held by a male who is particularly patronizing."

Trying to clarify, I asked, "Like men are brutes and women are victims?"

"Yeah. Like 'women good—men bad.' That kind of thing. It's condescending to protect. It's a chivalrous attitude."

Thayil was challenging a simplified conceptualization of sexism as neatly separating women and men. In fact, he suggested that it is sexist to divide people by gender identity. In his early twenties he believed that men and masculinity were the problem, that men were "assholes, and they're jerks, and rapists" and that women were the victims of men. When he was younger, gender identity was the most salient marker for sexism—men were sexist; women suffered. More recently, however, he had come to the conclusion that it was sexist itself to simplify the problem of gender relations as men being bad and women being good. Women could be sexist, and men could be nonsexist. Making room for the idea that women could be "assholes" and men could be "cool" necessitated a conceptual move from gender identity as the most salient feature of gender relations to behavior or practice as the marker of "good" and "bad." This emphasis on how one acts came through when he contrasted the kinds of bands and musicians he likes with glam rockers.

"The types of bands we've always dealt with [were] generally pretty decent guys," he noted. "We weren't hanging around the glam rock stars of the mid-eighties or whatever. It's just a different thing. They hated rock 'n' roll. They hated the way it was characterized. They didn't like popular music. They just innately knew what was cool and what wasn't. . . . And the relationship between [the music] and feminism just grew into 'do the right thing.'"

For Thayil, feminism translated into "do the right thing." Both men and women can do the right thing—that is, not engage in sexist behavior. More importantly, however, both men and women can do the *wrong* thing or reproduce male dominance. As was noted in chapter 4, Thayil mentioned in this interview the behavior he'd witnessed from both men and women on tour as Soundgarden became more popular; it seemed that the audiences were changing, and the women were becoming more like those he'd seen at other bands' shows. This included lifting their shirts to expose their breasts to band members.

When women lift their shirts to expose their breasts to a band, they are doing a sexist form of femininity that smacks of *groupie*, while the behavior of mainstream rock bands elicits and/or rewards women acting as sexual objects. The behavior of both the women in the audience and the male musicians sets up a sexist relationship between masculinity and femininity. Treating the woman in the audience as a sex object is uncool, but so is the woman's treating the band like sexist, sexually predatory men. By saying "we weren't that kind of band" but that he'd "seen that kind of behavior," Thayil explicitly marked individual behavior as his and others' point of departure from mainstream "glam-rock" bands. Importantly, his emphasis was not on being androgynous, but instead on avoiding behaviors that reproduce the old patterns of masculine sexual subject/feminine sexual object.

When I asked Donita Sparks how the crowds have changed since L7 became more popular she expressed a dissatisfaction similar to Kim Thayil's. "When we played in smaller places it seemed that the fans were more in tune with what we were about socially and politically," she said. Now, in the larger clubs, she noted, "You know, you just get more assholes."

The audiences did not share the band's political and social approach to the music and behaved in ways that reproduced traditional forms of masculinity (in this case it was violence). Sparks referred to this as a certain "sensibility." When I asked her what that sensibility was she said, "It's about being more enlightened, having a sense of fairness and not being a sexist pig. . . . " To clarify the sensibility or political and social approach to the music, she emphasized individual behavior. The sensibility is a way of acting. Kat Bjelland of Babes in Toyland similarly addressed this sensibility, saying about the band's fans that they had "similar minds."

Other musicians expressed similar approaches to feminism and to sexism. Feminism was a way to evaluate women's and men's behavior, and based on that evaluation, decide who was an ally and who was an enemy. For instance, when I asked Sparks if L7 consciously put feminism into their music her response captured this emphasis on gender performance rather than identity.

"Consciously? Well, it's part of me and the songs come out of my experience. But you know if you listen to our songs they're universal. Men and women can relate to them. Like "Shitlist," a guy could relate to that just as much as the gals can. It's not about girls against boys. It's about cool people against assholes. I'm not writing as a woman, I'm writing as a human being. . . . It's just hard music. I don't think of people as male or female. I think of them in terms of assholes and cool people. And it has nothing to do with being male or female. You know, I know a lot of men who are really cool and there are women who are real assholes. . . . I have more in common with a cool man than an asshole woman." For Sparks, what defined cool people versus assholes was not gender identity, but behavior.

It seemed that every time feminism came up, alternative hard rockers started talking about how it's not about "girls against boys."

Similarly, Kat Bjelland balked at calling herself a feminist.

I asked, "Do you consider yourself a feminist?"

She responded, "Everybody knows that labeling is a bad thing to do to yourself or to anybody else, so it's hard to say. All I know is I hate to separate people by if they're a feminist/not feminist, racist/not racist. It's just that either you have an open mind or you don't. You're halfway smart and open-minded or you're closed and afraid of stuff and dumb. You know what I mean? No. I don't consider myself a feminist or any '-ist.' No '-ists.' I'm just a human."

I pushed her a bit and asked, "So you don't use the word *feminist?*"

"I don't like labeling stuff. I know you need labels when you're writing, but you can really pigeonhole yourself like that." For

Bjelland, fitting people into identity categories or political labels is not useful. The only thing that really matters is whether one, a man or a woman, is open minded.

This was an explicit point of departure from the riot grrrl subculture. Most of the musicians I interviewed talked about riot grrrl as generally a good thing, but in some ways sexist or politically misguided for sometimes excluding men. Ian MacKaye of Fugazi talked about being a politically minded man in a patriarchal society. "We are a patriarchal society to some degree," he pointed out. "But I gotta say, it wasn't my choice and I try not to abuse that. But I feel like I'm entitled to having my opinions and I'm not particularly interested in stifling myself because I feel like men say too much. I just think men should think about what they're saying. Honestly, I was raised with very strong women all around me, so I don't have any problem taking orders from women at all. And I don't mean that in a negative way. . . . It's true, I am a man. That's kind of a tough problem sometimes. But on the other hand, it's obviously not as much of a problem as being a woman."

Later, while talking about being criticized for being a man and speaking out about sexism, he said, "I'm struggling with a lot of people in Washington. Friends of mine who are like superfeminists and they've focused a lot of criticism on the band, on me in particular, because they don't feel I have a right to speak about women's issues, that only women should talk about that. But fuck that. I am not interested in being censored by that kind of thinking. If I'm expressing things that I believe in, then I'm going to express them. To me, it's just too hard to follow all these rules. Why can't we just respond honestly to each other?"

"People are getting pissed off?" I asked.

"The whole riot grrrl thing is very tough. I guess I just feel unwilling to censor myself. . . . some people who consider themselves riot grrls who are very vocal, have criticized me in particular as someone who is exploiting women's problems. But I submit to them that I was singing about it in 1987."

When I asked Kat Bjelland about the riot grrrl phenomeonon she responded, "I know Kathleen [Kathleen Hanna of Bikini Kill], who sort of started the word and the whole 'zine thing . . . I thought it was a cool little fanzine movement. Speakin' their mind. People jumped on it and like, 'I'm a riot grrrl.' It's like, What's *that* supposed to mean? Be an individual. Shitty bands, and they can't even play good music. I don't know. It's just jumping on a bandwagon to feel a part of something, which is fine I guess. It might make shy girls feel a little stronger and that's beneficial, but it's just [that] the media throw something out and it gets so overused. It makes me sick."

"What about the idea of having all women bands and only allowing women in to see them?" I asked.

"How about we have an all-white-male band and have a bunch of white people go to see it? I think it's pretty obvious why it's stupid. It's segregating. It's totally like leaving out people. I don't like when guys do that. No. It's stupid."

At another show, I was talking with the lead singer of a local alternative hard rock band in Chicago. She also had a problem with gender segregated shows. "They're simply fighting bigotry with bigotry," she said. "Men are not the enemy so much as . . . I guess some men are, but so are some women too."

Drawing alliances along the lines of gender identity was perceived as sexist, and this made sense given these rockers' emphasis on individual behavior. The problem with drawing political lines between women and men was that it did not acknowledge the ways in which men can challenge male dominance or women can reproduce it through individual actions. This translates into the notion that women and men are equally culpable for sexism, and women and men can work equally well at challenging it.

This interpretation of feminism is particularly effective for encouraging men to participate in both cultural and interactive gender maneuvering. It is also a very effective way to construct a normative framework for rock culture that undermines male dominance. By constructing sexism as uncool and feminism as cool within the context of rock culture, this meaning frame is a strong incentive for newcomers to "get with the program."

Despite their relative success in encouraging women and men to do alternative gender performances and interactions and in constructing a social context in which alternative gender arrangements were the norm, these rockers do not, by any stretch of the imagination, create a feminist utopia. They do not check male dominance at the door as they enter. There are ways in which alternative hard rockers reproduce the gender order, and in highly problematic ways.

For the most part, they refuse to think in terms of men and women as members of social groups with competing interests. They believe that it is sexist to think of women as victims and men as victimizers. They also reduce feminism to a critique of individual behavior rather than a critical perspective for understanding and challenging the broader social structure. Feminism then, is not about women against men, but about sexist people against non-sexist people. Thus, while their efforts to undermine male dominance emphasize the everyday negotiations of gendered practices, they do not take into consideration the ways in which gender difference has real significance in broader male-dominant gender relations. They conceptualize gender relations as reducible to interpersonal interaction among individuals and ignore the importance of gender-group membership in terms of social privilege and disadvantage. This means that forms of male dominance for which group membership or structure matters go unnoticed, or worse, are legitimated.

For instance, on several occasions I heard men talk about how all-female bands were getting hired for gigs over more qualified all-male groups simply because they were made up of women. One would think that a feminist sensibility might make sense of this practice, if in fact, it were true. A feminist critique that takes into consideration gender identity as an important axis for distributing social and economic resources and opportunity might argue that there has been a long history of cultural, institutional, and interpersonal barriers to women becoming hard-rock musicians. These barriers tilt the playing field to the benefit of men who aspire to be hard-rock musicians. Though some all-female bands might not be as musically talented as some all-male bands, hiring young women over young men could be one way to even the playing field at the level of group membership. One could also argue that it is important for all-female bands to mentor or act as role models for other young women, and hiring all-female bands makes that possible.

However, because it is considered sexist to make any claims to women's subordinate status simply by virtue of their membership in the social group *women*, these lines of reasoning were never verbalized. Alternative hard rockers never made what Craig Calhoun calls claims to identity with "strategic considerations."[2] Gender identity has always mattered and continues to matter when it comes to getting gigs, dealing with record companies, and interacting with audiences. No matter how much we say it does not matter or how effectively we perform alternative genders, we are all still perceived as women and men, and people act accordingly. Explicitly hiring competent women bands is one strategy for dealing with this inequity. Strategically considering gender identity would open a space for alternative hard rockers to rethink hiring practices as part of a larger social pattern rather than an individual action. Instead, the assertion that women and men are equal and should be treated as such translates into the belief that women and men should be treated the same. This ignores the ways in which women and men are not treated the same up to the very moment of, and in many cases during, decision making about which bands to book.[3] In the end, the unchallenged story about the unfair hiring of women ultimately works to support male dominance. It reinforces the idea that men, on average, are better musicians than women. It delegitimates women's presence on stage to some degree, and it allows men to attribute not getting bookings to the "sexism" of those doing the hiring, not their own lack of ability.

At the same time, however, gender difference becomes a point of contention between the women and men within the subculture, especially when it comes to characterizing music. Men are far more likely to talk about and emphasize essential differences between women and men.

When I asked Eddie Vedder why he is committed to feminist politics in his own life, he said, "I just think there are inherent differences between women and men. And women are so fucking cool. There are so many good thing about women, about women's character. You know, like Perry Farrell's song 'Classic Girl.'" (Vedder then sang a few lines from the Jane's Addiction song: "She gives her man a great idea / He says, 'Hey man, why don't you listen to my great idea' / Men never can be, not like a girl / Such a classic girl. . . . ") He continued, "You know, women are mothers. They know how to nurture. Many men envy women's ability to give birth."

"Yeah, but they're afraid to speak up about it," I pointed out.

"Yeah, they'll lose all their drinking buddy friends," Vedder said. "I guess I didn't give a shit about losing those kinds of friends."

While Vedder was committed to forging a new sort of masculinity in rock and was willing to give up his place in the hegemonic masculinity occupied with his drinking buddy friends, he still relied on and reproduced essential gender difference as one reason why he is interested in fighting sexism.

Kim Thayil laid this same sort of essential difference framework on music itself. Talking about Soundgarden's sound, he said, "It's aggressive. It's loud. Being that it's visceral and I tend to associate visceral with masculine qualities. Testosterone. I do have a theory about estrogen rock. These aren't divided by the gender of the performer, but by the music itself. Women can play testosterone rock and there are a number of men who play estrogen rock."

"What is estrogen rock?" I asked.

"I always thought of it as being more, you know, minor keys and minor scales. Minor keys are more sympathetic. They're sadder. They're sort of floaty, and God, it's like drowning . . . most of the all-girl bands I can think of are preoccupied with testosterone rock."

"Like L7?"

"Yeah. Or . . . well, that's why I think some of them kind of stink. Well, L7 is great, but when all-female bands try to be preoccupied with testosterone aggression it seems inadequate because there's some really fucked-up, aggressive guys out there who can do the same thing."

I asked for clarification: " . . . because they're fucked up or just . . . ?"

"I'm not saying there aren't aggressive women. But when I think of an aggressive guy, he certainly has a few notches up on an aggressive woman because they grow up that way. They probably had to deal with it more with other men. Everything from sports to fighting to competition . . . "

While Thayil made a point to emphasize how these differences are a result of socialization and life experiences, he still comes to the conclusion that men, on average, will be better at testosterone rock than women. That he labels this distinction "testosterone" and "estrogen" lays an essentialist meaning on that difference.

The women in alternative hard rock have to maneuver within these arguments about gender difference in order to be taken seriously as musicians. In my conversations with them, they often verbally maneuvered to erase or diminish the importance of gender difference. When I talked with Donita Sparks of L7, I asked her what she thought about the differences between "estrogen" and "testosterone" rock.

She scoffed, "I like Kim. I really do. He's a great guy. But that is the biggest bunch of fucking bullshit I've ever heard in my life."

"Well, he said that L7 plays testosterone rock."

"Bullshit. Why is it so fucking hard for people to recognize that women can be angry and aggressive and it doesn't make them masculine? We're not trying to be like men. We're rock musicians. We're trying to be rock musicians. It's not the same thing. Being a man is one thing, being a rock musician is another. Testosterone, estrogen, parts, hormones. They have nothing to do with what kind of music you play. There are people who like to be aggressive and play aggressive music, and there are people who don't. End of story."

Later in our conversation, the topic of lumping women musicians together came up. I had read that L7 refused to participate in anything that was framed in terms of "women in rock," so I asked her about that. She responded, "Gender is not genre! You know lumping us in with Bikini Kill and Hole and Liz Phair, it's really sexist. Liz Phair is on the cover of *Rolling Stone*. She should be on the cover. She's really creative. She's doing really innovative things. But they have to make it 'women in rock,' like it's some kind of special case. No. She should be on the cover regardless of her gender. It's a way to set us apart from real rock. It belittles women to lump them all together. . . . No women-in-rock bullshit. We rock hard. That's all there is to it. But we always get the girl-band bullshit. We don't rock hard for women; we just rock hard. We won't do women-in-rock articles, and people say that's unsisterly. But I think it's sexist to think about it in that way."

When I spoke with other women musicians, they all wanted

to make sure my project wasn't another women-in-rock story, and they all talked about how they didn't want to be thought of as simply another "girl group."

Louise Post of Veruca Salt said, "You know, the press in Chicago talks about us like we're just another girl group, but we rock, like those things don't go together. They talk about Juliana Hatfield, Liz Phair, L7 whenever they talk about us."

I responded, "Those bands are all so different."

"Yeah, but we're all girl groups. The differences don't matter."

Within the context of rock culture, where the mainstream media continuously lumps women musicians together as if music by women is a separate kind of music, and within this specific subculture where men sometimes invoke gender difference to characterize different kinds of music, it becomes necessary for women to continuously play down gender difference as having any importance. Sparks's and other women's suspicions about gender difference is completely understandable.

However, this quite legitimate effort by women to deemphasize their gender in any kind of evaluation or categorization of their music is inextricable from the subcultural proscription against identifying gender-group membership as having significance in any context. This translates into an emphasis on individual empowerment through individual action. Even when the women I spoke with talked about clear disadvantages for women, they offered solutions based on individual action.

Lori Barbero of Babes in Toyland understood that gender-group membership matters. She said, "Most of the women I know, including myself, are a lot stronger, smarter, more intelligent than most of the men at the same level, and in all facets are treated way worse. Being a woman is basically a minority. I'm treated way different than your average white man and it makes me really uptight. I know for a fact that every woman I know who has any kind of job in an area with men, they probably naturally, because they have to, they work three times harder than any other men. Women work way harder than men, especially at professional things. You have to prove it. But also because women are more together. I'm not a man hater or bra burner—'down with men.' I love them, believe you me. But when it comes to professionalism, I think it's a crock of shit. I get really freaked out."

Barbero identified a systemic pattern of inequality between women as a group and men as a group. However, not two minutes later, when we were discussing how her audiences have changed over time, she suggested individual action as a remedy. "The whole audience in rock 'n' roll has changed," she noted. "It used to be like ninety percent men and then like the last three years it's balancing out. Women are going out. They can associate better. . . . Women are included and it is getting better, but it's not good enough. There should be more women. Women still get pushed back. . . . Music is male dominated . . . well, the world is male dominated. . . . Everyone understands music. . . . It shouldn't make any difference what gender you are. I wish women were more aggressive. . . . "

Another woman musician I spoke with emphasized individual behavior as a remedy for sexism in rock. We were talking about women musicians getting hassled by men in the audience and she said, "Some people are like, 'Why are you so negative?' Just because I'm screaming doesn't mean I'm actually very negative. I get angry about a certain subject, but I'm one of the happiest people I know right now. I'm not mad. Maybe it's just passion. It's not anger. Whenever a woman—this is something I hate—whenever women are screaming [people are] like, 'She's a bitch.' When guys do it, it's like, 'He's so passionate. He's a genius.'"

A bit later, however, when we were talking about a particular woman musician I had seen get really hassled by men in an audience a week earlier, she suggested that the woman's actions might have led to the harassment, saying, "I just think our audience has always been really great. They usually don't heckle us or anything. I just think we put off a vibe. I'm not really sure what it is. . . . We're not trying to all—'Look we're these fuckin' rock stars up here you should worship.' . . . We don't say stupid shit like 'my pussy this' or 'I'm going to fuck you,' so no one yells back at us. Once in awhile, of course, you get some idiot. Doesn't seem like very much. If you put yourself in the public eye that much, you're going to get people heckling you."

Although she knows that women are perceived differently because they are women, this woman was repeating the subcultural understanding of how gender inequality works: if you play a certain sort of femininity, you're going to get sexist treatment, so you don't play that femininity. Even though group membership matters in how one is treated, the strategy for addressing gender inequality is individual gender maneuvering.

This is in stark contrast to the riot grrrl subcultural emphasis on gender-group membership. The practice of setting up public spaces where young women could play only in the presence of other young women was grounded in a structural understanding of how gender operates in rock. Rather than denying gender matters, as those in the Chicago subculture did, riot grrrls defined themselves explicitly through an identity-based politics. Because of this, riot grrrl subcultures were somewhat more successful at getting young women into public places as fans and as musicians playing rock.[4] They were able to claim that gender identity and group membership *do* matter, that there are real, material consequences for women and men, and acted accordingly. I would argue that their ability to do so was fundamentally grounded in their more separatist approach to creating a subculture. Within the subculture in Chicago, the presence of men as central figures necessitated a deemphasis on gender-group membership. It was necessary, first, to keep men interested in the project of creating something new and to prevent any kind of ghettoization of women musicians in the subculture. It would be possible, I think, to construct a subculture in which gender-group membership was not an axis of evaluation and categorization of musical ability and style but was considered an important factor in hiring decisions; it would take a decidedly structural understanding of the workings of gender. It is the same structural process that relegates women to the side as a "special case" and systematically privileges men in booking decisions. However, for people in Chicago, these were individual actions, not structural processes, as Sparks suggested. Thus, the individual action of explicitly hiring an all-female band is flattened, equated with writing a "women-in-rock article." As individual actions, both are constructed as sexist because they draw attention to gender difference.

The most disturbing example of alternative hard rockers' legitimation of male dominance emerged during a conversation about intimate partner violence. In a conversation among six or seven people, one person said that a particular woman had declared that her boyfriend had physically assaulted her on different occasions. At first, the others were appalled: "What an asshole!" "I can't believe he would do that!" A man in the group said, "I know. He kind of told me about it." A woman said angrily, "What did you do about it? What did you say? What can we do about this?" Everybody got very uneasy and finally a man said, "What can we do? Why doesn't she kick his ass or get the fuck out of there?" Nobody challenged this conclusion. People were visibly uncomfortable, but had no response.

Although it is an all-too-common response to question the woman's involvement when people hear about a man's physical violence toward her, one would think that participants in a subculture that is based heavily on feminism would have a way to talk about how the violence is gendered, not the woman's fault, and the responsibility of everybody present. However, in a world where women as individuals fight back or are culpable, what else could be said? There can be no discussion about how men as a group benefit from the male dominant power relations enacted through individual men's violence toward women; the violence is reduced to the individual act of an "asshole." There can be no discussion of women's economic dependence on men. There can be no discussion about the tremendous pressure placed on women as a group to be partnered, make partnerships work, and to take care of others. There can be no discussion of how men as a group are encouraged to use aggression and violence to deal with conflict and to establish dominance. In other words, there can be no discussion of the larger structural context in which this individual man is physically assaulting an individual woman. The violence is not placed within the broader context of male dominance in which gender identity does matter immensely in issues of violence. In a world where women as individuals either participate in sexist interactions (and are thus equally responsible) or refuse to participate, what else can be said? It was very difficult to take into consideration a long history of social, political, and economic masculine privilege and feminine subordination, or of structural power relations that benefit men as a group and are disadvantageous to women as a group. The subcultural beliefs that invoking gender difference is sexist silences any kind of structural approach to violence. Ironically, alternative hard rockers are highly successful at eliminating violence and aggression as a mechanism of power in the mosh pit, but seemingly do nothing at all to challenge individual men's uses of violence outside of the rock club.

I do not want to suggest that adopting a structural perspective on violence or discrimination is somehow simple or a skill that most people learn and alternative hard rockers have somehow missed out on. We live in a culture that strongly encourages individualistic thinking, so thinking in terms of group membership is not commonsensical, especially when about issues of opportunity and violence. I also do not want to suggest that all alternative hard rockers do not understand male dominance in structural as well as individual terms. What I *do* want is to point out the fact that there is a strong subcultural norm for emphasizing individual behavior, and to identify women's and men's culpability. This subcultural norm makes it very difficult for any individual to assert a structural interpretation of any form of sexism, and thus, in this silence, certain forms and manifestations of male dominance go unchallenged and are thus reproduced.

Though feminist ideology strongly emphasizes moving from individual-level analysis to structural analysis, alternative hard rockers managed to individualize their own feminist sensibilities. As I mentioned above, there is a very strong, very dominant cultural emphasis on individualism in contemporary U.S. culture that no doubt contributes to alternative hard rockers' interpretation of feminism. This, however, is not the complete story. In addition to a general emphasis on individualism in American political history, there are also features of the particular sociohistorical context in which alternative hard rock developed that fuel this approach to feminism.

FROM "SISTERHOOD IS POWERFUL" TO "THE NEW VICTORIANS": BROAD SHIFTS IN THE CULTURAL CLIMATE OF FEMINISM

Alternative hard rockers' conscious efforts to undermine male dominance by transforming their everyday practices while simultaneously flattening gender difference as a point of stratification is embedded within broader sociocultural approaches to feminist ideology at the time. Alternative hard rockers grew up with the second wave of the women's movement, but they were in their teens during the Reagan-Bush years and during what Susan Faludi calls the "backlash" against feminism.[5]

The second wave of the women's movement, which began in the late 1960s and early 1970s put gender relations under the political microscope and brought women's subordination to the consciousness of most Americans. Everything from the gendered division of labor, women's labor-force experiences, interpersonal communication, violence against women in all forms, and women's political participation and exclusion were identified as examples of women's social, political, and economic inequality in relation to men. Feminism centered on the ways in which all aspects of social life were gendered and worked to maintain male dominance.

In practice, feminism took many different paths. Consciousness-raising groups for women sprung up all over the country: women gathered in small or large groups to talk about their lives and experiences, to identify the similarities in their experience, and to come to political consciousness by recognizing their personal experiences as part of the systematic social organization of male dominance. More traditional forms of political activism revolved around speak-outs, marches, demonstrations, picket lines, and legal and political reform.

Part of the broad feminist cultural critique was to question the normative expectations and behaviors attached to masculine and feminine gender identities. Men's adherence to a masculine gender identity, including all of the social expectations that come with masculinity, was cast as one of the core mechanisms by which women are subordinated, exploited, and sometimes brutalized by men. Masculine characteristics such as competitiveness, aggression, and inexpressiveness, as well as men's lack of involvement in family life were identified as fundamental problems contributing to male dominance and women's subordination. Femininity was problematized as debilitating to women and thus in need of transformation as well. Feminine characteristics such as being "other-centered" and passive made women easier targets for men's exploitation and violence. Feminists pointed out that femininity and masculinity set up the perfect victim/victimizer relationship between women and men, and men were all too willing to take advantage.

Because gender identity was cast as one of the fundamental problems of women's subordination, mostly white, middle-class feminists emphasized solidarity among women in opposition to men. By identifying the ways in which the gender order encouraged women to see each other as insignificant or as potential threats and enemies, feminist discourse encouraged women to form social, political, and emotional bonds with each other. Because the gender order benefits men at the expense of women, and because men as a group have a political interest in maintaining the gender order, many feminists encouraged women to form political alliances along the lines of gender identity. The slogan "sisterhood is powerful" was meant to reinforce the idea that women's solidarity with each other in opposition to men as a group would be empowering to women.

With this quite thorough critique of masculinity, some men's groups began to develop in tandem with women's groups. Profeminist men's groups focused on putting the spotlight on masculinity and male privilege in an effort to acknowledge their individual participation in exploiting or brutalizing women and, through group or individual therapy, eliminate the aspects of masculinity that are harmful to women, children, the environment, and themselves. The main focus was on individual men coming to terms with and eliminating all of the problematic aspects of their masculine identity so as to become better partners to women, better fathers to children, and better citizens of the planet. Although some individuals and some men's organizations worked at the level of social change,[6] the vast majority of men sympathetic to the women's movement focused on their individual participation in gender relations.

Feminism had a profound impact on perceptions of and actual gender relations creating, what R. W. Connell calls a "crisis in the gender order."[7] This crisis in the gender order resulted from feminists' critique and subsequent, widespread, cultural delegitimation of overt male dominance. However, as Connell points out, crises in the gender order are invariably met with reactionary cultural shifts in order to reestablish or ensure male dominance in light of changes in gender relations. Part of the reactionary cultural response to second-wave feminists' politicization of gender relations included an effort to undermine the legitimacy of feminism. Accusations of "male bashing" and a vociferous backlash blaming feminism and feminists for causing the problems in women's lives and for not being in touch with the interests and needs of "real" women put feminism and feminists under reactionary political fire.[8]

Connell argues that the therapeutic model for masculinity inevitably provided grist for the antifeminist mill. Though initially meant to be in tandem with feminist discourses, the argument that gender relations are harmful to men was used to launch an oppositional position to feminism. Suddenly, the focus shifted to how men are harmed by gender relations. Beginning in the early 1980s, "men's rights" groups and promasculinity rhetoric began to emerge in the cultural mainstream in direct dialogue with feminism. The focus was on how men are as much or sometimes more harmed by gender relations than are women, and that the feminist movement exacted unjust damage to men and masculinity.[9] Other critics challenged feminist assertions that masculinity was problematic and celebrated the essentially masculine.[10] According to these proponents of men's rights and traditional masculinity, the problem of gender relations was not, as feminists had theorized, that women were harmed or socially, economically, and politically disadvantaged by the social privileges conferred to men as a group. Instead, the problem with gender relations was that men and women (though the emphasis was straightforwardly on men) suffered psychologically as a result of existing gender relations. With a complete disregard for social structure, these authors claimed that feminists were perpetrating a lie when they claimed that gender relations were beneficial to men and disadvantageous to women. Instead of transforming masculinity, or any part of the social structure for that matter, the most important gender issue was to alleviate the psychological damage resulting from gender relations by encouraging men to accept, nurture, and celebrate masculinity.

In the late 1980s and early 1990s, on the heels of this cultural celebration of the essentially masculine, a handful of women published scathing critiques of feminism and received huge amounts of media attention. These critics agreed with the men's rights proponents that men were getting a bum deal and added that women should stop playing "victim." For example, Katie Roiphe, in her book *The Morning After: Sex, Fear, and Feminism on Campus*, presents a critique of feminists for making women victims.[11] Her argument focuses on sexual assault and claims that women are in fear not because of men's sexual violence, but instead because feminists are perpetrating a lie that convinces women that sexual violence is something to be concerned about; women are victimized by feminism to the extent that feminism encourages women to believe that they are helpless victims. Throughout her argument, Roiphe completely glosses over structural power and privilege based on gender identity. Roiphe reduces power to *individual* power and either chooses to ignore or is not aware of structural power. Her argument suggests that it is dangerous to talk about men having more power because it makes women seem like weak individuals. Gender identity as a point of social stratification that benefits men as a group and is disadvantageous to women as a group is somehow not within Roiphe's conceptualization of gender relations. Thus, *power* means *strength*, and to say that men have more power than women is to say that men are stronger than women. Social group membership based on gender identity is erased from gender relations.

Naomi Wolf makes a similar argument in her book *Fire with Fire: The New Female Power and How It Will Change in the 21st Century*.[12] Taking a decidedly antifeminist turn compared to her book, *The Beauty Myth*,[13] Wolf argues that feminists are wrong to continue to emphasize how women are unequal and suffer from gender inequality. Feminism's continued emphasis on women's disadvantages is what Wolf calls "victim feminism," which she juxtaposes to "power feminism," an emphasis on women's strengths and social, political, and economic gains. Like Roiphe, she suggests that "victim feminism" is responsible for women feeling disempowered and dissatisfied with their lives. It makes women *feel* less powerful and therefore they *are* less powerful. "Power feminism" tells women that they are not disempowered, that they are equal to men, and that they can do anything they put their minds to. This is, according to Wolf, a more appealing feminism to young women because it makes them feel powerful rather than weak and oppressed.

Both Roiphe and Wolf criticize feminism not only for making women victims, but also for unfairly and viciously blaming men for women's victimization. Much like their men's rights predecessors, they claim that men suffer emotionally when confronted with the feminist claim that traditional forms of masculinity are problematic and harmful to women. Renée Denfeld, in her book *The New Victorians: A Young Woman's Challenge to the Old Feminist Order*,[14] makes the same argument as both Wolf and Roiphe. She, too, criticizes feminism for making women victims and for not recognizing the gains that women have made. The main thrust of her book is that feminists are out of touch with the desires, interests, and needs of young women. She claims that feminists' obsession with sexuality and "extremist" claims that sex is male dominant, that pornography is problematic, that women forming sexual and emotional bonds with other women undermines male dominance, are throwbacks to Victorian ideas about women's sexual vulnerability and chastity and men's sexual aggression and irresponsibility (hence the book's title). This has resulted in young women's rejection of the identity label *feminist* and inactivity in terms of feminist activism. Denfeld suggests that young women are concerned about reproductive rights, child care, wages, and health care costs and availability, not who they develop sexual relationships with and how. In other words, Denfeld sets up a straw man (or straw woman, in this case) by claiming that feminists are only concerned about sexuality, and then criticizes feminism and the women's movement for not adapting to the current interests of women. Of course, there are few others besides feminists who are forcing public debate on reproductive rights, women's wages, child care, and health care for women. Denfeld's critique, in line with men's rights activists and Roiphe, includes feministbashing for their "malebashing." One of the reasons young women do not identify as feminists, according to Denfeld, is because they are not interested in questioning their relationships with men, nor in seeing men as the enemy. Once again, it is sexist to claim that gender identity is important in gender relations of power. Throughout the book, Denfeld presents the testimony of women (presumably gathered through interview, though this is not clear) who are disenchanted with the women's movement and feminism. These testimonies repeat the same general theme that it is sexist to make any claims that divide women and men in terms of oppressed and oppressor. Men are not to blame, and it is unappealing to young women when feminists suggest they are. Denfeld concludes her first chapter, "The Antiphallic Campaign," with, "In discounting the role that men play in women's lives, the women's movement today has made a serious mistake. As long as feminism stands for male bashing, mandated lesbian sexuality, separatism, and repressive sexual mores, countless women will turn their faces away from a movement that stands for hostility and discrimination."[15] Not only is it unfair, but it is discriminatory for feminists to draw any political lines based on gender identity. Like Roiphe and Wolf, Denfeld conflates feminist claims that, structurally, men benefit from and women are disadvantaged by existing gender relations and that hegemonic masculinity and femininity reinforce interpersonal and institutionalized male dominance on the one hand, and women's and men's feelings on the other.

Finally, Camille Paglia joins in the antifeminist chorus criticizing feminists for being unfair to men and masculinity. In fact, her book *Sexual Personae: Art and Decadence From Nefertiti to Emily Dickinson*,[16] gives any men's-rights manifesto a run for its money in terms of celebrating masculinity. Specifically, she chastises feminists for trying to make men more androgynous by encouraging them to incorporate feminine characteristics into their gender identity. It is, according to Paglia, problematic to encourage androgyny in men because it unfairly and mistakenly blames men for gender inequality. Paglia suggests to feminists that they stop being "small-minded" and accept not only that masculinity and male dominance are grounded in biology and thus immutable, but that we all benefit greatly from men's actions.

The theme running through most antifeminist rhetoric is that feminists are extremists who are not in touch with women's real

needs and interests, that they cast women as "victims," and that
they pit women against men and blame men unfairly for existing
gender relations. According to these writers, to claim that hegemonic masculinity is problematic and/or to claim that men do in
fact take advantage of masculine privilege conferred through institutionalized arrangements is the same thing as saying that men are
bad and women are good. Social privilege is conflated with individual strength, so to claim that men as a group have more social,
economic, and political power than women as a group is the same
thing as saying individual men are more powerful and stronger than
individual women—that men are strong and women are weak. By
conflating individual-level and structural-power relations, these critics are able to claim that feminists, in short, are sexist because they
are antimale and because they reinforce the idea that women are
weak, helpless, passive victims.

All of these women, claiming to be feminists while bashing
feminists, were given a tremendous amount of mainstream media
coverage. Their message was broadcast widely and often. It was
within the context of this cultural backlash against feminism that
alternative hard rock emerged. The ways in which alternative hard
rockers talked about gender inequality and feminism were remarkably similar to the antifeminist rhetoric in the mainstream media
at the time: It is sexist to claim women are victims. Women are
strong, powerful, and capable of kicking ass. It is sexist to draw political alliances along the lines of gender. Men are not the enemy,
"assholes" are. Women and men are equally responsible for reproducing the gender order. Gender relations are about how individuals act and feel, not about the ways in which the social structure
confers economic, social, and political power along the lines of
group membership.

At the same time, however, alternative hard rockers took seriously feminist critiques of interpersonal gender relations, especially
sexual relations. They did not buy the mainstream rhetoric that gender inequality is no longer a problem, nor did they buy that celebrating masculinity is the way out. Their approach to feminism
simultaneously reflects both the backlash rhetoric and feminist
rhetoric. The result is a conscious, critical perspective on mainstream rock's sexism, and a strategy that focuses on the individual

actions of both women and men. Within this context then, it makes perfect sense that Courtney Love's performance, described at the beginning of this chapter, had a feminist political agenda and included a scathing critique of both women's and men's behavior. It also included an individual woman not being the victim by fighting back. The moral of the story perhaps goes something like this: Sexual assault is about gender and it is intolerable. We're all part of the problem as long as we continue to reproduce old patterns of behavior. What women and men need to do is stop behaving in old ways. First, change the way you, as an individual, perform, enact, do gender. Second, call out people who repeat the old, sexist patterns, and if possible force them to do otherwise. On an individual level, manipulate masculinities and femininities in order to undermine male dominant patterns of gender structuration. If you don't do these two things, you're part of the problem. If you do, you're part of the solution. In other words, gender maneuvering is the be all and end all when it comes to feminism in alternative hard rock. In this way, Courtney Love's performance was anything but an aberration or simply a reflection of some individual experience or emotional state. The content reflected not only the subcultural norms for alternative hard rock but also the conflicting messages about feminism proliferating the culture more widely.

Why did Courtney Love set up an elaborate performance rather than simply talk about sexual assault or write lyrics that straightforwardly condemn sexual violence? Is it possible that the content of the performance made sense sociologically but that the form itself was reducible to her own idiosyncracies or artistic preferences? As you might have guessed, the answer to this question is "no." The form also reflected a more general subcultural characteristic, and like the content, the sociocultural context in which alternative hard rock had emerged.

FEMINIST POLITICS IN ALTERNATIVE HARD ROCK

In alternative hard rock, feminist politics are about doing feminism through one's performance of gender, one's rock performance, and one's interactions with others. Just as Courtney Love performed re-

sistance to sexual assault, Eddie Vedder performed this kind of antirape politics when he said, "Don't party on anybody's pussy unless they want you to," and then sang Fugazi's song "Suggestion"
(as described in chapter 1). Vedder also emphasized pro-choice politics during Pearl Jam's performance on *Saturday Night Live*, taking
out a thick, black marker and writing PRO-CHOICE up the full length
of his arm. His body became the sign; he himself became the political message through performance. When women alternative hard
rockers write SLUT on their stomachs they too became the message. Feminist politics are not about writing politicized lyrics or explicitly speaking out about gender inequality; they are about how
one behaves in performance and in interactions with others.

In fact, despite consciously trying to not reproduce the sexism
of mainstream rock, most alternative hard rockers balk at any suggestion that they are feminist activists or that their music is political.

For example, I asked Lori Barbero of Babes in Toyland if the
band consciously puts feminism into their music. Flatly, and without skipping a beat, she responded, "No. Not at all. We've never
preplanned anything. What we do is sit there with our instruments,
play something, and write a song. It's not prefabricated. Maybe Kat
will say, 'I have this guitar thing from last night.' But we don't say,
'Okay, we want to sound like this or we have to make sure we write
a political, PC song.' I'm not PC. I think PC is so un-PC."

When I first approached the women from the band 7 Year Bitch
about doing an interview, I told them that I was researching feminism and rock music.

Guitarist Roisin Dunne responded, "To be perfectly honest, we
don't consider ourselves a feminist band. . . . I don't think we'd give
a very good interview."

Later, when the bass player and drummer agreed to talk with
me, I brought up the issue of feminism, asking, "What role has
feminism played in your becoming a musician and/or in your
music?"

The drummer, Valerie Agnew, responded, "Nothing we do is
preconceived. We never set out to be a feminist band or to do any
sort of messages. But I think that with what you do, you can set
an example."

Bass player Liz Davis took over: "I wouldn't even say our lyrics are feminist. Probably the most feminist song would be "Dead Men Don't Rape." But the lyrics for our songs are more vague than that. They're not about men or women, they're about relationships and other stuff. I think it's more what we do that is a political statement. . . . [Feminism] is important in all parts of my life, like what men I have sex with. We didn't start in a band because we were feminists, but feminism gave us the balls, so to speak, to do it. It gave us the confidence to go up there and do it. If we didn't have feminism, we probably wouldn't do it."

Agnew continued, "It's part of the larger picture in my life. It's part of the larger picture in society. Women write their own music and produce their own music. That didn't happen until recently. So to a certain extent women can do what they want. As far as the band goes, we don't call ourselves a feminist band. The band doesn't agree on feminism. We [Agnew and Davis] are the most feminist, but we don't use it as a vehicle for the band. It's not the point of the band. [Guitarist Dunne and vocalist Selene Vigil] have all the advantages of feminism but won't use the F-word to describe themselves."

When Agnew said, "We are the most feminist" in comparison to the other women in 7 Year Bitch, she demonstrated that she was conceptualizing *feminist* not as an identity but instead as practice. If an identity, one would either be a feminist or not. By saying "most," Agnew indicated degrees of being feminist, suggesting that it is not an either/or but instead a continuum that, based on her earlier statement, is constituted by what one does rather than who one is. *Feminist* for Agnew is an adjective that describes behavior and performance, not a person. As an entity, 7 Year Bitch is not a feminist band because they do not explicitly put out feminist messages in their music; that is, the band is not feminist because the music is not feminist.

While she recognized structural changes resulting from feminism such as women writing and producing their own music, describing herself and the band Agnew said, "Nothing we do is preconceived. We never set out to be a feminist band," setting a boundary between what she does in terms of using feminism within "the larger picture in her life" and conveying "any sort of messages." Through her practices, she can set an example and encourage women and men to act in ways that do not reproduce hegemonic gender relations. She does not consider herself an activist in the traditional meaning of the term, but she does have a desire to undermine sexism and male dominance through her actions. Feminist ideology plays a central role in her life, but at the same time she is not interested in being a "feminist band."

Davis agreed. They did not start the band because they were "feminists," but feminism gave them "the balls . . . to do it." Like Agnew, Davis made a distinction between their being a feminist band and utilizing feminism as an ideological framework for their practices. For Davis, it was "what we do" that is a political statement—for instance, having the confidence to be hard rock musicians or using feminism to inform decisions about who to choose for sexual partners. Although she did not explicitly state what exactly a "feminist band" would be, her statements immediately following presented a contrast that is suggestive of her meaning: "The most feminist song would be 'Dead Men Don't Rape,'" a song that explicitly names and blames men for sexual violence. However, most of their songs are "more vague" than that; "they're not about men or women, they're more about relationships or other stuff." A feminist band with feminist lyrics then, would be one that draws political lines based on gender identity and would explicitly politicize gender relations through its lyrics.

Similarly, when I asked Kat Bjelland if she considered Babes in Toyland to be sympathetic to feminism, she responded, "Maybe just in action, because it's all of us in the band and it's just by what we're doing. Just showing that women can do it by themselves. You know, we didn't have a manager when we signed with Warner Brothers. Lori did a lot of the business at first. . . . So I guess we do kind of represent feminist stuff, but we all have different politics, so as a whole, we're just showing that people should do what they want to do and have a good time and not let anything get in the way."

Bjelland's discussion of oppression is remarkably similar to that offered by the early 1990s antifeminist feminists. Rather than seeing oppression as a systematic disadvantage resulting from one's position within the social structure,[17] oppression is a feeling that one chooses to experience or not. In addition, she is adamant about the music not being politicized. The only way in which Babes in Toyland can be construed as a feminist band is the extent to which they demonstrate to young women that they can do what they want if they try hard enough.

This emphasis on being a positive role model and example is the most common way in which alternative hard rockers talk about the relationship between their music and feminism. In our interview, Eddie Vedder said, "I don't consciously put feminist politics in the lyrics or the music. There aren't any explicit political messages in my songs. But when I think about specific songs, there are definitely strong women. You know, like 'Why Go Home?'—that's about a really strong young woman I know who was institutionalized because she didn't fit her parents' idea of what a good girl should be. She resisted and actually became stronger for it. When we did Rock for Choice, the song 'Once' took on a new meaning. You know, 'once . . . upon a time . . . I could control myself. . . . ' So, you know, they're not feminist songs per se, but when kids listen to them, maybe they'll get some ideas for themselves. You know, if they see examples of people resisting, maybe they'll resist themselves."

At the end of the interview, as I did with all of the musicians I interviewed, I asked Vedder if there was anything we hadn't covered that he'd like to talk about. He thought for a moment and then said, "It's all about the music. My art is the most important thing to me. I don't want to get bogged down in politics. I don't want people to focus on politics and forget about the music. I want to be known and respected for the music, not the politics. If some kid decides to act like a decent human being because he respects what I do, great. But in the end, it's about the music. That's it."

I asked Kim Thayil whether or not he would characterize Soundgarden as a feminist band. "I think that's something that wouldn't be represented by the band as a group, but maybe as individual members to different degrees," he said. "I would say Soundgarden is a feminist band, but the only way I can characterize us as feminist is by default, by not presenting or supporting a sexist paradigm. That's as close as we get to being feminist as a rock band. We don't advocate any feminist platforms or ideas, but at the same time we're trying not to be sexist. So it's kind of a neutral thing. Just do something entirely different. [Our music is] void of sexual content in regard to social and political issues generally."

Donita Sparks of L7 expressed a similar approach to feminism in the excerpt discussed earlier. In response to my question about whether or not she consciously put feminism into her music she said, "[Feminism] is part of me and the songs come out of my experience . . . [however] if you listen to our songs they're universal. Men and women can relate to them . . . I'm not writing as a woman, I'm writing as a human being." As it is for the women in 7 Year Bitch, feminism is part of Sparks's life and informs her experiences, but rather than making her lyrics explicitly political, her songs can appeal to both women and men, and are about "cool people against assholes," not "girls against boys."

At one point, I asked Sparks outright if she considered herself a feminist. She immediately responded, "Oh, I'm a feminist. I'm a member of NOW and I get my *Ms.* every month. . . . We started Rockers for Choice."[18]

Although she is more willing than others to adopt the identity label *feminist* for herself, it means getting a feminist magazine that focuses on social, economic, and political gender inequities and a straightforwardly activist effort to generate funds for prochoice organizations. In contrast, her participation in alternative hard rock means gender maneuvering to undermine male dominance and is about "cool people" versus "assholes." Cultural and interactive gender maneuvering is something different from being a feminist. Sparks draws a distinction between doing nonsexist rock and doing alternative gender on the one hand, and being a feminist on the other. For Sparks, they are quite compatible, but not the same thing.

For the Gen-Xers of alternative hard rock, it is important to not put explicitly political messages about gender in their lyrics or their performances. At the same time, all that I interviewed said that they were very much committed to doing rock music in a way that sets an example of how to incorporate feminism into everyday life. Talking with Jennifer Finch of L7 about the incorporation of feminism into rock culture, I asked her, "What do you think has led up to this movement?" Very quickly she snapped back, "This

is not a movement. It's a bunch of kids rocking. Individuals changing their behavior is not a movement."

She was absolutely right, but what is interesting was her immediate move to separate "kids rocking" from a movement. This
strikes a stark contrast with the ways in which people talked about
rock 'n' roll in the late 1960s and early 1970s. Rock culture was
then an inextricable part of the antiwar movement. Rock musicians
were vociferous in their opposition to the Vietnam War in their
stage performances and in their lyrics. In other words, rock music
was a voice for a political movement. Further, the cultural story
told largely by baby boomers is that it was done *well*—so well, in
fact, that as a political voice it will likely never again be matched.
The Vietnam War era was not only a chapter in rock history, but
in many ways the *defining* chapter in rock history. To try and repeat it would be trite, clichéd, inadequate, and—most importantly—
inauthentic.

Alternative hard rockers' form of gender politics is about rock
authenticity. To simply reproduce what has already been done, and
especially what has since been marketed to the masses, is to sell
out. In order to be authentic, rockers must do things differently
from whatever has been or currently is being served up by the mainstream media. Political activism through rock music had been done,
and had subsequently been co-opted by the mainstream media and
served up as product; alternative hard rockers thus had to do it differently in order to be authentic. Their point of departure from what
had been done included rejecting sexism and rejecting political activism. Rather than doing sexism or political activism, doing the
embodied feminist performance became a quite effective form of
rock authenticity. It had not been done before—not in this way,
as a genre-defining set of styles, practices, and performances. While
there are likely countless intervening factors that led to the forms
of politics alternative hard rockers adopted, within the broader cultural context of a consumer culture that constructs the body as the
site of political activism and within a political media culture that
consistently delegitimates any claims of structural inequality,[19]
it makes sense that the answer was to embody feminist ideals
and antiheterosexist politics by performing alternative genders and
sexualities.

Though this is, at least partially, about rock authenticity, alternative hard rockers also have a political motivation for not making their music about politics. Lori Barbero captured this when talking about how the whole riot grrrl phenomenon had become simply a trend. When I asked her what was wrong with trends she responded, "They go away. If it's a trend, it will go away. If it's an establishment, then it would be a different story. An establishment kind of stays or is remembered. But trends . . . people laugh at trends. You look back and trends come and go."

If their desire to eliminate the sexism in rock was explicitly attached to the music, once the music lost favor in the mainstream, so would the politics. Rather than making the music a message that would eventually be lost in the heap of past trends, alternative hard rockers have tried to change the rules of the game. And so, alternative hard rockers rarely speak or sing of their feminist politics. They perform and embody them, just as Courtney Love had the night I watched her politicize sexual assault. Far from being a manifestation of her own personal "issues," as the media suggested, it was alternative hard rock culture, and it was, like all subcultures, embedded within and in dialogue with, the much broader dominant culture of the time.

One interpretation of this might be that this represents a retreat of feminism into relatively insignificant cultural spaces, and/or feminism being reduced to a politics of performance. Another interpretation, however, is that this is a sparkling example of how feminism has filtered into all areas of social life—even the stubborn old boys club of rock 'n' roll. I believe it is a little of both.

On the one hand, if we think of gender structuration as a contextualized effort to transform the gender order in localized settings, then perhaps the work of alternative hard rockers *is* feminist politics, and perhaps one example of what might have been and continues to take place all over. Feminist politics are about developing specific strategies for transforming the gender order in very specified context—at particular jobs, within families, or in rock music—in addition to engaging in mass, collective strategies for broader structural change. In other words, feminist politics are not only about collective political action to change legislation, reduce the male-female wage gap, or grant subordinate groups equal footing in the opportunity structure. Perhaps we might start thinking about feminist politics as multiple and contextual (through cultural and interactive gender maneuvering) as well as collective and sweeping (through the more traditional forms of activism).

Alternative hard rock shows us that, with an eye to the social structure of specific cultural and institutional settings, it is possible to forge a feminist politics that is decidedly local and grounded in individual action. On the other hand, alternative hard rock also demonstrates how this can only work if the individual or group action is understood as not simply about the localized setting, but also as one part of gender structuration within the larger gender order of male dominance. The most disturbing and illustrative example of this is alternative hard rockers' ability to transform the meaning and uses of violence at a rock show while not connecting the violence of individual men to gender relations outside of the rock club.

I would like to see more research on gender maneuvering in different sorts of settings such as schools, the workplace, and the home, and research on how gender maneuvering impacts the lives of people outside the particular settings in which they're maneuvering. Most importantly, future research should focus on how microprocesses of gender maneuvering might be connected to or implicated in more traditional forms of activism.

In the end, neither gender maneuvering nor collective political action alone will dismantle male dominance. However, simultaneously working to transform macro institutional structures and the localized structure of specific settings and face-to-face interaction—and, importantly, identifying the connections between the two—just might in the long run do the trick. A resurgence in collective political movement, along with this kind of micromaneuvering, might mark the next wave of feminism.

So what can you, as an individual, do?

The first thing is to take a long, hard look at one or more of your daily or weekly activities. What do you do for fun? Where do you work? What organizations do you belong to? Identify how the heterosexual matrix takes shape: How are masculinity and femininity situated in relation to each other in a way that reproduces male dominance and/or heterosexism? What are the expectations and requirements for masculinity? What are they for femininity? How do those expectations get produced and sustained? And most importantly, how can you fuck with them? What can you do with your body, your words, your interactions with others, your participation in activities that might throw a small or big wrench in the usually smooth seamlessness of the gender order? In every situation, there are ways to maneuver. All you have to do is look around, figure out the localized, specific gender order, and refuse, on some level, to go along.

If you can get others to follow along with you, as many alternative hard rockers have, all the better. The goal is not to simply cause trouble; ultimately, it is to transform the gender organization of our daily lives and of the social structure more generally. This means also looking at the broader picture as well. Political representation, wage gaps, access to health care, the global labor market, poverty—these forms of inequality will not change through gender maneuvering. Changing these structures requires massive, collective activism. Ideally, feminist politics will come to mean and be embraced as both gender maneuvering and collective activism. They require shaking things up at all of these levels of social life— with our bodies, our activities, our interactions, and in the broader distribution of resources and power. Whatever the form, change will require action. So get to work; there is still much to be done.

NOTES

1. GENDER AND ROCK MUSIC: SO WHAT'S NEW?

1. See David Handelman, "Money for Nothing and the Chicks for Free," *Rolling Stone*, August 13, 1987, 34–36+.
2. See Gina Arnold, *Rolling Stone*, February 20, 1992, 19.
3. See Susan McClary, *Feminine Endings: Music, Gender, and Sexuality* (Minneapolis: University of Minnesota Press, 1991).
4. See James Scott, *Weapons of the Weak: Everyday Forms of Peasant Resistance* (New Haven: Yale University Press, 1985); James Scott, *Domination and the Arts of Resistance* (New Haven: Yale University Press, 1990).
5. In her piece "Not Just Weapons of the Weak," Laura Miller suggests that men sometimes adopt strategies to usurp women's authority. While she focuses on men's everyday resistance to women's authority and to challenges to male privilege, I will be focusing on men's everyday resistance to male privilege. See Laura Miller, "Not Just Weapons of the Weak: Gender Harassment As a Form of Protest for Army Men," in *Gender through the Prism of Difference*, 2d ed., ed. Maxine Baca Zinn, Pierrette Hondagneu-Sotelo, and Michael A. Messner (Boston: Allyn and Bacon, 2000).
6. I used the method developed by Paul Lichterman, which combines the grounded theory method and the extended case method. See Paul Lichterman, *The Search for Political Community: American Activists Reinventing Commitment* (Cambridge: Cambridge University Press, 1996).
7. For a very interesting documentary video treatment of the business of rock music in Chicago at the time, see *Out of the Loop*, prod. and dir. Scott Peterson, 86 min., Headache Productions, 1997, videocassette.
8. While I will be focusing on alternative hard rock, my conceptualization of "alternative" is not limited to hard rock. There are many bands and musicians, such as REM, Ani DiFranco, or Melissa Etheridge, who do sexuality and gender differently than the mainstream does in rock music.
9. It is interesting to me—and, I think, telling of the mainstream media, that riot grrrls received a tremendous amount of press that identified their feminist ideological underpinnings while all-male bands would talk about feminism and gender inequality but be ignored by the press. There is a tremendous fascination with riot grrrls' "separatist"

strategies. Although it is only occasionally that a group of women might set up an "all-grrrl" show and only allow women entrance, the mainstream media paints quite a negative picture of riot grrrls as angry, man-hating, out-of-touch young women. Meanwhile, compared to the coverage of feminism in riot grrrl circles, the mainstream media virtually ignored the feminist leanings of Pearl Jam and Soundgarden; feminism in rock remains marginalized by associating it with "angry young women" and ignoring angry young men.

10. See for instance, Chelsea Star, *BECAUSE: Riot Grrrl, Art Worlds, Social Movements, and Style* (UMI Archives, University of California-Irvine, 1999); Mavis Bayton, *Frock Rock: Women Performing Popular Music* (Oxford: Oxford University Press, 1998); Mary Celeste Kearney, "The Missing Links: Riot Grrrl—Feminism—Lesbian Culture," in *Sexing the Groove: Popular Music and Gender*, ed. Sheila Whiteley (London: Routledge, 1997).

11. I am thinking about gender maneuvering as a form of interaction as theorized by Georg Simmel. According to Simmel, sociology is the study of the forms of interaction that occur across contexts and are the building blocks of society. I view gender maneuvering, or maneuvering more generally, as a form of social interaction in which individuals actively use identity performance and construction to situate themselves and others in relations of power that either maintain the existing power structure or challenge it. The content of maneuvering (motives, actual practices, etc.) will vary by context, but the form can be identified *across* context. While my empirical focus is on gender maneuvering, I want to suggest that ethnic, racial, sexual, class, and perhaps age maneuvering are also variations on this form and might be empirically investigated as such. See Georg Simmel, *On Individuality and Social Forms*, ed. Donald N. Levine (Chicago: University of Chicago Press, 1971).

12. For a detailed social history of rock music, see David P. Szatmary, *Rockin' in Time: A Social History of Rock-and-Roll*, 3d ed. (Upper Saddle River, N.J.: Prentice Hall, 1996).

2.   THE GENDER ORDER OF MAINSTREAM ROCK CULTURE

1. See for instance, Simon Frith, *The Sociology of Rock* (London: Constable, 1978); Simon Frith, *Sound Effects: Youth, Leisure, and the Politics of Rock* (London: Constable, 1983); Simon Frith, *Music for Pleasure: Essays on the Sociology of Pop* (New York: Routledge, 1988); Will Straw, "Characterizing Rock Music Cultures: The Case of Heavy Metal," *Canadian University Music Review* 5 (1984): 104–22; Robert Walser, *Running with the Devil: Power, Gender, and Madness in Heavy Metal Music* (Hanover, N.H.: Wesleyan University Press, 1993); and Deena Weinstein, *Heavy Metal: A Cultural Sociology* (New York: Lexington Books, 1991).

2. Frith, *The Sociology of Rock, Sound Effects*, and *Music for Pleasure*.

3. See Michel Foucault, *The History of Sexuality: An Introduction, Volume 1*, trans. Robert Hurley (New York: Vintage, 1978).

4. As Gayle Rubin suggests, Foucault does not argue that there was no repression of certain forms of erotic desire, but that the ways in which normative sexuality was established was through the proliferation of discourse, not a clamping down on it. See Gayle Rubin, "Thinking Sex: Notes for a Radical Theory of Sexuality," in *Pleasure and Danger: Exploring Female Sexuality*, ed. Carol S. Vance (London: Pandora, 1984).

5. See George Chauncey Jr., "Christian Brotherhood or Sexual Perversion? Homosexual Identities and the Construction of Sexual Boundaries in the World War I Era," in *Hidden from History: Reclaiming the Gay and Lesbian Past*, ed. Martin Duberman, Martha Vicinus, and George Chauncey Jr. (New York: Penguin, 1989); John D'Emilio, *Sexual Politics, Sexual Communities: The Making of a Homosexual Minority in the United States, 1940–1970* (Chicago: University of Chicago Press, 1983); John Gagnon and William Simon, *Sexual Conduct: The Social Origins of Human Sexuality* (Chicago: Aldine, 1973); David Greenberg, *The Construction of Homosexuality* (Chicago: University of Chicago Press, 1988); Jonathan Katz, *Gay American History* (New York: Routledge, 1976); and Rubin, "Thinking Sex."

6. For a good discussion of sexual stratification, see Rubin, "Thinking Sex."

7. See Emile Durkheim, *The Rules of the Sociological Method* (1895), ed. Steven Lukes, trans. W. D. Hall (New York: Free Press, 1964); and Howard Becker, *Outsiders: Studies in the Sociology of Deviance* (New York: Free Press, 1963).

8. See Simon Reynolds, *The Sex Revolts: Gender, Rebellion, and Rock 'n' Roll* (Cambridge, Mass.: Harvard University Press, 1995).

9. Chrys Ingraham uses the term *heterogenders* to refer to "the asymmetrical stratification of the sexes in relation to the historically varying institutions of patriarchal heterosexuality." She uses this term to convey the importance of conceptualizing both gender and heterosexuality as simultaneously socially constructed within and through institutional arrangements. See Chrys Ingraham, "The Heterosexual Imaginary: Sociology and Theories of Gender," in *Queer Theory/Sociology*, ed. Steven Seidman (Cambridge, Mass.: Blackwell 1996), 169.

10. See Judith Butler, *Gender Trouble: Feminism and the Subversion of Identity* (New York: Routledge, 1990).

11. It is interesting that country music, hip-hop, and rap are not feminized, but are raced and classed. Though it is not the focus of this project, it would be interesting and useful to theorize the ways in which race, class, and gender are operating in and organizing the constructions of country (white, rural, and working-class), hip-hop and rap (black, urban, and working-class), rock (white, working-class, and masculine), and pop (feminine) and how this organization as a whole reflects and maintains race, class, and gender hierarchies.

12. See for instance, Frith, *The Sociology of Rock, Sound Effects*, and *Music for Pleasure*; Straw, "Characterizing Rock Music Cultures"; Walser, *Running with the Devil*; and Weinstein, *Heavy Metal*.

13. See Walser, *Running with the Devil*.

14. See Stuart Hall and Tony Jefferson, eds., *Resistance through Rituals: Youth Subcultures in Post-War Britain* (London: Hutchinson, 1976); and Stuart Hall, "Encoding/Decoding," in *Culture, Media, Language*, ed. Stuart Hall (London: Hutchinson, 1980).

15. This is not to say that rock is not also raced and classed. For a discussion of the symbolic construction of rock as raced, see Walser, *Running with the Devil*, and as classed see Frith, *The Sociology of Rock* and *Sound Effects*.

16. I will hereafter frequently italicize the words *musician, groupie, teenybopper*, and *real fan* to signify an identity label or social position rather than a specific person.

17. Carl Couch emphasizes the relational aspect of social identities. Not only do identities define an individual's position, but they also define others' relationships to that person. Over time, as people continue to act out particular identities, enduring relationships between people are established and sustained. See Carl Couch, *Social Processes and Relationships* (Dix Hills, N.Y.: General Hall, 1989).

18. I'm thinking especially of the crew having sex with the groupie as "payment" for getting her backstage.

19. See Peter Lyman, "The Fraternal Bond As a Joking Relationship: A Case Study of the Role of Sexist Jokes in Male Group Bonding," in *Changing Men*, ed. Michael Kimmel (Newbury Park, Calif.: Sage, 1987).

20. See for instance, Frith, *The Sociology of Rock, Sound Effects*, and *Music for Pleasure*; Straw, "Characterizing Rock Music Cultures"; Walser, *Running with the Devil*; and Weinstein, *Heavy Metal*.

21. See R. W. Connell, *Masculinities* (Berkeley and Los Angeles: University of California Press, 1995).

22. See Tricia Rose, "'Fear of a Black Planet': Rap Music and Black Cultural Politics in the 1990's," *Negro Education* 60 (1991): 276–90.

23. It is not clear what the relationship between real fans and groupies is, but I would argue that in the realm of ideology, the groupie is defined as inferior. It is entirely possible, however, that the dominant hierarchy works to the advantage of the groupie in face-to-face interaction. Ultimately, this is an interesting empirical question. Further research might focus on whether or not rock ideology defines groupies as of a higher status than real fans and, as a separate question, how the hierarchy manifests itself in interactions between real fans and known groupies.

24. The label *invert* for homosexuals signifies the belief that sexuality, gender identity, and genital structure should match up, and when they do not the natural order is inverted. Some researchers even went so far as to search for masculinized genital structure in lesbians. See Jennifer Terry, "Anxious Slippages between 'Us' and 'Them': A Brief History of

the Search for Homosexual Bodies," in *Deviant Bodies*, ed. Jennifer Terry and Jacqueline Urla (Bloomington: Indiana University Press, 1995), 129–69.

25. For discussions of how gender order and sexuality are connected, see Charlotte Bunch, "Lesbians in Revolt," in *Feminist Frameworks*, ed. Alison M. Jaggar and Paula Rothenberg Struhl (New York: McGraw-Hill, 1978); Suzanne Pharr, *Homophobia, a Weapon of Sexism* (Inverness, Calif.: Chardon Press, 1988); and Adrienne Rich, "Compulsory Heterosexuality and Lesbian Existence," *Signs* 5 (1980): 631–60.

26. For more complete discussions of this sexual hierarchy see Seidman, ed., *Queer Theory/ Sociology*; and Michael Warner, ed., *Fear of a Queer Planet* (Minneapolis: University of Minnesota Press, 1993).

27. See Cheryl Cline, "Essays from *Bitch: The Women's Rock News Letter with Bite*," in *The Adoring Audience*, ed. Lisa A. Lewis (London: Routledge, 1993).

28. Gender as a social system organizes the material relations in rock culture. Not only is male dominance reproduced in the meanings attributed to rock and the positions within rock, but it is also reproduced in the concrete workings of producing and performing rock music. There has been a long history of a gendered division of labor in rock music, with men holding most positions, including most positions of power. The vast majority of musicians, producers, owners, managers, disc jockeys, programmers, journalists, and fans have been men. As in most male-dominated occupations and social contexts this has changed somewhat over the decades, but progress has been slow. It has and continues to be difficult for women to gain positions of power or to reap the economic benefits that men already have. Given the gendered division of labor, control over the rules and content of production and performance has been in the hands of men, thus making the power structure of rock gendered and male dominant. See Mavis Bayton, *Frock Rock: Women Performing Popular Music* (Oxford: Oxford University Press, 1998); Lucy O'Brien, *She Bop: The Definitive History of Women in Rock, Pop and Soul* (New York: Penguin, 1995).

29. Butler's focus is on the symbolic construction of the heterosexual matrix, and the vast majority of scholarship using Butler's framework has focused on the production of this relationship through discourse, much like I have done with rock music ideology, as discussed above. However, as a sociologist, I find Butler's framework particularly useful for analyzing the relationships among established social positions, the expectations for how people occupy social positions, and the concrete workings of those positions in the practice of social life.

30. See Sara Cohen, "Men Making a Scene: Rock Music and the Production of Gender," in *Sexing the Groove: Popular Music and Gender*, ed. Sheila Whiteley (London: Routledge, 1997).

31. For a discussion and description of occupational gender segregation and stratification see Barbara Reskin and Irene Padavic, *Women and Men at Work* (Thousand Oaks, Calif.: Pine Forge, 1994).

32. See Robin Leidner, "Serving Hamburgers and Selling Insurance: Gender, Work, and Identity in Interactive Service Jobs," *Gender and Society* 5 (1991): 154–77.

33. Barrie Thorne presents compelling evidence that the salience of gender difference and the relative importance of doing gender vary by context. I am not contradicting her assertion. While I would agree that the salience of gender difference varies, there are few, if any, contexts in which gender is absent. See Barrie Thorne, *Gender Play: Girls and Boys in School* (New Brunswick, N.J.: Rutgers University Press, 1997).

34. For a good discussion of gender as something we *do* in addition to what we *are*, see Candace West and Don Zimmerman, "Doing Gender," *Gender and Society* 1 (1987): 125–51.

35. While Anthony Giddens includes *resources and rules* in his definition of social structure, I am adopting William Sewell's definition of social structure as *rules only*. See William H. Sewell Jr., "A Theory of Structure: Duality, Agency, and Transformation," *American Journal of Sociology* 98 (1992): 1–29.

36. According to Sheldon Stryker, people have many different identities that make up the self. Depending on context, one identity will become more salient or central to one's sense of self than will other identities. He calls this an *identity salience hierarchy*. See Sheldon Stryker, *Social Interactionism: A Social Structural Approach* (San Francisco: Benjamin/ Cummings, 1979).

3. THIS IS ALTERNATIVE HARD ROCK: ROCK CULTURE AS GENDER MANEUVERING

1. Stuart Hall, ed., *Culture, Media, Language: Working Papers in Cultural Studies 1972–79* (London: Hutchinson, 1980) and Stuart Hall, ed., *Representation: Cultural Representations and Signifying Practices* (London: Sage, 1997).

2. At the time of my research, there were still only two area codes in the Chicago area. All of the suburbs had the area code 708, while the area code within the city limits was 312.

3. Lauraine Leblanc, *Pretty in Punk: Girls' Gender Resistance in a Boys' Subculture* (New Brunswick, N.J.: Rutgers University Press, 1999); and Greil Marcus, *Lipstick Traces: A Secret History of the Twentieth Century* (Cambridge, Mass.: Harvard University Press, 1989).

4. Although sociologists of rock have done well to document this ideological dichotomy between fans of the music and fans of the musicians, they have at the same time reproduced it in their theoretical and empirical analyses. Simon Frith first identified this dichotomy between real fans and teenybopper or groupie fans as one component of rock ideology. However, Frith buys into the ideology when he simplifies female participation in rock and pop music as teenybopper culture. Teenybopper culture is defined by Frith as the bedroom culture in which adolescent girls listen to their favorite records alone or with one or two other young girls. Their favorite records are chosen by how the musicians look and act and the extent to which the lyrics set up an opportunity for young girls to develop imagined romantic relationships with the artists. Boys, in contrast, participate in rock more publicly and find interest in the skill of musicians and the sound of the music. According to Frith's analysis, then, not only is the gender split between real fans and teenybopper or groupie fans ideological, but it generally holds true in women's and men's actual participation in rock culture.

   With few exceptions, the sociological literature on rock audiences has followed Frith's lead, and has continued to reproduce this dichotomy. The most telling reproduction is the omission of any analysis of female participation in the vast majority of studies that analyze rock audiences; see, for example, Dick Hebdige, *Subculture: The Meaning of Style* (New York: Methuen, 1979); Will Straw, "Characterizing Rock Music Cultures: The Case of Heavy Metal," *Canadian University Music Review* 5 (1984): 104–22; and Deena Weinstein, *Heavy Metal: A Cultural Sociology* (New York: Lexington Books, 1991). By focusing on rock audiences and excluding women from their analyses, these studies infer implicitly that women fall out of the realm of real rock fans.

   Other studies that do include women and provide some discussion of their experiences often recapitulate the notion of women as primarily interested in the boys in the bands. For example, Robert Walser includes an analysis of female fandom of heavy metal music, but ends up reproducing the dichotomy when he speculates, with no empirical evidence, that women's interest in heavy metal was initially an outcome of the sexual attractiveness of Jon Bon Jovi and his fusion of metal music and the romantic sentiments of pop; see Robert Walser, *Running with the Devil: Power, Gender, and Madness in Heavy Metal Music* (Hanover, N.H.: Wesleyan University Press, 1993).

   This assumed model of female fandom leads sociologists to conclude that women's involvement in rock culture, particularly as audiences, is capitulation in their own gender subordination. For example, Simon Frith ties women's participation to domesticity; see Simon Frith, *Music for Pleasure: Essays on the Sociology of Pop* (New York: Routledge, 1988). Because it is embedded within hegemonic gender discourses, teenybopper culture enculturates women into romanticism, passivity, and domesticity, which ultimately prepares them for gender subordination in traditional marriage. Others who analyze the content of rock lyrics and videos (see, for example, Jane Delano Brown and Kenneth C. Campbell, "Race and Gender in Music Videos: The Same Beat but a Different Drummer," *Journal of Communication* 36 [1986]: 94–106; Kathleen Endres, "Sex Role Standards in Popular Music," *Journal of Popular Culture* 18 [1984]: 9–18; Colleen Hyden and N. Jane McCandless, "Men and Women as Portrayed in the Lyrics of Contemporary Music," *Popular Music and Society* 7 [1983]: 32–36) and women's involvement as musicians (see, for example, Stephen B. Groce and Margaret Cooper, "Just Me and the Boys? Women in Local-Level Rock and Roll," *Gender and Society* 4 [1990]: 220–29; Mary Ann Clawson, "When Women Play the Bass: Instrument Specialization and Gender Interpretation in Alternative Rock Music," *Gender and Society* 13 [1999]: 193–210) arrive at similar conclusions.

To argue the point about capitulation through participation, some feminist critics have shifted the focus from content and how others view young female fans of rock to the female fans themselves and suggest that what might appear to be capitulation from an outsider's perspective serves quite resistive functions for young women (see, for example, Barbara Ehrenreich, Elizabeth Hess, and Gloria Jacobs, "Beatlemania: Girls Just Want to Have Fun," in *The Adoring Audience*, ed. Lisa A. Lewis [London: Routledge, 1993]; Sheryl Garratt, "Teenage Dreams," in *On Record: Rock, Pop, and the Written Word*, ed. Simon Frith and Andrew Goodwin [New York: Pantheon, 1990]). The resistive function of young women's participation in rock and pop lies in the meanings the music and the musicians hold for the young women.

Although these scholars have reframed teenybopper and groupie culture in terms of resistance rather than acquiescence to gender subordination, the gendered dichotomy between male and female audience practices and interests remains unchallenged. Young women still approach the music differently than young men, and they emphasize the attractiveness and sex appeal of musicians, although the meanings of these attractions can be resistive.

The dominant gender discourses of female inferiority and female sexual objectification circulating in the mainstream culture undergirds groupie culture, whether deployed within mainstream rock culture or theorized by sociologists.

5. In mainstream rock, there is a normative set of practices and beliefs that set the performing musician apart from the fans and audience. See, for instance, Simon Frith, *The Sociology of Rock* (London: Constable, 1978); Simon Frith, *Sound Effects: Youth, Leisure, and the Politics of Rock* (London: Constable, 1983); and Frith, *Music For Pleasure*. See also Straw, "Characterizing Rock Music Cultures"; Walser, *Running with the Devil*; and Weinstein, *Heavy Metal*.

4.   GENDER MANEUVERING IN FACE-TO-FACE INTERACTION

1. This concept was first developed by W. I. Thomas and further developed by Erving Goffman. See Erving Goffman, *The Presentation of Self in Everyday Life* (New York: Doubleday, 1959).
2. See Erving Goffman, *Frame Analysis: An Essay on the Organization of Experience* (New York: Harper Colophon, 1974).
3. See Jessie Bernard, *Women, Wives, Mothers: Values and Options* (Chicago: Aldine, 1975); and Scott Coltraine, "Household Labor and the Routine Production of Gender," *Social Problems* 36 (1989).
4. Candace West and Don Zimmerman, "Doing Gender," *Gender and Society* 1 (1987): 125–51. This is not a point of departure from Giddens's work. In fact, Giddens's concept *structuration* was developed in order to bridge structural sociology with interactionist sociology.
5. Barrie Thorne, *Gender Play: Girls and Boys in School* (New Brunswick, N.J.: Rutgers University Press, 1997).
6. This might have gotten rid of the men, but I would argue that the men would have had an immediate response to put Maddie and the other women back into a subordinate feminine position. As I will discuss in more detail in chapter 7, in the early 1990s we were in the midst of a cultural backlash against feminism. The mainstream media, with much help from young women calling themselves feminists while bashing feminism, were painting a pretty nasty picture of feminists as "politically correct," repressed, prudish, "feminazis." To say "You sexist asshole" is feminist-speak, and in the cultural climate of the time, there were too many possible returns supplied by antifeminist rhetoric. The men could easily volley back this rhetoric in order to put Maddie back in her place. Maddie and the other women in this subculture are well aware of the criticisms of feminism and the currency antifeminist jargon carried. Committed to undermining male dominance, and living in a world hostile to feminist rhetoric, they rely on strategies other than explicitly naming sexism. Thus, given the cultural climate, Maddie and the other women chose a fourth option—to gender maneuver.
7. For a discussion of masculinities performed by women, see Judith Halberstam, *Female Masculinity* (Durham, N.C.: Duke University Press, 1998).

8. Goffman, *Interaction Ritual*.
9. Michel Foucault, *The History of Sexuality: An Introduction, Volume 1*, trans. Robert Hurley (New York: Vintage, 1978).
10. This is a slight shift in how Max Weber conceptualizes power relations between social positions. According to Weber, power is conferred on the basis of structural position and social status. While this is a relational conceptualization of power, there is still the sense that one person has power over another person. The high-status person has power while the low-status person does not. Foucault, building on this Weberian model for power, suggests that power is created and manipulated between positions. Both individuals are active participants in the power dynamic. See Max Weber, *Economy and Society*, ed. Guenther Roth and Claus Wittich (Berkeley and Los Angeles: University of California Press, 1978).
11. There is much research on the ways in which socially subordinate groups and individuals use individual and collective action to resist domination; see for instance, James Scott, *Weapons of the Weak: Everyday Forms of Peasant Resistance* (New Haven: Yale University Press, 1985). To build on this literature, I am suggesting that power relations can be *negotiated* through the ongoing process of face-to-face interaction. Structural domination can be subverted by subordinates taking over the position, sabotaging an individual's ability to perform in a superordinate position, redefining the meaning of the position itself, redefining the meaning of the relationship between superordinate and subordinate positions, or laying meaning on an individual's performance that undermines her legitimacy. As the research on resistance has demonstrated, all of these challenges to power relations can be done covertly or overtly by individuals or groups. I am viewing resistance as an interactive process rather than a set of acts, and focusing on the play of volley and response. This is a microprocess of resistance whereby individuals attempt to shift power relations by overtly or covertly redefining the meaning of the masculine and feminine positions, challenging another's legitimacy and competence in a masculinity or femininity, and redefining the meaning of the relationship between masculinity and femininity through face-to-face interaction.
12. In this instance, the particular form of the hegemonic structuration and the maneuvering were specific to the rock music setting and *when* this interaction took place. If we were at school or at work or in some other setting, the "alone" question probably wouldn't arise. Even if it did, however, it would probably take on a completely different meaning because the activities by which people produce gender would be different.
13. In his own empirical work, R. W. Connell concludes that resistive masculinity is restricted to a shift in how individual men understand and define their masculine identity and that it does not translate into practice. He found that when men talk about resisting sexism, they often talk about their own personality or identity characteristics, and they do not talk about a transformation of institutional arrangements by doing masculinity differently. I would argue that Connell's conclusions might be a result of relying on interview data rather than observational data. Given my findings, it is entirely possible that an antisexist perspective might translate into alternative practices even if the men themselves do not focus on this when they talk about being antisexist.
14. As suggested by feminist theories of the intersection of gender with race, ethnicity, class, sexual orientation, and so on, there are multiple femininities as well as multiple masculinities. In a previous work, Connell outlines *complacent femininity* or *emphasized femininity* as the hegemonic counterparts to masculinity; see R. W. Connell, *Gender and Power* (Stanford, Calif.: Stanford University Press, 1987). He defines complacent femininity as the practices that are defined as feminine and maintain male dominant power relations. Unlike his work on masculinities, however, Connell's conceptualization of femininity does not include multiple configurations. Because his theoretical project was to focus on the social organization of masculinity, it is perhaps unfair to criticize Connell for his oversimplified conceptualization of femininity. At the same time, this oversimplification becomes problematic when one tries to apply the theory to empirical research. It flattens hierarchical relations among femininities. It also provides no analysis of how marginalized, complicit, or subordinate masculinities relate to or match up with various femininities. Because Connell only focuses on the relationship between masculinities, we're left wondering how multiple femininities organize social relations and, importantly, how

marginalized, subordinate, or complicit masculinities are situated in relation to various femininities making an analysis of power relations difficult. For instance, it is difficult to distinguish the practices of marginalized class, race, or ethnic groups that reproduce male dominance and those that do not. While mapping the social organization of femininity is not my goal here, I want to suggest that focusing on the relationship between masculinities and femininities in a particular social context is a step toward understanding how multiple femininities and multiple masculinities take shape in relation to each other and how power might operate among them. This sort of analysis calls for a conceptualization of how the symbolic meaning of gender difference and gender hierarchy takes shape through social action in a specific context and among specified groups of women and men. By specifying the contextual form of gender structuration, the relationship between and among various masculinities and various femininities will become more visible and better understood. With the exception of work done on the intersection of gender, race, and class, gender sociologists have done little to build on Connell's theory to develop a conceptualization of multiple femininities. The interaction between Maddie and the stranger suggests that there are multiple femininities, and that the relationship between masculinity and femininity becomes quite complex when multiple femininities are introduced. As with Connell's multiple masculinities, there are practices that are feminine and therefore deemed inferior to the masculine, yet are also defined as inferior or subordinate to other feminine practices—for instance, being sexually promiscuous versus being sexually restrained. It would do gender sociologists and students of gender in other disciplines well to map the social organization of femininity, especially if we're interested in understanding and transforming power relations among and between women and men.

15. Of course, the flexibility for deploying different masculinities and femininities will depend on the institutional setting and the structural power relations between interactants. For instance, Maddie might be less likely to use subordinate masculinity in relation to someone who has institutional power over her, such as a boss or teacher, for instance. I would, however, expect for there to be different forms rather than an absence of maneuvering in more rigid institutional settings.

5.   THE BODY IN ALTERNATIVE HARD ROCK

1. This public badge of masculinity could be tied to the class position of truck drivers. Research suggests that for men who are subordinated by class, race, or ethnicity, masculinity becomes a very important mechanism of social status and dominance. In response to their subordination to other men, these men emphasize their domination over women to maintain their masculinity. See, for example, David L. Collinson, "'Engineering Humor': Masculinity, Joking and Conflict in Shop-Floor Relations," *Organization Studies* 9 (1988): 181–99; R. W. Connell, "Disruptions: Improper Masculinities and Schooling," in *Beyond Silence Voices*, ed. Lois Weis and Michelle Fine (Albany, N.Y.: State University of New York Press, 1993); Manuel Peña, "Class, Gender and Machismo: The 'Treacherous Woman' Folklore of Mexican Male Workers," *Gender and Society* 5 (1991). For an alternative perspective on this, particularly in terms of machismo and Mexican immigrant men, see Pierrette Hondagneu-Sotelo and Michael Messner, "Gender Displays and Men's Power: The 'New Man' and the Mexican Immigrant Man," in *Theorizing Masculinities*, ed. Harry Brod (New York: Sage, 1994).

2. While Laura Mulvey suggests that women can occupy the sexual subject position in relation to the feminine sexual object, she argues that this does not subvert but reinforces hegemonic gender. Though the person in the sexual subject position is a woman, she is still occupying the masculine position in relation to the feminine object. Masculinity and femininity are still locked in a subject/object relationship. Others disagree, and argue that women's desire for other women, even if enacted by visually consuming women's bodies, disrupts the gender order by dislocating maleness from masculine sexual subjectivity. See Mary Ann Doane, "Film and the Masquerade: Theorizing the Female Spectator," in *Issues in Feminist Film Criticism*, ed. Patricia Erens (Bloomington: University of Indiana Press, 1990); Kathy Myers, "Towards a Feminist Erotica," in *Looking On: Images of Femininity in the Visual arts and Media*, ed. Rosemary Betterton (London: Pandora, 1987).

3. See Iris Marion Young, "Breasted Experience: The Look and the Feeling," in *The Politics of Women's Bodies: Sexuality, Appearance, and Behavior*, ed. Rose Weitz (New York: Oxford University Press, 1998).
4. As part of their political stance against the commercialism and capitalist market of mainstream rock, Fugazi refuses to sell band merchandise, including concert T-shirts, at their shows.
5. That grunge grew up in the state of Washington perhaps makes this more likely.
6. Laura Mulvey relies on psychoanalytic theory to explain why and how viewing the feminine sexual object from a masculine subject position is a source of sexual pleasure. According to Mulvey, the position of looker is always necessarily masculine. Because masculine sexuality and gender identity is developed through distancing from the feminine, sexual pleasure in looking at the feminine sexual object is derived through the separation or space from the feminine. See Laura Mulvey, "Visual Pleasure and Narrative Cinema," in *Issues in Feminist Film Criticism*, ed. Patricia Erens (Bloomington: University of Indiana Press, 1990). See also Annette Kuhn, *The Power of the Image: Essays on Representation and Sexuality* (London: Routledge, 1985).
7. See Elaine Hatfield and Susan Sprechter, *Mirror, Mirror: The Importance of Looks in Everyday Life* (Albany: State University of New York Press, 1986).
8. See Luce Irigaray, excerpt from *"Ce sexe qui n'en est pas un,"* in *New French Feminisms: An Anthology*, ed. and trans. Elaine Marks and Isabelle de Courtivron (New York: Schocken Books, 1981), 110.
9. See, for instance, Susan Bordo, *The Male Body* (New York: Farrar, Straus and Giroux, 1999); Joan Jacobs Brumberg, *The Body Project: An Intimate History of American Girls* (New York: Vintage, 1997); and Fred Davis, *Fashion, Culture, and Identity* (Chicago: University of Chicago Press, 1992).
10. By *gendered dress* I mean the relationship between feminine and masculine styles. An analysis of gendered dress will differ from an analysis of men's and women's styles in two distinct ways. First, the analytic focus of gendered dress is styles that are symbolically defined as masculine or feminine, not the styles worn by women or men. Second, the focus is on the relationship between the styles. How do feminine styles articulate femininity in relation to masculinity? How do masculine styles articulate masculinity in relation to femininity?
11. See Adrienne Rich, "Compulsory Heterosexuality and Lesbian Existence," *Signs* 5 (1980): 631–60.
12. Susan Bordo, *Unbearable Weight: Feminism, Western Culture, and the Body* (Berkeley and Los Angeles: University of California Press, 1993), 294.
13. bell hooks, "Madonna: Plantation Mistress or Soul Sister?" in *Black Looks: Race and Representation* (Boston: South End Press, 1992), 29.
14. I would assume that people of different races and classes, and in different cultural contexts, would maneuver in completely different ways. Knowing *how* is largely an empirical question for further research.

6. SEXUALITY AND GENDER MANEUVERING

1. Building on the empirical work of social scientists and historians who demonstrate the importance of sociohistorical context and social processes in the construction of sexual scripts, sexual identities and communities, and sexual desire; on Gayle Rubin's groundbreaking conceptual separation of sexuality and gender; and on Michel Foucault's conceptualization of sexual discourse as social control, some theorists conceptualize sexuality as not simply one feature of broader gender relations but as a separate organizing principle in its own right, and equally central to the workings of power and material inequality as gender.
2. See, for instance, Judith Butler, *Gender Trouble: Feminism and the Subversion of Identity* (New York: Routledge, 1990); Eve Kosofsky Sedgwick, *Epistemology of the Closet* (Berkeley and Los Angeles: University of California Press, 1990); Steven Seidman, introduction to *Queer Theory/Sociology*, ed. Steven Seidman (Cambridge, Mass.: Blackwell 1996); and Michael Warner, introduction to *Fear of a Queer Planet*, ed. Michael Warner (Minneapolis: University of Minnesota Press, 1993). I say "partially" here because Gayle Rubin, a

foundational theorist for queer theory, suggests that the marginalization of homosexuality is simply one form of sexual stratification. Other forms of erotic desire, such as sadomasochism, fetishism, and sex for money are also marginalized within the current sexual order but are not necessarily encompassed within the relationship between heterosexuality and homosexuality. See Gayle Rubin, "Thinking Sex: Notes for a Radical Theory of Sexuality," in *Pleasure and Danger: Exploring Female Sexuality*, ed. Carol S. Vance (London: Pandora, 1984).

3. See Sedgwick, *Epistemology of the Closet*.

4. See Seidman, *Queer Theory/Sociology*.

5. I would argue that doing homophobe is doing sexuality. As queer theory suggests, sexuality is an organizing feature of social relations and is not limited to genital contact or even to sexual desire. Thus, actions that reproduce the sexual order, whether they consist of genital contact, sexual desire, or assumptions about sexuality constitute doing sexuality.

6. Queer theory and queer politics are a move away from understanding homosexuality as constituting a minority group composed of subjects who are oppressed and need to be liberated. Instead, queer theorists and activists favor analysis of and resistance to the social construction of sexualities that, among other things, indicate homosexuality and heterosexuality as a stable, unified identity. This is quite similar to Judith Butler's and R. W. Connell's conceptualizations of gender identity discussed previously. While Butler and Connell focus on masculine and feminine identities and queer theorists focus on homosexual or heterosexual identities, in both cases the identities result from social relations; they are not an essential, internal essence that is brought by individuals to social relations.

7. Sexuality can be queered at any or all of the levels of social organization. Sexuality can be queered at the level of individual practice when a person engages in actions that challenge or undermine the fixed or hierarchical construction of sexual identities. The social organization of any face-to-face interaction can by queered by constructing and enacting the relationship between people in a way that disrupts the meaning of sexuality as fixed, stable, hierarchical identities. Finally, the sexual structure of an institution or an organized group such as a subculture can be queered to the extent that the overarching normative structure or rules for thinking about and doing sexual desire do not reproduce the construction of sexuality as hierarchical, stable identities.

8. Though the man did not say this, a common response to this maneuver might be "All you need is a good fuck." This, I would argue, would be a sort of hegemonic maneuver to resituate the women into the sexual object position in relation to masculinity, and back into the heterosexual line. That is, this would simply be another move in the ongoing process of constructing the gender and sexual organization of interaction.

9. Here I am talking about mainstream rock. This excludes the subcultures that combined queer sexuality, punk, and hard rock in the 1990s to create "queer-core" music.

10. As Sedgwick suggests, the silence when not speaking desire signifies heterosexual desire because heterosexual desire is the unmarked norm.

11. I'm thinking of the macroorganization as the larger, dominant culture in which alternative hard rock is embedded. The microorganization of sexuality will refer to the normative framework for face-to-face interaction and individual practices. The mesoorganization, then, is in between, is the middle-level organization. It is the overall normative framework for the subculture.

My goal was to demonstrate the importance of conceptualizing and analyzing sexuality at multiple levels of analysis. Without a multilevel analysis, I might conclude that alternative hard rockers have successfully developed a rock music subculture that does not reproduce male dominance nor heterosexual dominance. At the level of practice, identity talk, and interaction, they have rejected compulsory heterosexuality and male dominance. However, the same practices and talk that undermine compulsory heterosexuality and work as effective gender resistance depend on the hegemonic sexual order. This leads to more questions unanswered by this analysis: What is the relationship between the different levels of sexuality as they intersect with gender? Are certain levels more likely than others to influence beliefs, practices, broader institutional features of social life? What is the relative importance or weight of each, and how might this vary by social context? How do the different levels of sexuality produce power relations in terms of both sexuality and gender? What levels of sexuality are more important or effective in terms of strategies for social change? Further multilevel theorizing and empirical analyses are needed to begin addressing these and other questions.

12. I found a dissonance between how alternative hard rockers talked about sexuality and how they enacted sexual desire. These findings suggest that focusing only on the way people talk about sexuality will leave hidden some of the most important aspects of sexuality, namely how it is enacted and negotiated in face-to-face interaction. This is significant because it suggests that, while alternative hard rockers were facile in and willing to think about sexualities in terms of stable homosexual and heterosexual identities, their everyday experience of sexuality, at least to some degree, undermined identity demarcations. My guess is that if asked on a survey or in an interview, alternative hard rockers would be more willing to "buy into" identity markers and choose one—and importantly, in most cases they would choose a heterosexual identity. A survey or interview question, however, because it relies on language, would be framing and therefore boxing alternative hard rockers' sexualities into an identity framework even though in their practices this sometimes is not the case. Importantly, there are ways in which sexuality is enacted and constructed in face-to-face interaction that stepped out of that framework and would likely disappear empirically if alternative hard rockers were asked to talk about sexuality. This suggests that ethnographic methods or a more innovative formulation of survey and interview questions would greatly enhance our efforts to map and understand sexuality and its relationship to gender and male dominance.

13. Lawrence Grossberg, "Putting the Pop back in Postmodernism," in *Universal Abandon? The Politics of Post-modernism*, ed. Andrew Ross (Minneapolis: University of Minnesota Press, 1988).

14. For a discussion of young women's erotic uses of dance, see Angela McRobbie, "Dance and Social Fantasy," in *Gender and Generation*, ed. Angela McRobbie and Mica Nava (London: Macmillan, 1984).

15. It is interesting to consider the ways in which rock music itself is masculinized and associated with phallic representation. In this sense, women's desire to fuck a voice or the music could very much be in line with normative heterosexual desire. However, as Gayle Rubin suggests, "normal" sexual desire is directed toward *persons* of the opposite gender. Sexual desire directed toward nonhuman entities or objects falls outside of the realm of acceptable sexuality. This is why, even if rock music itself is a masculine, women's desire to fuck it cannot be simply reduced to "normal" heterosexuality.

16. These data suggest that empirical investigations of queer sexuality must be extended to people who identify as heterosexual. Alternative hard rockers' expressions of sexual desire and sexual practices blur or in some cases render meaningless the lines between heterosexual and homosexual despite an overall norm for heterosexual identities. There has been little attention paid to the queer practices of people who identify as heterosexual, and further research in this area is needed. For instance, researchers might compare the queer practices of self-identifying heterosexual people and those of self-identifying gay, lesbian, bisexual, or queer people to better understand the play of gender and sexual hegemony and resistance at different levels of analysis. It would also be fruitful to further explore the workings of hegemony and resistance as men and women negotiate and practice sexual desire as they interact with each other. Mixed-gender, collaborative ethnography might be one way to get at these multiple vectors of gender and sexual relations.

17. This was something quite different from how people who identify as bisexual construct their sexuality, for instance. Amber Ault found that both lesbians' and bisexual women's constructions of bisexuality reproduce sexual binaries by conceptualizing bisexual people as having sexual desire for both men and women. Ault concludes that though the bisexual women she spoke with claim a more "queer" sexuality than lesbian women or gay men because they are "bisexual" instead of "monosexual", they are still bound to sexual identity binaries in their thinking. They construct their sexuality as both halves of the hegemonic sexuality whole and therefore not necessarily "queering" sexuality. See Amber Ault, "The Dilemma of Identity: Bi Women's Negotiations," in *Queer Theory/Sociology*, ed. Steven Seidman (Cambridge, Mass.: Blackwell, 1996).

18. Adrienne Rich, "Compulsory Heterosexuality and Lesbian Existence," *Signs* 5 (1980): 631–60.

19. These findings demonstrate that queering sexuality can be an effective form of gender

resistance. There is much debate among feminists about whether or not deconstructing identities is politically expedient; see, for instance, Linda Alcoff, "Cultural Feminism versus Post-Structuralism: The Identity Crisis in Feminist Theory," in *Culture/Power/History: A Reader in Contemporary Social Theory*, ed. Nicholas B. Dirks, Geoff Eley, and Sherry Ortner (Princeton: Princeton University Press, 1994); Amber Ault, "The Dilemma of Identity"; Judith Butler, *Gender Trouble*; Christine Di Stefano, "Dilemmas of Difference: Feminism, Modernity, and Postmodernism." in *Feminism/Postmodernism*, ed. Linda J. Nicholson (New York: Routledge, 1990); Nancy Fraser and Linda J. Nicholson, "Social Criticism Without Philosophy: An Encounter Between Feminism and Postmodernism," in *Feminism/Postmodernism*, ed. Linda J. Nicholson (New York: Routledge, 1990); and Diana Fuss, *Essentially Speaking: Feminism, Nature and Difference* (New York: Routledge, 1989). While these findings do not provide any kind of answer to those questions, they do suggest that gender resistance and the subversion of identities are not necessarily incompatible. Further research in other social settings might begin to map the costs and benefits of queering sexuality to undermine male dominance and how social context mediates its effectiveness. It is entirely likely that queering sexuality at a rock concert will have a very different outcome than queering sexuality in a work, school, or family setting. Whether queering sexuality in these settings would be more or less effective is an important empirical question.

20. See R. W. Connell, *Masculinities* (Berkeley and Los Angeles: University of California Press, 1995).
21. See Rubin, "Thinking Sex."
22. See Chrys Ingraham, "The Heterosexual Imaginary: Sociology and Theories of Gender," in *Queer Theory/Sociology*, ed. Steven Seidman (Cambridge, Mass.: Blackwell 1996); and Rubin, "Thinking Sex."
23. See, for instance, Combahee River Collective, "The Combahee River Collective Statement," in *Home Girls: A Black Feminist Anthology*, ed. Barbara Smith (New York: Kitchen Table, 1983), 272–82; Patricia Hill Collins, "Moving beyond Gender: Intersectionality and Scientific Knowledge," in *Revisioning Gender*, ed. Myra Marx Ferree, Judith Lorber, and Beth B. Hess (Thousand Oaks, Calif.: Sage, 1999), 261–84; bell hooks, *Talking Back* (Boston: South End Press, 1989); Evelyn Nakano Glenn, "The Social Construction and Institutionalization of Gender and Race: An Integrative Framework," in *Revisioning Gender*, Myra Marx Ferree, Judith Lorber, and Beth B. Hess (Thousand Oaks: Sage, 1999), 3–43; and Valerie Smith, "Split Affinities: The Case of Interracial Rape," in *Conflicts in Feminism*, ed. Marianne Hirsch and Evelyn Fox Keller (New York: Routledge, 1990), 271–87.
24. See bell hooks, "Feminism: As a Transformational Politics" in *Talking Back: Thinking Feminist, Thinking Black* (Boston: South End Press, 1989).

7. FEMINIST POLITICS

1. According to C. Wright Mills, the sociological imagination connects individual experience to the history of society. Using my sociological imagination meant connecting the individual action taken by Courtney Love and situating it in the larger sociohistorical context in which she was acting. See C. Wright Mills, *The Sociological Imagination* (London: Oxford University Press, 1959).
2. Craig Calhoun, "Social Theory and the Politics of Identity," in *Social Theory and the Politics of Identity*, ed. Craig Calhoun (Oxford: Blackwell, 1994).
3. Joan Scott draws a distinction between *equivalent treatment* and *the same treatment*. Equivalent treatment takes into consideration variance in experience and adjusts for inequities, while the same treatment is simply as it sounds—treating people or groups the same despite differences in experience. See Joan Scott, "Deconstructing Equality-versus-Difference, or, The Uses of Post-structuralist Theory for Feminism." *Feminist Studies* 14 (1988): 33–50.
4. See Mavis Bayton, *Frock Rock: Women Performing Popular Music*.
5. Susan Faludi, *Backlash: The Undeclared War against American Women* (New York: Doubleday, 1991).
6. An example of two of the men's orginizations are the National Organization of Men against Sexism, and Men Stopping Rape.

7. R. W. Connell, *Masculinities* (Berkeley and Los Angeles: University of California Press, 1995).

8. Faludi, *Backlash.*

9. See for instance, William Farrell, *Why Men Are the Way They Are: The Male-Female Dynamic* (New York: McGraw-Hill, 1986); William Farrell, *The Myth of Male Power: Why Men Are the Disposable Sex* (New York: Simon & Schuster, 1993); and Herb Goldberg, *The Hazards of Being Male: Surviving the Myth of Masculine Privilege* (New York: Nash, 1976).

10. See for instance, Robert Bly, *Iron John: A Book about Men* (New York: Vintage, 1990); and Jack Kaufman and Richard L. Timmers, "Searching for the Hairy Man," *Social Work With Groups* 6 (1983): 163–75.

11. Katie Roiphe, *The Morning After: Sex, Fear, and Feminism on Campus* (Boston: Little, Brown, 1993).

12. Naomi Wolf, *Fire with Fire: The New Female Power and How It Will Change in the 21st Century* (New York: Random House, 1993).

13. Naomi Wolf, *The Beauty Myth: How Images of Beauty Are Used against Women* (New York: Anchor, 1992).

14. Renée Denfeld, *The New Victorians: A Young Woman's Challenge to the Old Feminist Order* (New York: Warner Books, 1995).

15. Ibid., 57.

16. Camille Paglia, *Sexual Personae: Art Decadence from Nefertiti to Emily Dickinson* (New York: Vintage, 1990).

17. For a good discussion of the meaning of oppression, see Marilyn Frye, "Oppression," in *The Politics of Reality: Essays in Feminist Theory* (Freedom, Calif.: The Crossing Press, 1983), 1–16.

18. Rockers for Choice, organized by the women in L7, was a coalition that organized a series of benefit concerts. All proceeds were donated to organizations dedicated to maintaining women's access to safe and legal abortion.

19. For an interesting discussion of the commodification of the body, see Mike Featherstone, "The Body in Consumer Culture," in *The Body: Social Process and Cultural Theory*, ed. Mike Featherstone, Mike Hepworth, and Bryan S. Turner (London: Sage, 1991), 170–208. See also Susan Bordo, *Unbearable Weight: Feminism, Western Culture, and the Body* (Berkeley and Los Angeles: University of California Press, 1993).

Index

"slut," subcultural use of term, 45, 112–113, 115–118, 125–127, 131
Smart Bar (Chicago club), 4
Smashing Pumpkins, 12, 43
Smell the Magic (L7), 4
Smith, Patti, 11
Smith, Valerie, 202n23
Sonic Youth, 55–56
Soundgarden, 3–4, 9, 12–13, 15, 62, 91, 109, 159–160, 166, 184, 192n9
Sparks, Donita, 62, 71, 118–119, 154, 160–161, 167–168, 170, 185
Spenser, Jon, 60
Sprechter, Susan, 199n7
Star, Chelsea, 192n10
Stipe, Michael, 34
Straw, Will, 192n1, 193n20, 196n5
structuration, x–xii, 33–38, 74, 106–107, 116, 119, 123, 187, 196n4, 197n11
Stryker, Sheldon, 194n36
"Suggestion" (Fugazi), 2
Szatmary, David, 192n12

"teenybopper," subcultural use of term, 19, 27–28, 31–32, 35, 38, 44, 59, 61, 173, 195–196n4
Ten (Pearl Jam), 3
Terry, Jennifer, 193–194n24
testosterone rock, 166–167
Thayil, Kim, 9–10, 62, 91, 109, 159–160, 166–167, 184
Thelma and Louise (film), 49, 105
Thomas, W. I., 196n1
Thorne, Barrie, 82, 84, 89, 194n33, 196n5
Timmers, Richard L., 203n10
Tribe 8, 136–138, 145, 153

Truth or Dare (documentary film), 126

University of Wisconsin, 4–5

Vedder, Eddie, 2–3, 6, 16, 64, 111, 165–166, 181, 184
Velvet, 58–59
Veruca Salt, 12, 19, 42–44, 69, 168
violence toward women, 171–172

Walser, Robert, 192n1, 193nn13, 20, 195n4, 196n5
Warner, Michael, 194n26, 199n2
Warrant, 1, 20, 64
Weber, Max, 197n10
Weinstein, Deena, 192n1, 193nn12, 20, 195n4, 196n5
Wesley Willis Fiasco, 44, 47, 53, 67, 72, 75, 109–110
West, Candace, xi, 81–84, 86, 88, 194n34, 196n4
Whitely, Sheila, 192n10
White Snake, 1
"white trash," subcultural use of term, 55, 127
Wicker Park (section of Chicago), 6–7, 42–43, 45, 50
Wilson, Ann, 28
Wilson, Nancy, 28
Wolf, Naomi, 176–177, 203nn12, 13

Young, Iris Marion, 199n3
"yuppie," subcultural use of term, 6–7, 46

Zimmerman, Don, xi, 81–84, 86, 88, 194n34, 196n4

ABOUT THE AUTHOR

Mimi Schippers completed her Ph.D. in sociology at the University of Wisconsin-Madison and is currently assistant professor of sociology at Albion College.